"This remarkable book breaks new ground in exploring the critical role those American Christian institutions and individuals played in shaping the development of Protestantism in China in the first half of the twentieth century."

—**Alister E. McGrath**, professor of science and religion, Oxford University

"Christopher Sneller is a gifted storyteller. Based upon meticulous research of published and unpublished sources, he traces the previously largely untold story of the history of the impact Union Theological Seminary in New York had on the Protestant church in China in the first half of the twentieth century. This is a fascinating narrative which missiologists, historians, sociologists, and theologians will find helpful."

—**Glenn R. Kreider**, professor of theological studies, Dallas Theological Seminary

"Focusing on the developments of Chinese Christianity, Christopher Sneller provides an insightful book that gives a window to wider Christian movements over the last century. Sneller draws the story of Union Theological Seminary and Chinese Christianity together with the likes of Bonhoeffer and the Modernist-Fundamentalist debates, resulting in an accessible and engaging account of how these cross-cultural interactions continue to influence events today. You'll learn as much about American Christianity as that of Chinese Christianity."

—**Ben C. Blackwell**, professor of early Christianity, Houston Theological Seminary

"Modern histories of Chinese Christianity largely ignore any influence by Union Seminary (NY). Christopher Sneller not only demonstrates the profound impact of the seminary on the shaping of modern Chinese Christianity, but he also makes a persuasive case for intentionality. More than enlightening history, this book is a clarion call to the vital role of seminaries in shaping leadership, culture, and the direction of the church."

—**E. Randolph Richards**, research professor of New Testament, Palm Beach Atlantic University

"This seminal work, based on archival research, unpacks for the first time the complex relationships between theological education at Union Theological Seminary in New York and its formative impact on diverse expressions of emerging Chinese Protestant Christianity in mainland China, especially the Three-Self Patriotic Movement. It demonstrates how these 'Sino-American relationships' sustained, enlivened, and even expanded Chinese Christianity during revolutions; now Chinese Christianity is vibrant and enhances world Christianity. This book deserves highest recognition."

—**Daniel Jeyaraj**, professor emeritus of world Christianity, Liverpool Hope University

"Powerful, unseen currents carry water across oceans and regulate global climate. In the same way, Christopher Sneller demonstrates the unmistakable effect of Union Seminary on both Chinese Christianity and geopolitics since the early twentieth century. This influence has largely gone unnoticed until now. Sneller's research not only has breadth and depth; it is accessible to a wide range of readers. I recommend this book to anyone interested in learning how similar forces may contribute to the shaping of Christianity around the world in the century ahead."

—**Brad Vaughn**, author of *Reading Romans with Eastern Eyes*

"Christopher Sneller has written the definitive study of how Union Theological Seminary in New York became instrumental in shaping several generations of China's leading Christian intellectual voices. It demonstrates the way Union produced some of the major progressive Chinese Christian thinkers of the first half of the twentieth century and, in the second half of the century, nurtured the two most important leaders of the newly formed Three-Self Patriotic Movement. An essential read for anyone interested in the history of Christianity in China."

—**Alexander Chow**, co-director, Centre for the Study of World Christianity, University of Edinburgh

"Though scholars often highlight how indigenous cultural influences shape forms of local Christianity, in this exciting study, Christopher Sneller draws our attention to the significant ways outside forces profoundly influenced local forms of Chinese Christianity. Sneller argues convincingly how the influential connections between Union Seminary and prominent Chinese have been underspecified and how an account of modern Chinese Christianity must take such influences into account. This is an excellent resource to demonstrate the complexities and often overlooked types of influences that create contemporary majority world Christianities."

—**Christopher Flanders**, professor of missions, Abilene Christian University

"Social networks and social capital generate real and visible changes in world Christianity. Christopher Sneller reveals why Union Theological Seminary in New York has played a formative role in Chinese Christianity. It wasn't just what was taught there, but also who was introduced to whom and how ties to a common institution mobilized groups on both sides of the Pacific. This book demonstrates the power of relationships and invites deeper investigations into the networked nature of global Christianity today."

—**Daryl R. Ireland**, research assistant professor of world Christianity, Boston University

"This excellent volume is impeccably researched and sheds new light on Sino-American relations through the oft-neglected lens of religion. The eye-opening realization that Christopher Sneller discovers is that Christianity's influence was never unidirectional between the two countries and how certain small nexus points (e.g., Union Seminary and K. H. Ting) had an exponential effect in creating a web of influences that inextricably linked them. These findings are truly groundbreaking and stunning in their implications."

—**Allen Yeh**, professor of intercultural studies and missiology, Biola University

"For those interested in historical missions, the legacy of Union Theological Seminary, or Chinese Christianity, Christopher Sneller's *Exporting Progressivism to Communist China* is a valuable study. What's more, this book will *raise* interest in the history of missions in China, one of the most important countries on the global stage. Sneller's careful work charts the intersection of two worlds that deserve better understanding: protestant liberalism and Chinese Christianity."

—**Philip Tallon**, dean of the school of Christian thought, Houston Christian University

"Christopher Sneller's study shows convincingly how New York City's Union Theological Seminary intentionally exported its liberal or progressive theology to twentieth-century China through a network of its American and Chinese students—and how this has had a lasting impact on China's Three-Self Patriotic Movement in particular. It is a necessary read for all wishing to understand the TSPM."

—**Glen L. Thompson**, professor emeritus of New Testament and historical theology, Asia Lutheran Seminary

"Christopher Sneller offers an engrossing account of Union Seminary's oversized influence on Protestant Christianity in China. Though this is a specialized study, there are several compelling implications that will make it of interest to a wide variety of readers."

—**David George Moore**, host of *Moore Engaging*

"The aim of this outstanding volume by Christopher Sneller is to historically document the connections between (a) Chinese Protestantism in Mainland China and (b) Union Seminary, New York. The strength of this scholarly work comes from Sneller's wise use of interdisciplinary approach, weaving together information and insights gleaned from the integration of research methodologies from the fields of history, education, sociology, and theology."

—**Enoch Wan**, director of PhD, EdD, and DIS programs, Western Seminary

"This book addresses the contributions of Union Seminary in New York to the formation of Protestant churches in China, especially through the Three-Self Patriotic Movement (TSPM), the Cross and Sword Secret Society, the Sino-Foreign Protestant Establishment (SFPE), and the Chinese Students' Christian Association. I strongly recommend this book not only to those who are interested in the churches in China and its relations to Union Seminary, but also to those who are interested in the intersection between churches and theological institutions in various other contexts."

—**Sebastian Kim**, professor of renewal in public life, Fuller Theological Seminary

# Exporting Progressivism to Communist China

**Evangelical Missiological Society Monograph Series**

Anthony Casey, Rochelle Scheuermann, and Edward L. Smither
Series Editors

---

A Project of the Evangelical Missiological Society
www.emsweb.org

---

The EMS Monograph Series publishes the best book length works of EMS members. The monographs may be reworked dissertations or original works based on missiological research focused on aspects of history, theology, culture, strategy, or spiritual formation all relating to the academic and practical nature of the missionary enterprise. EMS monographs are peer reviewed and authors work with an editing team from Pickwick Publications (Wipf and Stock). Typically, 3–5 monographs are published each year.

# Exporting Progressivism to Communist China

## How New York's Union Seminary Liberalized Christianity in Twentieth-Century China

Christopher D. Sneller

FOREWORD BY
Alister E. McGrath

PICKWICK *Publications* · Eugene, Oregon

EXPORTING PROGRESSIVISM TO COMMUNIST CHINA
How New York's Union Seminary Liberalized Christianity in Twentieth-Century China

Evangelical Missiological Society Monograph Series 16



Pickwick Publications
An Imprint of Wipf and Stock Publishers
199 W. 8th Ave., Suite 3
Eugene, OR 97401

www.wipfandstock.com

PAPERBACK ISBN: 978-1-6667-5927-3
HARDCOVER ISBN: 978-1-6667-5928-0
EBOOK ISBN: 978-1-6667-5929-7

*Cataloging-in-Publication data:*

Names: Sneller, Christopher D., author. | McGrath, Alister E., 1953–, foreword.

Title: Exporting progressivism to communist China : how New York's Union Seminary liberalized Christianity in twentieth-century China / by Christopher D. Sneller ; foreword by Alister E. McGrath.

Description: Eugene, OR : Pickwick Publications, 2023 | Series: Evangelical Missiological Society Monograph Series | Includes bibliographical.

Identifiers: ISBN 978-1-6667-5927-3 (paperback) | ISBN 978-1-6667-5928-0 (hardcover) | ISBN 978-1-6667-5929-7 (ebook)

Subjects: LCSH: Missions—China. | Missions—East Asia. | Christian education—East Asia.

Classification: BV3415.2 .S57 2023 (print) | BV3415.2 .S57 (ebook)

06/21/23

To the two most important women in my life:
Shirley Sneller (1945–2022), my mom, who was my
biggest cheerleader throughout her entire life,
and to Monica Sneller, my wife, who gladly moved our (then) family
of six to London in 2010 and keeps me laughing, mostly at myself.

# Contents

# Foreword

THIS REMARKABLE BOOK BREAKS new ground in exploring the critical role that American Christian institutions and individuals played in shaping the development of Protestantism in China in the first half of the twentieth century. Christopher Sneller focuses on Union Theological Seminary in New York, which is well known for its pivotal role in the American controversies over fundamentalism and modernism in the 1920s. Through detailed analysis of archival material, however, Dr. Sneller has discovered another, perhaps even more significant role played by Union around this time—its decisive role in the shaping of Chinese Protestantism, above all its slow transition from an alien presence within China to an indigenized Chinese Christianity.

Dr. Sneller's detailed study of Union's archives shows that nearly two hundred Union alumni went to serve in China over the period 1911 to 1949, of which thirty-nine were Chinese nationals. Many of these Chinese students went on to develop key leadership roles within Chinese Protestantism, especially in the educational sector. Yet in addition to providing leadership for Christian colleges in Republican China, Union graduates also played significant roles in the Chinese Young Men's Christian Association, and the important Three-Self Patriotic Movement, which helped consolidate Christianity in this region.

This innovative and thoroughly researched work opens with an account of the development of Christianity in China, focusing particularly on Protestant missionary work in the region until the collapse of the Qing Dynasty. This milestone in Chinese history opened up a new chapter in the Protestant presence and engagement in the region, as the "Golden Age" of missions in China dawned. Dr. Sneller draws on James Davison Hunter's concept of a "dense social network" to explore how this group of Union graduates were able to have such an impact on the transformation of this region, gradually enabling "Christianity in China" to transition to "Chinese Christianity."

This important work casts new light on the role of Union Theological Seminary in the shaping of Christianity in China, and helps clarify the importance of social relationships and networks established at Union in this process, as well as in influencing Sino-American relationships. Dr. Sneller's careful analysis of the identity and function of Union's network of prominent Americans at this time—such as Henry R. Luce, John D. Rockefeller, Harry Emerson Fosdick, and Henry Pitney van Dusen—is highly illuminating. While this major work will be an invaluable resource for historians of missions, Dr. Sneller's emphasis on the importance of social networks has implications for understanding and advancing the role of American colleges and seminaries in the twenty-first century in the shaping of international Christianity. While Dr. Sneller offers us an essentially historical exploration of an important slice of missionary history, his work has importance for all concerned with the present and future roles of Christian seminaries and colleges.

Alister E. McGrath
Oxford University

# List of Abbreviations

| | |
|---|---|
| Cands | Cross and Sword Secret Society |
| CCH | *Cheng Zhi Hui* (Association for Accomplishing Ideals) |
| CCP | Chinese Communist Party |
| CIM | China Inland Mission |
| CMS | Church Missionary Society |
| CSCA | Chinese Students Christian Association |
| D&J | David and Jonathan Secret Society |
| HYISIS | Harvard-Yenching Institute Sinological Index Series |
| IWM | Interchurch World Movement |
| KMT | *Kuomintang, Guomindang* (Chinese Nationalist Party) |
| LMS | London Missionary Society |
| MIT | Massachusetts Institute of Technology |
| PRC | People's Republic of China |
| SFPE | Sino-Foreign Protestant Establishment |
| SCM | Student Christian Movement |
| SCC | Society of the Catholic Commonwealth |
| SVM | Student Volunteer Movement |
| TSPM | Three-Self Patriotic Movement of the Protestant Churches in China |
| UFWD | United Front Work Department |
| UTS | Union Theological Seminary (NY) |
| YDSL | Yale Divinity School Library |
| YMCA | Young Men's Christian Association |
| YWCA | Young Women's Christian Association |

# Part I
# The Historical Backdrop

# I

# Introduction

THE TWO MOST IMPORTANT leaders in the Three-Self Patriotic Movement of the Protestant Churches in China, Y. T. Wu (吴耀宗 *Wu Yaozong*, 1893–1979) and K. H. Ting (丁光训 *Ding Guangxun*, 1915–2012*)*, both attended Union Theological Seminary in New York. This observation provoked the underlying questions of this research. Why did Wu and Ting attend the same theological school? How is Union Seminary connected to Chinese Christianity? Does the seminary's influence go deeper than these two men? In the following pages I will demonstrate that Union played a seminal, though unnoticed, role in the Sino-Foreign Protestant Establishment and the Three-Self Movement in the People's Republic of China.[1] The New York school influenced Chinese Protestantism through a dense network of leaders who brought a progressive Christianity to the Middle Kingdom.

## The Growth of Christianity in China

Christianity has surged across the globe in the past century. Its epicenter has shifted from the West to the South and East.[2] In 1900 Europe and North America accounted for 82 percent of the world's Christians (423 million Christians compared with 94 million in the rest of the world). A century later Christians in Europe and North America represented 35 percent (758 million Christians versus 1.4 billion in the rest of the world). Contra Hilaire Belloc, Europe is no longer the faith. More people have converted to Christianity since the end of colonialism than in the entire period of

1. Hereafter, the Sino-Foreign Protestant Establishment may be referred to as SFPE, the Three-Self Patriotic Movement as TSPM, and the People's Republic of China as PRC. See "List of Abbreviations" preceding this chapter for abbreviations used throughout this work.

2. See Sanneh, *Whose Religion Is Christianity?*, and Jenkins, *Next Christendom*. I prefer Sanneh's term "world Christianity" over "global Christianity."

colonial rule.[3] China is playing and will play a vigorous role in the future of world Christianity. Today there are at least 70 million Christians in China, accounting for 5 percent of the population. In their 1993 book, *Protestantism in Contemporary China*, Hunter and Chan estimated 40–50 million Protestants.[4] Lian Xi suggested the number of Christians to be 50 million Protestants and 17 million Catholics.[5] In 2010 the World Christian Database inflated the number to 119.5 million.[6] An estimate of 70 million Christians in China seems reasonable but the actual figure could be greater. This century Chinese Christians will represent, in the words of Thomas Alan Harvey, "the vanguard of the church."[7]

Many observers expected Christianity to weaken and eventually die in Communist China. The Chinese church did indeed navigate treacherous times throughout Mao Zedong's rule. It was one thing for Christianity to exist in Communist nations where the church had existed for centuries and played an important state function, such as the Soviet Union, but in China, hope seemed futile.[8] The Cultural Revolution confirmed these fears. Between 1966 and 1976 the church in China seemed to disappear. Lee Ming Ng described the apparent failure of Chinese Christianity in his 1971 dissertation: "[It] appears as though the missionary effort of almost a century and a half has again come to naught in China." Ng voiced the general consensus among scholars that the church in China is "lost," the missionary enterprise in China has been a "debacle" or a "fiasco," and, what is perhaps the most comprehensive judgment of all, Christianity has "failed" in China.[9] Three years later John King Fairbank, a prominent sinologist at Harvard, echoed Ng's concerns of the apparent failure of Christianity in China: "Nearly a century and a half after Morrison arrived, it was evident that the missionaries'

3. Sanneh, *Whose Religion Is Christianity?*, 41.

4. A. Hunter and Chan, *Protestantism in Contemporary China*, 70.

5. Xi, *Redeemed by Fire*, 2.

6. Sanneh, *Disciples of All Nations*, 266.

7. T. Harvey, *Acquainted with Grief*, 159.

8. "If it is so difficult for an old established church just to maintain itself in the face of Communist atheism, what hope may we have for the 'younger churches,' churches with no long tradition of Christian life to hold their loyalty? If these young churches are subjected to a long period of Communist domination, will they be able to maintain even a bare existence, or must we reconcile ourselves to seeing them blotted out completely?" Jones, *Church in Communist China*, 4.

9. L. Ng, "Christianity and Social Change," 1.

long-continued effort, if measured in numbers of converts, had failed."[10] Yet the Chinese church did not die during the Cultural Revolution.

Instead, it survived and found ripe ground. Today Christianity of many kinds is flourishing there. Christianity fever (基督教热 *Jidujiao re*) has infected the nation. More Chinese have become Christians in the Communist era than all the missionary eras combined. Chinese Christianity has expanded through unregistered "house" churches and through the registered churches within the Three-Self Patriotic Movement. Churches across China were closed during the Cultural Revolution so Christians began meeting in homes. Freed from the constraints of church buildings and ordained clergy, the "underground" church thrived. And it is here, in the house church movement, that Chinese Christianity is growing the fastest. Based on the principles of self-support, self-government and self-propagation, the TSPM forms the state-sanctioned Protestant church in Communist China.[11] The TSPM has acted to both protect and persecute the house churches. Despite the awkward relationship between the registered and unregistered churches in China, the two make for interesting partners and it is through both forms of the church that Christianity has taken root in China. The Middle Kingdom has what the Nestorian, Catholic, and Protestant missionaries of the past longed for: an indigenous church. After centuries of failed attempts, "Christianity in China" has become "Chinese Christianity." Lamin Sanneh notes, "China looks set to become the next frontier of the post-Western Christian resurgence."[12] China will indeed play an important role in the future of world Christianity. Though the unregistered churches provide intriguing research opportunities, this book will focus on the TSPM and the leadership network therein.

## The Aim of this Book

My research centers on how Union Theological Seminary (NY) influenced a group of Chinese Christians in Republican China. The New York seminary played a seminal but unnoticed role in the formation of the TSPM. From its founding, Union's eyes were on the globe. The school's founders sought to create a moderate seminary in the heart of America's most important

10. Fairbank, *Missionary Enterprise*, 1.

11. The Catholic counterpart, the Chinese Patriotic Catholic Association, is outside the scope of this book.

12. Sanneh, "Prospects for Post-Western Christianity," 120.

city that would touch not just the United States but also the entire world. Historians have emphasized the liberalizing role Union played on American Christianity. However they have failed to appreciate Union's influence on the world. Union influenced Christianity in the Middle Kingdom in planned and unplanned ways. The school intended to send missionaries to China and to educate Chinese Christians. But the school could not plan how instrumental it would become in the traffic of liberal Protestantism between the United States and China. The school linked important people and ideas, both Chinese and American, during a tumultuous period of Chinese history: 1911–49. During this time the New York school exported a progressive Christianity, which was both ecumenical and adaptable, to China through the Christian colleges in China and the Young Men's Christian Association (YMCA). In so doing Union helped pour the theological foundations of China's official Protestant organ. Christians connected to Union, the Christian colleges, and the YMCA provided a leadership core in both Republican and Communist China. Few historians—neither Western nor Eastern, religious nor secular—have recognized the breadth and depth of Union's influence. Union propagated a distinct theological vision, but few scholars have recognized this theology as coming from Union.

Union impacted Christianity in Republican China through the publications of its professors and students, through the growing number of Americans who went to China as missionaries, and, most importantly, through the Chinese students trained at the school. I will utilize the social theories of James Davison Hunter and Mark Granovetter to explain Union's influence on China. Hunter suggests that cultures change through a dense network of leaders and Granovetter, that weak social ties play an important role in social networks. This dense leadership network, or nexus, became the core of the SFPE in Republican China and the TSPM in Communist China. Union attracted, funded, and trained many of the key figures in Chinese Protestantism. The broader research question concerns Union's role in the quest for an indigenous Chinese Christianity. The indigenization effort experienced centuries of failure until the end of the twentieth century. Between 1911 and 1949 thirty-nine Chinese Christians attended Union. These men and women had access to the highest echelons of power in both Republican and Communist China. I will explore the role some of these leaders played in indigenizing Chinese Christianity.

## Chapter Structure

To make the connections between Chinese Protestantism and Union Seminary I employ an interdisciplinary approach—weaving through history, education, and theology. Chapter 1, this introduction, sets the stage: examining the surprising growth of Chinese Christianity and the relatively unnoticed connection between Union Seminary and Chinese Christianity. I close the introduction by explaining the historical, sinological, and sociological tools that I use to make my case: Bays's explanation of the Sino-Foreign Protestant Establishment and Hunter's paradigm for social change. Chapter 2 provides a brief survey the history of Christianity in China, so I can appropriately set the context for Christianity in modern China. In chapter 3 I explore Union's history and unique characteristics. Chapter 4 examines Union Seminary's impact in Republican China. I explain its role in the fundamentalist-modernist controversy and the large number of its alumni who went to China as missionaries. These missionaries often served Christian higher education or the Young Men's Christian Association. YMCA leaders and graduates of the Chinese Christian colleges would themselves steam across oceans to attend seminary at Union, such as the founder of the TSPM: Y. T. Wu.

Chapter 5 describes the way Union exerted its most significant impact on China: the formation of a dense social network of Christian leaders. The school linked influential Chinese and American Christians. In short Union generated social capital for its graduates. I examine four influential Americans who were part of that social capital and who were deeply connected with China. This group includes two wealthy businessmen, Henry R. Luce and John D. Rockefeller, Jr., and two Union professors, Harry Emerson Fosdick and Henry Pitney Van Dusen. In describing Rockefeller's connection to China, I rely on Mary Brown Bullock's 2011 *The Oil Prince's Legacy: Rockefeller Philanthropy in China.* While Bullock's study examines the history of Rockefeller's philanthropy in science and medicine in China, I will focus on Rockefeller's involvement in the SFPE via Union Seminary.

Chapters 6 through 8 examine influential Chinese Christians who were educated at Union. Chapter 6 is devoted to K. H. Ting. Born in 1915 in Shanghai, Ting lived at the intersection of China and Western imperialism, and all the agony and advantages that went with both. Much happened in China between Ting's birth in Republican China, his years in North America and Europe, and his return to Communist China in the 1950s. He held leadership positions in many important Christian organizations in twentieth-century China: the Christian Colleges, YMCA, the Episcopal Church in China, Nanjing Union Theological Seminary, the TSPM, and the China Christian Council. Ting represents well the complexity of liberal Chinese Christianity. He sought to be faithful to both the Christian message, as he understood it, and to China.

Chapters 7 and 8 explore two societies of Chinese Christians in the United States: Cross and Sword and the Chinese Students Christian Association. Both societies demonstrate the ambition and interconnectedness of Chinese students in American between 1911 and 1949. This social network included Timothy Tingfang Lew (劉廷芳 *Liu Tingfang*, 1892–1947), William Hung (洪业 *Hong Ye*,1893–1980), Andrew Y. Y. Tsu (朱友渔 *Zhu Yuyue*,1885–1986), and Siu-may Kuo (郭秀梅 *Guo Xiumei*, 1916–95). The case of Lew demonstrates the strong connections between Union and China. While pursuing a PhD from Teachers College from 1918 to 1920, Lew taught at Union, becoming the first Chinese national to teach a subject other than Chinese studies in an American seminary.[13] Lew returned to Manhattan to teach at Union from 1927 to 1928. His classes emphasized principles of indigenization; one lecture examined the three components of "The Indigenous Church in China": self-support, self-government, and self-propagation.[14] This is the earliest instance that I have found of a Chinese scholar teaching the three-self principles in the United States. And it occurs in lectures at Union Theological Seminary by a former Union student.

Chapter 9 assesses the theological influence of Union on Chinese Christians who studied there. I describe three types of Chinese graduates of Union: those who embraced Union's theology, those who rejected it, and those who denied its influence. In the concluding chapter I return to the question of why this research matters, explain the unique contribution herein, and suggest future lines of research. These chapters will describe an important but neglected story in Sino-American relations and in church history. By the end I demonstrate that Union provided key personnel and theological ideas in the two-way traffic of Christianity between China and the United States. Far from being an isolated instance, Ting's education at Union was part of a deliberate effort of the school to engage China. Yet the existing scholarship scarcely mentions this connection. Flip through any

13. Boorman, "Timothy Tingfang Lew," 101. MRL 6: Timothy Tingfang Lew Papers, ser. 1, box 1, folder 2, Burke Library, Union Theological Seminary, NY.

14. 1927–28 lecture notes. MRL 6: Timothy Tingfang Lew Papers, ser. 3, box 1, folder 3, Burke Library, Union Theological Seminary, NY.

history of Christianity in modern China and there is no mention of Union Seminary.[15] If mentioned it is in relation to the controversy surrounding Chinese evangelist John Sung (宋尚節 *Song Shangjie*, 1901–44). Based on my archival findings, the current historiography regarding Sung's time at Union and in the Bloomingdale Asylum needs to be reassessed. In chapter 9 I will offer a new account of his Sung's time in New York. The extent of Union's influence has gone unnoticed because the correlation is difficult to explain. Like an iceberg, Union's role in Chinese Christianity is substantial but difficult to see from the surface. Even Ting's close friend and biographer, Philip L. Wickeri, downplays Union's role.

## Sources of Information

This book relies on Wickeri's historical research; however, I disagree with his analysis of Union's impact on Ting. He first met Ting in 1979 in New Jersey when he was a doctoral student at Princeton Theological Seminary. After Wickeri served as interpreter at an international conference, Ting invited him to come to Nanjing University to teach English. He went to Nanjing in 1981. During his two years there he met with Ting weekly. Wickeri's research in Ting's home and in the library at Nanjing Union Theological Seminary became the core of his doctoral thesis.[16] In 1991 Wickeri became the only non-Chinese to be ordained in the TSPM. I am indebted to Wickeri's personal advice and his research. While leaning heavily on his scholarship, I do so cautiously.

The strength and weakness of Wickeri's research stems from his long friendship with Ting. Wickeri admits that his "close working relationship" with Ting has shaped his views but he attempts to be "sympathetic, but not without critical assessment."[17] The other monograph of Ting's life, Jia Ma's *Discerning Truth through Love* (*Ai shi zhenli*), is based on nine interviews with Ting between 2000 and 2005. Ma provides a good analysis of Ting based on Ting's recent writings. However, the backbone of his research is conversations with a calculating public figure with his legacy in mind.

15. Bays, *New History of Christianity;* A. Hunter and Chan, *Protestantism in Contemporary China.*

16. Wickeri, *Seeking the Common Ground.* This book examines the crucial role of the United Front Work Department (UFWD) in setting religions policy in a communist state.

17. Wickeri, *Reconstructing Christianity in China*, 9.

Wickeri's book provides deeper and more personal insight. But his analysis suffers from this close proximity to his subject. Wickeri glosses over important questions regarding Union: he seems satisfied with Ting's dismissal of Union's influence. I argue later that Ting himself did not fully appreciate how Union impacted him. The influence came largely through a dense social network long before Ting arrived in New York City. Additionally, Wickeri seems to view the Chinese Communist Party as benevolent and to scorn house churches and their conservative theology. Hunter and Chan suggest that Wickeri "gives a far more positive assessment of the CCP and its religious policies than most analysts."[18]

Wickeri argues that other factors diminished any deep contribution made by Union. He believes that Ting's Anglican formation, his involvement in the Student Christian Movement, and his theological views in relation to his social setting "mitigated against the theological outlook that Union had to offer." Wickeri adds: "He was interested in what his teachers had to say, but there is no evidence that he was particularly attracted to the thinking of Union's leading Protestant theologians, or to van Dusen's ecumenical vision."[19] No existing scholarship can match Wickeri for his insight into Ting. However, I think he is wrong on this point regarding Union. This book contends that Union impacted Ting's theological views long before he even arrived in New York, largely through Union's dense social network in China's Christian colleges and the Chinese YMCA. The seminary helped train leaders of these institutions who imparted a particular theological framework even before Ting walked onto Union's campus in Manhattan's Upper West Side. Later in this introduction I will offer a sociological framework to help position Union at the center of a web of influential Christians in China and, in chapter 4, I will use archival data to make this case. Despite being missed by most scholars, one scholar has recognized Union's role in the TSPM.

Xu Yihua of Fudan University in Shanghai argues that Union—"one of the best and most liberal Protestant seminaries in the United States"—played a vital role in the development of twentieth-century Chinese Protestantism.[20] In the area of theological education Union was the most influential of American institutions on China. Before the formation of the People's Republic of China in 1949, Union accepted more Chinese students

18. A. Hunter and Chan, *Protestantism in Contemporary China*, 58.

19. Wickeri, *Reconstructing Christianity in China*, 72.

20. Y. Xu, "Union Theological Seminary," 11.

than any other theological seminary or divinity school in the United States. These Union-trained Chinese theologians became the leaders in the TSPM. Union exerted "an extensive impact on the Christian church in China" through its training program for foreign missions, prestigious faculty, and recruitment of Chinese students.[21] Despite Union's deep connections with the Protestant movement in Republican China, the link between Union and China is "barely mentioned in the previous literature on Union."[22] I agree with Xu: Union "strengthened the liberal wing of Chinese Protestantism, which was primarily responsible for forming the TSPM after Communist take over."[23] But up to this point this fact has not been properly studied. Xu alerted the academic community to the need and importance of this research, which I now pick up.

Even the institutional histories of Union Theological Seminary fail to appreciate the depth of the seminary's impact in China. To date, three histories have been written of the New York school, all by Union faculty members: George Lewis Prentiss (1889), Henry Sloan Coffin (1954), and Robert Handy (1987).[24] Not surprisingly, Prentiss emphasizes the key reasons for the founding of the seminary. Union wanted to be an institution that grappled with the greatest social and scientific problems of its time "armed with such Christian moderation, both of opinion and feeling."[25] Even in 1889, Prentiss lists the Union alumni who become missionaries between 1838 and 1884. Coffin's 1954 history also emphasizes Union's role in world service. Because he served as president of Union from 1926 to 1945, Coffin offers a perspective relevant to my research. The most thorough and helpful history, however, is from church historian Robert T. Handy. Handy explains how many Union professors in the nineteenth century studied in Germany and then brought this continental theology to the United States. As I later demonstrate, a stream of nineteenth-century German theology flowed to twentieth-century China through Union Seminary. Since all three histories come from the pens of Union faculty, they suffer from a lack of critical and distanced evaluation. All three books highlight Union's ambition to influence the world. My study analyzes the fulfillment of that vision in the case

21. Y. Xu, "Union Theological Seminary," 23.
22. Y. Xu, "Union Theological Seminary," 11.
23. Y. Xu, "'Patriotic' Protestants," 114.
24. Prentiss, *Union Theological Seminary*; Coffin, *Half-Century*; Handy, *History*.
25. Prentiss, *Union Theological Seminary*, 85.

of China. I use particular sinological and sociological tools to make my argument. And it is to those tools that I now turn.

## Methods of Analysis

### Collecting Primary Historical Data

To explain how Union Seminary impacted Chinese Christianity, I utilize an interdisciplinary approach. Fundamentally this research is historical theology but it straddles the fields of history, theology, education, and sociology. My interest in Union Seminary's connection to China began in 2002 when I taught English at Nanjing University. One of my colleagues in the School of Foreign Studies happened to be Bishop Ting's son, Stephen Yenren Ting (丁言仁 *Ding Yan Ren*, 1948–), who was born in New York City. When I realized that both K. H. Ting and Y. T. Wu had studied at Union, my curiosity soared. I began this study intending to focus on how Union influenced just one Chinese Christian: K. H. Ting. In my optimism and naïveté, I imagined that I would find historical treasures in Union's archives to document how the seminary influenced Ting. I contacted the staff at Union's Burke Library. Their response transformed the direction of this book in two important ways.

First, I realized that Ting's student records at Union were not accessible. This information is protected both by the Family Educational Rights and Privacy Act (FERPA) in the United States and by the seminary's policy. Union will release student records upon inquiry only if the person attended seventy-five or more years ago and has since died. So, Ting's records at Union were not yet available. Second, the school emailed me a digital edition of its alumni directory spanning 1836 to 1958.[26] The digital format allowed me to quickly search the entire directory for any mention of China. I identified any Union alumni connected with China, focusing on those graduating between 1911 and 1949. I transferred this list to a spreadsheet then ranked each alumni on a scale of 1–5.[27] My research then centered on individuals rated 4 or 5, Chinese and American Christians who spent most of their careers in China and held prominent roles in the SFPE. This

26. Union Theological Seminary, *Union Theological Seminary Alumni.*

27. My rating system followed these criteria: 1—alumni in China for one year or less; 2—alumni in China for two to three years; 3—alumni in China for three to five years; 4—alumni in China for five to twenty years; 5—alumni who were Chinese nationals or others who lived in China for over twenty years.

rating system focused my data collection in archives around the world. I gathered the most important and relevant data in the Special Collections at Yale Divinity School Library and the Burke Library Archives (Columbia University Libraries) at Union Theological Seminary, New York. But I also found helpful documents in the Rare Books and Manuscript Collection at Columbia University, the Shanghai Municipal Archives, the Archives at the University of Toronto, the China Inland Mission Archives at the School of Oriental and African Studies in London, the Archives of the Episcopal Church in Austin, and the Kautz Family Archives at the University of Minnesota. My research findings, including the limitations regarding Ting's records, transformed my fundamental research question. I began with a focus on one Chinese Christian and ended with an intricate network of influential Chinese and American Christians. To explain this network and its influence I utilized insight from Daniel Bays, James Davison Hunter, and Mark Granovetter.

## Locating Union Sinologically: Bays

In 2012 Daniel H. Bays summarized a lifetime of research in one short volume, *A New History of Christianity in China.* The former professor at Calvin College covered the entire field of Christianity in China, addressing current and past scholarship in the field. While his work lacks the philosophical sophistication of Jacques Gernet's *China and the Christian Impact: A Conflict of Cultures* (1985) or, to a lesser extent, Bob Whyte's *Unfinished Encounter: China and Christianity* (1988), Bays makes up for this in breadth and accessibility. Bays excels in his study of twentieth-century Chinese Protestantism. While much of the research has centered on foreign missionaries in China, Bays highlights the need for greater attention to be given to the native Christians.

> But the other, and arguably more important, piece of the picture was the rise of Chinese Christians in the joint Sino-foreign endeavor to establish and nurture the faith in Chinese soil. This process was characterized by a persistent, overriding dynamic: the Chinese Christians were first participants, then subordinate partners of the foreign missionaries, then finally the inheritors or sole "owners" of the Chinese church. It was also a "cross-cultural

> process," the result of which has been the creation of an immensely varied Chinese Christian world in our day.[28]

Bays coined a helpful phrase to describe the Chinese Christians and foreign missionaries who interacted in this "joint Sino-foreign endeavor": the Sino-Foreign Protestant Establishment. At the turn of the nineteenth century, certain missionaries rose to positions of prominence—"due to factors of status, tradition and force of personality, eloquence and persuasiveness, or control of resources or access to resources"—and formed an elite policy-setting and decision-making body.[29] By 1910 the Protestant missionary establishment had solidified in China. The SFPE, most notably Henry Venn (1796–1873) and Rufus Anderson (1796–88), emphasized indigenous leadership, or "native agency." Anderson suggested that the Chinese church should be self-supporting, self-governing and self-propagating. Western missionaries, though, operated under no urgent timetable to transfer power to their Eastern subordinates.

The process of indigenizing the Protestant establishment in China had four distinct phases from 1) foreign establishment to 2) foreign-Sino to 3) Sino-foreign to 4) Chinese. For Chinese Christians to enter this process they needed to be incorporated into the foreign establishment. Within China the network of Christian schools and the YMCA provided an entry point into that establishment. Bays notes: "It is true that steadily after 1910 annually several brilliant Chinese graduates of the missions school system went abroad, mainly to the US, and gained PhD or DD degrees, returning to prestigious positions in the Christian colleges and middle schools."[30] Bays recognizes the important role of American institutions of higher education in giving Chinese access and respect within the SFPE. However, he only mentions Union Theological Seminary in connection with the mental and spiritual crisis of the evangelist John Sung. In this latest work on Chinese Christianity, Union Seminary's important role has, once again, gone unnoticed. The following pages will demonstrates the school's role in educating key American and Chinese leaders in the SFPE. To describe Union's influence on China, I utilize Bays's historical framework of the SFPE. To analyze Union's influence on China, however, I utilize the work of two sociologists: James Davison Hunter and Mark Granovetter.

28. Bays, *New History of Christianity*, 1.

29. Bays, *New History of Christianity*, 100.

30. Bays, *New History of Christianity*, 101.

## Describing Union's Influence Sociologically: Hunter and Granovetter

In his 2010 book *To Change the World*, Hunter critiqued the common view that the history of the world is the biography of great men. Instead, he argued: "*the key actor in history is not individual genius but rather the network* and the new institutions that are created out of these networks."[31] These networks are more influential, more world changing, when they are more active and interactive (or, dense). Mark Granovetter's 1973 article, "The Strength of Weak Ties," broke new ground in how relational networks were understood. He demonstrated how weak ties play a crucial social role in linking groups of close friends. Weak ties allow disparate groups of people to connect into a broader, more global network of relationships.[32] In chapters 5 through 8, I apply these theories to Union to explain the depth of the seminary's influence on Chinese Protestantism. In this book I use Hunter and Granovetter's ideas to demonstrate how a network of elites clustered around the Christian Colleges in China, the YMCA, and Union Seminary. These leaders brought profound change into Chinese Protestantism.

## Final Research Considerations

The source material I collected in archives around the world has driven my research. As I photographed and, to a lesser extent, photocopied thousands of pages of letters, class notes, articles, lists, grade reports, and other materials, the connections between Union Seminary and prominent Chinese and American Christians became clear. The ideas of Bays, Hunter, and Granovetter provided a framework to explain the connections. I combined their theories, borrowing key ideas to apply to my archival findings. In so doing, the impact of Union came to light and allowed me to select prominent figures in Chinese Christianity as case studies. I limited my selection to those for whom I had relevant, and at times new, source data. I conducted my research primarily using documents in English, for this is where the data led me. Chinese was used to a lesser extent. Throughout this book, Chinese names and proper nouns will be Romanized into the now-standard *pinyin* except when individuals were known to prefer the older Wade-Giles style. K. H. Ting will be identified as such rather than as *Ding*

31. J. Hunter, *To Change the World*, 38 (emphasis his).

32. Granovetter, "Strength of Weak Ties" (1983), 202.

*Guangxun* but Peking will be called Beijing; Canton, Guangzhou, and so forth. Upon first usage, Chinese names, places, and historical events will be written both in Chinese characters and an alternate form of Romanization in parenthesis in the body of the text. Appendix A is a list of prominent Chinese names in this book.

### *Summary*

Union-educated leaders rose to positions of prominence and exerted a large influence on Chinese Protestantism because they held cultural and symbolic capital. Scholarship on Christianity in twentieth-century China has failed to recognize the extent of Union's influence because researchers have not been looking from the right perspective. I am not suggesting that the connections are difficult to see. Just a bit of historical digging and the archival shovel soon hits the connections, as Xu Yihua has demonstrated. Hunter's cultural theory is not the only lens through which we can see Union's importance in the SFPE. However, his suggestion that change comes via a dense, interconnected network of leaders helps explain Union's importance far more than previous histories. Bays's idea of the SFPE provides a historical framework and Hunter's ideas offer a cultural lens to sharpen the picture. Union sat, intentionally, at the intersection of two-way traffic between Chinese and American Christianity

Union's influence on the SFPE fills in a missing piece of the Sino-American puzzle. W. H. Griffith Thomas wrote about Union's influence on Chinese Protestantism in 1921.[33] The seminary impacted China through sending missionaries, especially into China's schools and colleges; through educating Chinese Christians in those schools and in New York; through the writing and teaching of its professors and alumni; and in providing a dense social network. My distinct contribution lies in this last point. Union's theological impact on Chinese Christians makes for an interesting study but both Y. T. Wu and K. H. Ting were loath to admit any influence from the New York seminary. Admittedly, there is a level of ambiguity in assessing how an institution "impacts" the thinking of certain individuals, especially if they do not explicitly acknowledge this influence. In these pages I explore how Union's progressive theological framework enabled Wu and Ting to adapt Christianity to adhere to the CCP's United Front ideology. From Union directly and indirectly from the Christian colleges

33. Thomas, "Modernism in China."

and Ys, Chinese Christians absorbed a particular theological framework that allowed them to reconstruct Christian belief. The Three-Self Movement might be self-governing, self-supporting, and self-propagating but is it self-theologizing? Or does it borrow from other theological traditions? I contend that the TSPM owes a greater debt to Union Seminary and its liberal interpretation of Christianity than previously recognized. In the next chapter I will set the context of twentieth-century Chinese Protestantism by summarizing the history of Christianity in China.

# 2

# Christianity in China

THROUGHOUT THE MILLENNIA CHINA has been one of the world's greatest empires. Two thousand years ago the Middle Kingdom rivaled the Roman Empire in wealth and civilization and, seven hundred years later, the expanse and greatness of the Arabs. In the eleventh century China flourished in art, philosophy, and trade. In 1600 the Chinese population of 120 million far exceeded that of all the European countries combined, making China the "largest and most sophisticated of all the unified realms on earth."[1] This chapter examines the history of Christianity in China. I will describe the various attempts and subsequent failures to establish an indigenous Chinese church. Christianity has struggled to endure in Chinese soil. This backstory makes the growth of Christianity in modern China all the more fascinating. Later I demonstrate how Union Seminary helped "Christianity in China" become "Chinese Christianity."

## Tang Christianity: Alopen and the Nestorians Arrive in AD 635

China's "religious" history stretches back to AD 150.[2] Buddhist monks from Northern India and Tibet brought their religion as they spread throughout China. The Himalayas are steep so the migration was slow. Buddhist ideas seeped into the Chinese hinterland and formed an alloy with traditional Chinese thinking (Daoism). Lars Laaman identifies the characteristic elements of Chinese religion as respect and fear of nature and the souls of ancestors and an awareness that all life is separated between life on earth

1. Spence, *Search for Modern China*, 7.

2. Translating the Latin concept of *religere* into Chinese is not easy. The Chinese term 教 (*jiao*) does not distinguish between religion and philosophy. *Jiao* means "the teaching of a particular person." Thus, there is not a simple demarcation in Chinese between religion and philosophy.

(地 *di*) and above earth (天 *tian*).[3] There was no concept of God but only of heaven. Only the son of heaven, the emperor, could sacrifice to heaven. The "Three Teachings" (三教 *San Jiao*) of Daoism, Buddhism, and Confucianism provided China's religious and philosophical bedrock. Into this environment missionaries from the Church of the East (Nestorians) arrived in Xi'an in AD 635.[4]

Emperor Taizhong ordered the Christian Scriptures, which Bishop Alopen's band had carried along the Silk Road from Persia, to be translated. The emperor read the translated text and issued an edict in 638 praising Alopen "the man of great virtue" and his mysterious message, which is "wonderful beyond our understanding." Taizhong believed the teaching would "benefit all" and should be "practiced throughout the land."[5] Tang Christianity had a 107-year lifespan. In the first half of the eighth century Confucianists sought to curtail the growing power of the Buddhist monasteries. The throne issued a decree in 845, the "Edict of the Eighth Month," castigating Buddhism for "instilling its infection with every opportunity, spreading like a luxuriant vine, until it has poisoned the customs of our nation."[6] The emperor decided to eradicate Buddhism. The emperor added: "We have ordered more than 2,000 men of the Nestorians and Mazdean religions to return to lay life and to cease polluting the customs of China."[7] Tang Christianity had aligned itself too closely with the Tang state. The Nestorians' faith was a marginal religion that never achieved a prominent role in Tang society. When it fell out of imperial favor, it vanished. Tang Christianity was not indigenous; it did not endure.

3. Laaman, "Christianity in China."

4. Discovered in the 1620s near Xi'an, a nine-foot marble stele told the story in 1800 Chinese characters of the Nestorian church in the Tang dynasty. The title at the top of the stele reads "A Monument Commemorating the Propagation of the Da-Qin (Syrian) Luminous Religion in China" or, in Bays's translation, "The Story of the Coming of the Religion of Light from the West to China." The stele, capped with a cross rising from a lotus blossom, describes the arrival in Xi'an of Bishop Alopen and his delegation. Bays, *New History of Christianity*, 7.

5. Palmer, *Jesus Sutras*, 43. Cited in Bays, *New History of Christianity*, 9.

6. de Bary and Bloom, *From Earliest Times*, 585.

7. de Bary and Bloom, *From Earliest Times*, 586.

## Yuan Christianity: The Khans Marry the Christian Keraits

Nestorian Christianity returned to the Middle Kingdom via the Mongols in the thirteenth and fourteenth centuries. As Persian Christians plied the trade routes between the Mediterranean world and China, they brought their faith to the Keraits, a Turko-Mongolian tribe. Within a century most of the 200,000-member clan had become Christian. They formed alliances with other Mongol tribes, including the subclan of Genghis Khan (1162–1227). Genghis turned the disparate Mongol tribes into a fierce war machine and their territory grew. He took three daughters of the Kerait royal family, marrying one himself and giving the other two in marriage to his oldest and fourth sons. The Christian wife of Genghis's fourth son became the mother of Kublai Khan (1215–1294), the founding emperor of the Yuan dynasty (1271–1368).

Between 1245 and 1253 Pope Innocent IV commissioned two Franciscan missions to the Mongols. The friars made it to the Mongolian capital and returned to Rome two years later, where they explained the prevalence of Nestorian Christianity among Mongol leaders. Roman Catholic emissaries would not return to China for fifty years. By this time Kublai Khan had defeated the Song dynasty and established the Yuan, placing his capital in Khanbaliq (Dadu, the site of modern-day Beijing). Between these Catholic visits to China in the thirteenth century Nestorians controlled Christianity in China. But the Nestorian's faith remained a Mongol religion. Venetian traders, such as Marco Polo's father and uncle, traveled to China during Kublai Khan's reign.[8] Eventually Catholic missionaries arrived. Giovanni da Montecorvino arrived in the Yuan capital in 1293. By 1305 he claimed six thousand baptisms. Montecorvino's success caught Rome's attention. They began sending more missionaries, evoking the ire of Chinese Nestorians. Both Nestorian and Catholic Christianity existed until the collapse of the Yuan dynasty in 1368. And then it disappeared: "Ming dynasty sources have no reference whatsoever to Yuan Christian's fate."[9] The Mongol rulers had protected Christianity in Yuan China. When the xenophobic Ming began it died out. As in the Tang dynasty, Yuan Christianity left little enduring mark on China. No indigenous church remained. Christianity's third foray into

8. Marco Polo's stories of China, *Description of the World* (1298), gripped European imagination.

9. Bays, *New History of Christianity*, 14.

China would not come for two hundred more years but this time it would become fixed into Chinese culture.

## Ming Christianity: The Jesuits Engage the Highest Levels of Society

In 1534, as the Roman Catholic church struggled to respond to Martin Luther in Germany, Ignatius of Loyola (1491–1556) gathered with six other students at Montmartre in Paris. Inflamed by a drastic conversion experience Ignatius wanted to rescue Catholicism from Luther. These seven students from the University of Paris called themselves the Company of Jesus. Six years later Pope Paul III officially regularized the group as the Society of Jesus. The Jesuits, as they would be known, had three primary goals: education, missions, and stopping the spread of Protestantism. The Spanish and Portuguese Empires had divided the world into two spheres: the West belonged to Spain; the East, to Portugal. In 1515 Pope Leo X granted rights of patronage, control over missions, to Portugal in the route East, and to Spain in the Western route. Silver in Japan lured Portuguese fleets to Asia. A founding member of the Jesuits, Francis Xavier (1506–1552), sailed to the East Indies on one of these Portuguese ships.[10] After a time in Goa he pioneered the Jesuit mission to Japan in 1549. But Xavier died three years later on Shangchuan Island (上川岛 *Shangchuandao*). He never entered the land of his dreams, mainland China. While the Jesuit mission flourished in Japan, they could not even enter the Middle Kingdom. All this changed in 1582. Michele Ruggieri (1543–1607) won permission to reside outside Guangzhou and to learn Chinese.[11] Eventually a fellow Italian Jesuit joined Ruggieri. This man, Matteo Ricci (1552–1610), would become the most famous Western missionary in Chinese history.[12]

Possessed of a brilliant mind Ricci carried out the Jesuit policies—accommodation to Chinese culture and evangelization from the top of society down—to perfection. Ricci shaved his head and beard and donned the

10. "[Spanish and Portuguese] ships not only dominated the trading routes, but the (at least simulated) piety of the rulers and the ship owners and captains as well meant that when needed, transportation for missionaries to get to their assigned mission field would be available." Bays, *New History of Christianity*, 20.

11. Y. Liu, "True Pioneer," 362.

12. See Spence, *Memory Palace*; and "Madness of the Wise: Ricci in China," in Leys, *Burning Forest*, 35–46.

robes of a Chinese intellectual. He used his impressive intellect to win favor of the elite, dazzling the literati at dinner parties with his memory skills. He would examine a list of five hundred Chinese characters once and then repeat the list in reverse order or recite volumes of Chinese classics after scanning them once.[13] Ricci set his sights on the imperial court and made it to Beijing in 1602, the first for a Western missionary in Ming China. Ricci presented European clocks, a steel-string fiddle, and a world map to the Emperor Wan Li. The Jesuit community in Beijing translated Western works of astronomy, geography, and mathematics into Chinese. Life in the capital city gave Ricci access to the highest of Chinese officials where he converted "three pillars" of the church: Xu Guangqi (徐光啟,1562–1633), Li Zhizao (李之藻, 1565–1630), and Yang Tinyun (杨廷筠, 1562–1627). Other Catholic orders began sending missionaries to China. In the 1630s the Jesuit dominance ended. When the Manchu's overthrew the Ming rulers in 1644, the change had little effect on the Catholic mission. Adam Schall von Bell demonstrated Western advances in science and astronomy to the new Qing leaders, winning their favor. Some Jesuits attainted official positions in the Office of Astronomy, where they helped revise the calendar. The number of Catholic missionaries grew under the open-minded and inquisitive Kangxi emperor in the 1680s and 90s, spurred by Kangxi's 1692 edict of toleration for missions and Christianity. By the end of the seventeenth century Christianity in Japan and China had switched places: an eradication campaign had destroyed Christianity in Japan but there were over 150,000 Catholics in China. This growth came to a sudden halt in 1704 with the devastating Rites Controversy.

The core of this bitter conflict involved the Chinese names for God and the rituals used to honor ancestors. Should God be described as Heavenly Ruler (天主 *tian zhu)*, Emperor on High (上帝 *shang di)*, or Spirit/God (神 *shen*)? And could Christians partake in ancestor veneration (令牌 *ling pai*)? The internecine conflict pitted the accommodating Jesuits against the mendicant Catholic orders, who were opposed to ancestor worship and believed the indigenous Chinese names for God tainted the God of the Bible. "Intermingled on both sides with the higher motives of sincerity, good intentions and spiritual commitment were the baser attitudes of jealousy, vindictiveness and European chauvinism," explains D. E. Mungello. "Impelled by powerful cultural and political forces arrayed against the Jesuits,

13. Spence, *Memory Palace*, 9.

the papacy ruled against accommodation."[14] Pope Clement XI dispatched Charles-Thomas Maillard de Tournon (1668–1701) to deliver *Ex illa die.* Tournon's attitude, displaying arrogance toward the missionaries and disrespect of the emperor, and his message infuriated the Son of Heaven.

The pope miscalculated how personally vested Kangxi had become in this issue. Edward J. Maletesta argues that the controversy happened because the emperor deeply cared about the issues. While he could have dismissed the whole rites affair as nonsense and expelled the Dominicans and Franciscans, instead he "agonized, argued, cajoled, engaged himself actively in the matter while complaining about his poor health and physical pain."[15] The frustration and anger that the Kangxi emperor felt at the pope's decision led to a turning point in the history of Sino-Western relations. In 1706 Kangxi decreed that all missionaries would be examined and only those who agreed with "the policies of Matteo Ricci" would be able to remain in China. Everyone else would be deported. Tournon responded with a decree to the missionaries dictating exactly how they were to respond. In 1724 Kangxi's son, the Yongzheng emperor, rescinded the 1692 edict for the toleration of Christianity. Yongzheng outlawed Christianity, labeling it an "evil cult" that subverted Chinese culture. Catholic Christianity had established a foothold among the Chinese but Western missionaries, this time Protestant ones, would not return until the nineteenth century.[16]

## Qing Christianity: Protestant Missions into China

During the long eighteenth century Britain surpassed Spain, Portugal, and France to become the world's naval superpower. In 1807 Robert Morrison (1782–1834) of the London Missionary Society arrived in Guangzhou.[17]

14. Mungello, "Introduction to Chinese Rites," 4.

15. Spence, "Claims and Counter-Claims," 22. Transcription of speech by Edward J. Malatesta, SJ.

16. I want to acknowledge, while not going into detail, the presence of Russian Orthodoxy in China in the mid-seventeenth century. The Russian Orthodox Church focused on cities in northern China, such as Heilongjiang and Beijing. In 1715 the Russian Czar sent a mission to Beijing, which was led by Archimandrite Ilarion. The Beijing Mission became official after the Treaty of Kiakhta in 1727 and served as Russia's unofficial diplomatic mission in China until 1864. See Widmer, *Russian Ecclesiastical Mission*, and Doubrovskaia, "Russian Orthodox Church."

17. See Hancock, *Robert Morrison*; Daily, *Robert Morrison*; Doyle, *Builders of Chinese Church.*

Unlike the free rides offered to Jesuits on Portuguese vessels, the British East India Company offered Morrison no such favor. He traveled on an American ship. After arriving he began compiling a Chinese-English dictionary and translating the Bible into Chinese. The Canton System limited Morrison and other foreigners to Guangzhou for certain periods of the year and forbade them from learning Chinese. Mainland China felt little of Morrison's impact during his lifetime. But he introduced China to the West, especially Victorian England. Other Western missionaries followed Morrison to China but not many.[18] From 1807 to 1839 fifty missionaries were assigned to China and only a few stayed for any length of time.[19] But after 1839 the number of Western missionaries in China changed drastically. The Middle Kingdom opened to the West in unprecedented ways. Sadly it was the Opium Wars and the ensuing unequal treaties that pried China open.

In 1810 the Qing leaders declared opium to be a poison that undermined morality and banned the drug. The decree had little effect and opium trade rose steeply. China wanted the British East India Company to stop selling opium in China. But they refused. Over time the opium trade had become critical in Victorian foreign policy. It provided vast revenue for Britain and played an important part in the nation's international balance-of-payments. War loomed between the superpowers over the opium trade. China's leaders underestimated the power of Britain's navy. Britain's force of arms easily outmatched the Qing response. The British imposed a treaty in 1842 that fundamentally altered how China related with foreign powers. China's emperors had always dictated terms for foreigners on their soil but no more. The Treaty of Nanjing ended the Canton System; opened the door for more opium trade; ceded territory (such as Hong Kong); granted extraterritorial rights to foreigners in China; and set tariffs at a low, fixed rate.[20] Bob Whyte assesses 1839–42 correctly: "The scandalous trade in opium, pushed by the East India Company with the open connivance of the British Government, was the excuse used for the forcible opening of

18. The London Missionary Society sent William Milne (1785–1822) to join Morrison in 1813, the Netherlands Foreign Missionary Society sent Karl Gützlaff (1803–51) in 1827, and the American Board of Commissioners for Foreign Missions sent Elijah Coleman Bridgman (1801–61) in 1830.

19. Bays, *New History of Christianity*, 46.

20. See Wood, "Treaty of Nanking," 181.

China to foreign trade."[21] The First Opium War poisoned Chinese views of the Christian West.[22]

Western nations turned, naturally, to those fluent in Chinese to help as translators on the treaties: the missionaries. Robert Morrison served as the Chinese secretary and chief interpreter of the Treaty of Nanjing, with assistance from the controversial German missionary Karl Gützlaff.[23] One of the first American missionaries to China, the physician Peter Parker, served as the Chinese interpreter to the American delegate at the Treaty of Wangxia, the first Sino-American Unequal Treaty, in 1844.[24] Bays correctly notes: "It is striking how natural it was for missionaries to enlist themselves in a project that essentially put China permanently in a handicapped position of inequality, unable to pursue her own national goals."[25] Article 17 of Wangxia limited missionaries to five treaty ports in China: Shanghai, Guangzhou, Fuzhou, Ningbo, and Xiamen. Even though missionaries were not allowed into China's interior, in 1854 Father Auguste Chapdelaine traveled into Guangxi Province to celebrate Mass.[26] In February 1856 he was arrested by a local official, then beaten and killed. France, eager to extend their empire in China, used Chapdelaine's murder to initiate war with China. Another opium war followed from 1856 to 1860 with similar results. This time France, and its Treaty of Tianjin, humiliated China.

The various unequal treaties shamed China on a global stage.[27] But these treaties allowed missionaries to penetrate China's interior. For many Chinese, even today, missionaries "served colonialism and the forces of colonialism supported the missionary work with their armed might."[28] The

21. Whyte, *Unfinished Encounter*, 102.

22. Sneller, "Take Away Your Opium," 20.

23. See Lutz, *Opening China*.

24. See Gulick, *Peter Parker and Opening*; Anderson, "Peter Parker and Introduction."

25. Bays, *New History of Christianity*, 59.

26. In 1900 the Roman Catholic Church beatified Chapdelaine. Exactly one hundred years later Pope John Paul II canonized Chapdelaine, along with 120 other Christian marytrs in China.

27. In the nineteenth century the treaties included the Treaties of: the Bogue (1843), Wanghia (1844), Whampoa (1844), Canton (1847), Kulja (1851), Aigun (1858), Tientsin (1858, 1861, 1885), Saint Petersburg (1881), Peking (1887), Maguan (1895), and Li-Lobanov (1896); and the Conventions of Peking (1860) and Chefoo (1876).

28. Luo, *Religion under Socialism*, 42. Using a Marxist viewpoint and guided by the CCP's Third Plenum, a group of Chinese academics at the Institute for Research on Religion of the Shanghai Academy of Social Sciences produced this study of religion in China.

Unequal Treaties stirred deep anti-foreign sentiment that would explode in 1900 when "the spears of the peasant insurgents were directed against the imperial powers who had made use of religion to invade China."[29] In due time I will describe the Boxer Uprising but, first, the missionaries. Despite crippling the Chinese psyche the Unequal Treaties opened up doors for Western missionaries in unprecedented ways.

Now foreigners were able to travel through the entire country and buy property in China. The number of missionaries in China leapt from 100 in 1860 to 3500 in 1905. While China slumped in the nineteenth century Great Britain surged to the height of its imperial power. Victorian England proved eager to spread Protestantism to the far corners of its empire. British Christians had the passion and, following the Industrial Revolution, the funding to become overseas missionaries.[30] The missionary movement started through societies established by the institutional churches in England, such as the London Missionary Society (LMS) and Church Missionary Society (CMS). But in 1865 a physician from northern England changed missions. J. Hudson Taylor (1832–1905) went to China in 1854 after being inspired by Karl Gützlaff. Taylor returned to England in 1859 and founded China Inland Mission (CIM) six years later. CIM differed from other mission societies. They appointed unordained laypersons as missionaries (including single women), focused on the unreached parts of rural China, wore native dress, and did not directly solicit funds. Enflamed by deep conviction—"The Great Commission is not an option to be considered; it is a commandment to be obeyed"—Taylor urged British Christians to become missionaries to "China's millions." Admitting unordained Christians of all social classes provided Taylor with a broad recruiting base. Taylor's first group of twenty-two people joined him in China in 1866, expanding to 322 missionaries in 1888 and 825 by 1905 (almost three times larger than the next biggest in England, the CMS).[31] In 1884 he recruited seven aristocratic Cambridge graduates to join CIM.[32] The story of the "Cambridge Seven," *The Evangelisation of the Word: A Missionary Band*, became a national

29. Luo, *Religion under Socialism*, 42.

30. Jessie Lutz makes an intriguing point: "There is a striking correlation between those nations which were industrialized earliest and most completely and those nations which were leaders in mission work." Lutz, *China and Christian Colleges*, 5.

31. Jesus's instruction in Matt 28:18–20 to "make disciples of all nations."

32. C. T. Studd, M. H. P. Beauchamp, S. P. Smith, A. T. Polhill-Turner, D. E. Hoste, C. H. Polhill-Turner, W. W. Cassels. See Austin, *China's Millions*.

bestsellerer and helped influence the Student Volunteer Movement for Foreign Missions (SVM) in the United States.

Organized in 1886, the SVM sought to recruit student volunteers for overseas missionary service.[33] Young men and women vowed: "It is my purpose, if God permit, to become a foreign missionary." Tapping into a surge of piety and a deep sense of religious duty on college campuses, the SVM captivated a whole generation of young American Christians with a global vision.[34] Between 1890 and 1920, 33,726 students volunteered to join the SVM. Student volunteers accounted for half of all the American Protestant missionaries of this period. Skilled communicators, like John R. Mott (1865–1955) and Sherwood Eddy (1871–1963), led the SVM to thirty years of rising success. Recruiters grabbed the imaginations of young American Christians by appealing to a sense of adventure and sacrifice. They avoided zealots or fanatics, for there were always more recruits than positions. Terrill E. Lautz comments: "The SVM represented a true impulse of idealistic internationalism, one that was profoundly disillusioned by the narrow nationalisms of the Great War and the destructive horrors to which it gave rise."[35] Potential volunteers were warned of the dangers and seriousness of foreign missions. Yet students applied in droves because they believed it was the noblest thing they could commit their lives to. The CIM in England and SVM in the United States represented a new surge of missionaries going to China at a critical time in history. SVM leaders came from universities and YMCA/YWCAs in the West and, in reverse fashion, the SVM provided leadership to the Ys and Christian colleges in China.

While the number of missionaries skyrocketed in late Qing China, Christianity remained on the periphery of Chinese society. Foreigners were able to travel and buy property but the Chinese elite despised them. The number of Protestant Chinese Christians numbered in the hundreds in 1860; by 1900, this number had grown to 100,000. Gary Tiedemann identifies three reasons Chinese converted to Christianity: material incentives (jobs, education, medical care), sociopolitical incentives (new social networks), and spiritual incentives (peace, eternal happiness).[36] Generally

33. For a history of the SVM see Parker, *Kingdom of Character*; or, for an emphasis on the end of the movement, see Showalter, *End of a Crusade*.

34. Bays and Widmer, "Call," 1.

35. Lautz, "SVM and Transformation," 3.

36. Tiedemann, "Indigenous Agency, Religious Protectorates," 232. Tiedemann acknowledges that motives to conversion are "complex, mixed, and not always apparent," so we cannot decisively categorize them into these three categories.

those who converted were on the margins of Chinese society. Paul Cohen describes nineteenth-century Chinese converts to Christianity as "confined almost entirely to poor peasants and townspeople, criminal elements and other unsavory types, and deracinated individuals in the treaty ports."[37] Mainstream Chinese saw Christianity as an unattractive nuisance. Christianity troubled Confucian scholar-elites for many reasons: the historical collusion of missionaries in the unequal treaties, deep-seated xenophobia, and philosophical differences between Christianity and Confucianism. Something else, though, troubled the Chinese elite in the 1880s and 1890s. Missionaries arrived in China in these decades with no cultural memory but not so for the Chinese. For them the stench of Taiping Rebellion (1850–64) lingered.

Hong Xiuquan (洪秀全 *Hung Hsiu-chuan*, 1814–64) led a rebellion against the Manchus to establish the Taiping Heavenly Kingdom (太平天国 *Taiping Tianguo*). Hong united the Hakka, "guest peoples" who were 5 percent of China's population, against the ruling Manchus, 2 percent of the population. Hong failed twice in his efforts to obtain the coveted *shengyuan (*生員 also called 秀才 *xiucai)* degree, which would have won him a place among the literati. The rejection humiliated the young Hong. But it did nothing to stifle his ambition. Before retaking the exam Hong came into contact with a Protestant missionary and was given a simple tract entitled "Good Words for Exhorting the Age." After a third examination failure in 1837 he had a vision in which a bearded man with gold hair gave him a sword and a younger man explained how to slay evil spirits. Six years later, after failing the exam for the fourth time, Hong read the Christian tracts more carefully and believed that the beings in his vision were God and Jesus. Therefore he must be a son of God and the younger brother of Jesus. In 1847 he studied the Bible for two months with Isaachar Roberts, an American missionary in Hong Kong. Hong organized a church, the God Worshippers' Society, which began attracting disinherited Chinese, especially Hakkas, from throughout Southwest China. The God Worshippers shared common property and followed articles of faith written by Hong.

Convinced he was God's Son, Hong became determined to rid China of idolatry and false religion. In Hong's rhetoric the Manchus were foreign demons who "poisoned China" with an "offensive odor" and needed to be eliminated. A force gathered around Hong. From their base in the Thistle Mountain area the force won a string of military victories. In January

37. Cohen, "Christian Missions," 10:560.

1851 Hong Xiquan declared himself "Heavenly King" of a new dynasty, the "Heavenly Kingdom of Great Peace" (太平天国 *Taiping Tianguo).* Two years later growing Taiping forces captured Nanjing and made it their capital. Though most scholars doubt that Hong's ideology was essentially Christian, his impact on China was considerable.[38] Aside from the brutal death toll—over twenty million people died, making it one of the deadliest wars in history—the rebellion challenged and transformed the Qing rulers. Confucian libraries across the Lower Yangtze Valley (江南 *Jiangnan* or, more commonly, *Zhangnan*) burned down in the fighting. In the midst of the fighting between the Taiping and Qing forces in the 1850s, the *Zhangnan* elite fled to the safest nearby city, Shanghai. Western missionaries considered the Taipings to be "outrageously un-Christian," in Bays's estimation, but these Confucian scholars saw them as authentically Christian. Contained in Taiping thinking was a fundamental critique of the imperial state, for the emperor usurped from God the title *di* (帝). These literati equated Taiping with Christianity thus anything Christian threatened China's wellbeing. Zeng Guofan (曾国藩 *Tseng Kuo-fan*, 1811–72) proclaimed in 1854:

> The [Taiping] bandits have stolen a few scraps from the foreign barbarians and worship the Christian religion. . . . Scholars may not read the Confucian classics, for they have their so-called teachings of Jesus and the New Testament. . . . This is not just a crisis for our Ch'ing dynasty, but the most extraordinary crisis of all time for the Confucian teachings.[39]

For the ruling literati, it was a war of civilizations.

Between 1898 and 1900 the Confucian scholars would have ample outlet for their anti-Christian fury in the Boxer Uprising. Drought and famine hit parts of China in the 1890s. Millions of people migrated in search of food. Popular agitators blamed growing foreigner intervention for disrupting China's *fengshui* (风水), the harmony between heaven and earth. The "Boxers United in Righteousness," who combined martial arts with a militaristic mysticism and claimed to be impervious to bullets and swords, wanted all foreigners to die or leave because they had upset cosmic forces. The group rallied popular support on the North China plain in Shandong around this anti-foreign and anti-Christian rhetoric. Empress Dowager Cixi (慈禧 *Tz'u-his*, 1835–1908) threw her support to the Boxers.

38. Interestingly, Daniel Bays bucks this general trend, suggesting that the "formal Taiping articles of faith [are] Christian enough" (*New History of Christianity*, 54).

39. Cheng et al., *Search for Modern China*, 147.

Their slogan became "Revive the Qing, destroy the foreign." In 1900 Cixi issued a de facto imperial decree to kill all the missionaries, even though this went against imperial law. In and around Beijing the Boxers lived up to their "Fist of Righteousness" name, killing any foreigner or Chinese Christian they could get their hands on; 250 foreigners and 30,000 Chinese Christians were killed.[40] An eight-nation expeditionary force entered Beijing in August 1900. As the empress dowager fled to Xi'an the Qing Court switched sides and issued an edict for the protection of foreigners. Over the following months foreigners, both military and civilian, including missionaries, looted much of Beijing.[41] One would assume that terrible days were ahead for Protestant missions in China. But, strangely, the opposite proved true. The fervor of the Boxer Uprising reflected a growing dissatisfaction with Qing policy.

After the Boxer Uprising of 1900 social change roared through China. In 1905 the 1,300-year-old imperial examinations were terminated. Six years later the mandate of heaven ended for the Manchus, who had ruled since 1644. For four thousand years emperors had ruled China but in 1912 China transitioned to a Republic. The Qing dynasty collapsed. The great Chinese civilization had been crippled in the nineteenth and early twentieth centuries. Throughout this agonizing period foreign nations humiliated the once-great nation. Karl Marx predicted that China would disintegrate when it met the glare of foreign light, like "any mummy carefully preserved in a hermetically sealed coffin."[42] The Middle Kingdom was changing in ways she never had in her long history. Surveying the twentieth century in China, Latourette rightly notes: "Upon this ancient people with its memorable past the revolutionary age thrust itself with shattering force."[43] Over and over again China was shamed by and before the world. The imperial system had been built on the indigenous Chinese philosophies of Confucianism and Legalism. These systems had survived twenty dynasties but even they came under attack.

40. See Cohen, *History in Three Keys*.

41. "Mr. Ament's [ABCFM missionary] financial feat of squeezing a thirteen-fold [Boxer] indemnity out of the pauper peasants . . . concrete a blasphemy so hideous and so colossal that, without doubt, its mate is not findable in the history of this or of any other age." Twain, "To the Person Sitting," 164.

42. Cited in Fenby, *Penguin History*, xxxi.

43. Latourette, *Twentieth Century outside Europe*, 371.

## Christianity in Republican China (1911–49)

China's literati wanted to restore their kingdom to a place of prominence. Hu Shih (胡适 *Hu Shi*, 1891–1962), Chen Duxiu (陈独秀 1879–1942), and other scholars trained in the classical tradition sought to create a new Chinese culture based on science and Western concepts of human rights. The New Culture Movement (新文化运动 *Xin Wenhua Yundong)* revolted against Confucianism because it violated the cornerstone of democracy, the freedom of the individual. "The basic task is to import the foundation of Western society, that is, the new belief in equality and human rights," wrote Chen in *New Youth* in 1916. "We must be thoroughly aware of the incompatibility of Confucianism and the new belief, the new society, and the new state."[44] Chen proposed China turn to "Mr. Science" and "Mr. Democracy" to build a new culture. Unfortunately the aftermath of World War I would find China, once again, humiliated by the world's true superpowers.

China entered the First World War in 1917 with an agreement from the Allies that German-held territory in China would be returned to Beijing. Even though Chinese forces had done no actual fighting in the war, China sent 100,000 laborers to assist the Allies in digging trenches on the Western front. After the war the Chinese delegation came to the peace treaty in France hoping for the return of rights and territory in Shandong and the abolition of extraterritorial rights of foreign nations in China. But a bitter disappointment waited them. At the Treaty of Versailles the Western allies implemented a secret wartime agreement with Japan, granting Tokyo the former German concessions in Shandong. The Western nations demonstrated their commitment to Japan as their most strategic ally in the East. The treaty stung Chinese people with deep embarrassment. The world knew of China's weakness whether or not the Middle Kingdom would admit to it. Shamed, young Chinese rallied in angry protests on May 4. In Paris Chinese blocked the route of their delegates to Versailles so China never signed the treaty. In Beijing three thousand students protested. Demonstrations spread to cities across China. The May Fourth Movement, as it would be known, revealed the repressed frustration and deep yearning of intellectuals embarrassed by the state of their once great nation. But the Movement did far more than boycott and destroy Japanese goods. What followed was a unique period of national introspection. Convinced that

44. Y. Lin, *Crisis of Chinese Consciousness*, 76. Cited in Spence, *Search for Modern China*, 315.

other nations would soon destroy China, educated Chinese instigated, in Spence's words, a "concentrated outpouring of intellectual exuberance and doubt [that] had not been seen in China for over two thousand years."[45] Chinese intellectuals demanded changes.

They exempted nothing politically, socially, philosophically, economically, or educationally from robust critique and analysis. The writer Lu Xun (鲁迅 *Lu Hsün*, the nom de plume for Zhou Shuren, 1881–1936) wrote an episodic story that captivated the Chinese imagination. In *The True Story of Ah Q*, an uneducated peasant and petty thief named Ah Q terrorizes the weak but trembles before the authorities. Ah Q is obsessed with his own image and plagued by an inferiority complex. Eventually he is mistaken for a revolutionary and executed. Chinese readers in the 1920s understood Lu Xun's point all too well. In case anyone missed it, he wrote elsewhere: "Our vaunted Chinese civilization is only a feast of human flesh prepared for the rich and mighty. And China is only the kitchen where the feasts are prepared."[46] Many Chinese intellectuals continued to blame Confucianism as they had done at the start of the New Culture Movement. Iconoclasm swept across China. Chen Duxiu, who had advocated science and democracy as the cure for China's maladies, turned to Marxism. In 1921 the Communist International, or Comintern, sent an agent, Hans Sneevliet, to Shanghai for a secret meeting with alleged Communists. In July the Chinese Communist Party was established. Chen Duxiu became the party secretary. As a reforming spirit gripped China its people become open, like never before, to Christianity. Daniel Bays labels the period of 1902–27 as the "Golden Age" of missions in China.[47] This era witnessed the institutionalization of the Sino-Foreign Protestant Establishment. Two key entities in the SFPE, the Young Men's Christian Association and the Christian colleges, had deep connections to Union Theological Seminary.

In 1895 David Willard Lyon (1870–1949) founded the first student YMCA in Tianjin. Lyon chose Tianjin over Beijing because of its location and role as the center of the missionary enterprise in North China. He saw Christians in Tianjin as more enthusiastic and open to interdenominational work. Lyon had a grand vision for Chinese Protestants: he saw the nondenominational YMCA as the key to uniting disparate denominations across the Middle Kingdom. From the beginning, the Y sought to be an

45. Spence, *Search for Modern China*, 272.

46. Cited in Fenby, *Penguin History*, 143.

47. Bays, *New History of Christianity*, ch. 5.

indigenous organization. Lyon insisted on Chinese leading meetings. In an 1896 YMCA quarterly report, Lyon wrote:

> Instead of its being conducted always by a foreigner I urged the importance of the Chinese boys themselves undertaking the leadership. They objected to it on the ground that it would not be as interesting or profitable if conducted by Chinese, and that command of English was not sufficient enough among the boys to conduct the meeting properly. I urged them to give the new plan a trial, at least, and the results have proven the wisdom of the plan.[48]

Rather than receiving land as a free donation, the YMCA bought property with members all making small donations. Su Chen contends that Lyon employed the "right approach with the right people at the right time."[49] The Y quickly developed large numbers of Chinese leaders and spread throughout the country. Modern Chinese social scientists critique the motive of the Ys. They argue: "The goal in disseminating modern Western bourgeois culture in China was to carry out cultural imperialism by raising up a generation of comprador Christians with a sense of national inferiority."[50] Regardless of the validity of this statement, Western missionaries came to China with various motives. They also used various methods to engage the Chinese masses.

Some missionaries turned to the establishment of schools as the most effective way of reaching China. Jessie Lutz, in her unparalleled study of the Christian colleges, contends that missionaries founded the schools out of "dismay over the indifference of the Chinese to the Christian message."[51] Christian schools were started in major cities throughout China: St. John's University (1879), Lingnan University (1888), Hangchow Christian College (1897), Shantung Christian University (*Cheeloo*, 1902), University of Shanghai (1906), the University of Nanking (1910), Soochow University (1911), Yenching University (1912), Ginling College (1913), West China Union University (1913), Fukien Christian University (1915), Hwa Nan College (1921), and Huachung University (1922).[52] In 1922 these thirteen

48. Lyon, Quarterly Report, First Quarter 1896, box 1, folder 1. Kautz Family YMCA Archive, University of Minnesota.

49. Chen, "Lyon and His Comrades."

50. Luo, *Religion under Socialism*, 29.

51. Lutz, *China and Christian Colleges*, 1.

52. A description and brief history of each of the Christian colleges in China can be found at http://www.library.yale.edu/div/colleges/descriptions.htm.

institutions came together under the umbrella of the Central Office of the China Union Universities.[53] Chinese gentry were loath to offer science, mathematics, and Western languages in Chinese schools so the missionary schools occupied a unique space in the market of higher education. The mission schools, hospitals, and printing presses served as both "purveyors of information" and "examples of Western methodology and organization."[54] The schools taught Christian doctrine, Newtonian science, and English language but they also carried particular Protestant emphases such as individualism and belief in progress. These ideas contrasted the Confucian stress on family and stability. Both the Christian colleges and the YMCA became key transmitters of Western liberalism to China in a critical period of Chinese history.[55] In size and influence they were key entities in the Sino-Foreign Protestant Establishment.

In the 1920s the growing Protestant enterprise and increasing nationalism caused the question of indigenization to take center-stage in the psyche of Chinese Christians. Wang Chengting wrote an article in 1921 entitled "Making Christianity Indigenous in China" in *The Chinese Recorder*. "In order to have the Chinese people accept Christianity, we must make it indigenous, that is, we must make it a native plant growing in Chinese soil."[56] Western missionaries and Chinese Christians puzzled at how to make Christianity native to China. The how-to question plagued indigenization efforts. In 1926 Zhixin Wang captured the crux of the challenge: "The word 'indigenous' (*pen-se*) essentially has the meaning of 'home-grown', but since Christianity has been imported from the West, how is it possible to become a product of China?"[57] Using the analogy of a Western peanut growing in Chinese soil, Wang argues that Christianity will only become "indigenous" or "home-grown" when it absorbs Chinese nutrients and develops in Chinese soil. Many Chinese felt like Christianity remained potted in Western soil. Addressing the National Christian Conference in 1922, T. C. Chao explained: "The (Chinese) Church is weak because she is still foreign, both in thought and form, and is divided

53. In 1945 this coalition of Christian colleges because known as the United Board for Christian Colleges in China (UBCCC). Then, after being forced out of China in 1951, it became the United Board for Christian Higher Education in Asia (UBCHEA). http://www.unitedboard.org/about_history.asp. See also Fenn, *Ever New Horizons*, and Lauby, *Sailing on Winds*.

54. Lutz, *China and Christian Colleges*, 10.

55. Barwick, "Protestant Quest for Modernity."

56. C. Wang, "Making Christianity Indigenous," 323.

57. Z. Wang, "Indigenous Church." Cited in P. Ng, *Chinese Christianity*, 87.

by Western denominationalism."[58] For decades Western missionaries had discussed the importance of native agency.

The long-serving leaders of two of the largest missions societies, Henry Venn (1796–1873) of the CMS and Rufus Anderson (1796–1880) of the ABCFM, emphasized indigenous leadership. They believed native converts should lead their churches so foreign missionaries should step aside sooner than later. Anderson stressed the three-self principle: churches should be self-supporting, self-governing, and self-propagating. At a Christian conference in Shanghai in 1892 the missionaries unilaterally agreed that the well-being of the Chinese church depended on establishing native agency and Chinese forms of worship. The Shanghai conferees drafted the "Three-Self Principle" as an expression of their long-term goal. The trouble came however with finding reliable Chinese leaders. Converts to Protestant Christianity came from the periphery of Chinese society; not many were well educated. Often Western missionaries did not trust Chinese clergy, viewing them as lazy and unreliable. Tiedemann notes: "Although most missionaries recognized the importance of native agency, their relations with and attitudes toward Chinese workers were contradictory and fraught with tensions."[59] Despite talk of native agency missionary practice differed. With notable exceptions, such as the Chinese Ys, missionaries found it difficult to release control to Chinese Christians. Some missionaries grew tired of this superficial commitment to indigenous leadership.

In 1912 Roland Allen (1868–1947) accused Western missionaries of violating Paul's principles of establishing churches. Allen's books, *Missionary Methods: St. Paul's or Ours?* (1912) and *Spontaneous Expansion of the Church and the Causes Which Hinder* (1927), challenged Western missionaries in China to follow the example of the apostle Paul in entrusting newly formed churches to the Holy Spirit. He urged the missionary enterprise to develop an indigenous church from the outset, a self-reliant church nourished and spread by native leaders. To do so Western missionaries must leave and the sooner the better. Allen's books contained a "radical criticism of missionary policy and practice current at that time and set forth an alternative vision of what might be done to establish truly indigenous, self-supporting churches."[60] The perennial question Allen cast before the church was "Do you deliver?" Is the Christian message and the Christian

58. T. C. Chao, "On Strengths and Weaknesses." Cited in Ng, *Chinese Christianity*, 87.

59. Tiedemann, "Indigenous Agency, Religious Protectorates," 239.

60. Long and Rowthorn, "Roland Allen, 1868–1947," 383.

church handed over, or delivered, to indigenous Christians? David Paton (1913–92), an authority on Allen and editor of his writings, offered a biting response to this question. For Paton the answer in the case of China was no; Western Christians had not delivered the church to Christians of the East.

In 1953 Paton reiterated Allen's accusation. He charged missionaries in China as being agents of the imperialist West. Missionaries carried and promoted capitalism and Western culture. In *Christian Mission and the Judgment of God*, Paton argued that regardless of the missionaries' stated policy, their actual policy precluded the development of a genuine self-governing, self-supporting, and self-expanding church. Paton believed that the expulsion of missionaries from China in the early 1950s was God's judgment for not developing a truly indigenous church. Paton wrote: "God's judgment is being executed upon His Church by political movements which are anti-Christian. Of this almost worldwide movement, the Communists are the spearhead."[61] Just as God used the Babylonians to judge Judah, He was using the Communists to judge the failed missionary enterprise in China. Before moving to Beijing Paton spent a month in Shanghai in 1940. In that month he met a young YMCA leader named K. H. Ting.[62] For the most part Allen and Paton were right regarding the lack of indigenous leaders. But there were exceptions.

In addition to drafting the "Three-Self Principles" the 1892 Shanghai convention established the Chinese Christian Church. The missionary establishment gave no funding and no Western leadership to this new denomination. The Chinese Christian Church saw little growth until 1911, when C. Y. Cheng (誠靜怡 *Cheng Jingyi*, 1881–1939) emerged as a leader. Cheng's father, a Manchu, had been converted through LMS missionaries in Beijing. He sent his son to missions schools where "his aptness and diligence marked him for special notice."[63] After helping LMS missionary George Owen revise the Chinese translation of the New Testament in 1906, Cheng studied in Glasgow for two years. He returned to China to pastor a newly formed church in Beijing. It was back in Scotland, however, that the world took notice of this dynamic Chinese pastor. At the World Missionary Conference in Edinburgh in 1910 Cheng electrified the delegates with his seven-minute speech. He challenged missionaries in China and worldwide

61. Patton, *Christian Mission and Judgment*, 49.

62. Ting and Paton remained friends until Paton's death, fifty years later. Wickeri, *Reconstructing Christianity in China*, 51.

63. Bitton, "Cheng Ching-Yi," 513.

to give more control over to native Christians. Western Christians need to "view us from our standpoint," explained Cheng, "and if you fail to do that, the Chinese will remain always as a mysterious people to you." He expressed hope to see an indigenous Chinese church that was united "without any denominational distinctives" because the Chinese Christian "finds no delight" in denominationalism and it "has never interested the Chinese mind."[64] Cheng became general secretary of the National Christian Council when it was established in 1922 and general moderator of the Church of Christ in China, an ecumenical organization unifying sixteen denominations, in 1927. C. Y. Cheng epitomizes Chinese Christians who would lead in twenty-century Chinese Protestantism: raised in a Christian home and educated in missionary schools in China and universities in the West. Though fluent in English and friendly to Western missionaries Cheng was fiercely committed to indigenous Chinese Christianity. Devoted to a united church, he opposed denominationalism.

## Summary

This chapter began with the Nestorians bringing Christianity to Xi'an in AD 635 and ends at a Christian missionary conference in Edinburgh in 1910. The strange years in between saw Christianity rise and fall in the Middle Kingdom. In the seventh century the Taizhong Emperor praised the "mysterious and transcendent" teaching of Alopen that "saves creatures" and "should be propagated under heaven." But two centuries later the Wuzong Emperor banned all foreign religions. The Nestorian faith returned, through marriage to the Khans, in the thirteenth century. But it faded as a new dynasty emerged. That new empire, the Ming, eventually welcomed Matteo Ricci and other Jesuit missionaries in the seventeenth century. Men of vast learning, the Jesuits sought for and attained influence in the imperial court. Theological and political conflict between the Jesuits and the mendicant Catholic orders led to the Rites Controversy and eventual expulsion of missionaries in 1724. By the end of the eighteenth century the community of converts declined in "numbers and morale" and Christianity "seemed to be on the way to extinction."[65] One hundred years later the seaborne British Empire used opium to pry China open. Protestant missionaries poured into China following the Unequal Treaties. As the missionary enterprise grew in

64. Stanley, *World Missionary Conference Edinburgh*, 107–11.

65. Latourette, *History of Christian Missions*, 182.

China, Western Christians struggled in turning churches over to Chinese to govern for themselves. "The Three-Self Principle" became a mythical goal in Chinese Protestantism. While Protestants in nineteenth-century China remained confined to the margins of Chinese society, seeds were sown to bring Christianity into China's mainstream. With local evangelization throughout China and the establishment of Christian institutions, such as schools and hospitals, the Christian church was well placed to address the social foment in the first decade of the twentieth century. As the children of Chinese Christians attended missions' schools and studied in the West, young Chinese Christians were positioned to become the indigenous leaders so sought after. These indigenous leaders would be expected to provide answers to difficult questions following the May Fourth Movement.

# 3

# Union Seminary (NY)

*It is the design of the founders to provide a Theological Seminary in the midst of the greatest and most growing community in America, around which all men of moderate views and feelings, who desire to live free from party strife, and to stand aloof from all extremes of doctrinal speculation, practical radicalism, and ecclesiastical domination, may cordially and affectionately rally.* (1836)[1]

THIS CHAPTER MOVES FROM the history of Christianity in China to that of Union Theological Seminary in the city of New York. I intend to demonstrate four distinct "lines" that characterized the seminary: Union sought to be urban, liberal, international, and influential. This four-stranded institutional DNA made the seminary what it was and will explain why so many important Chinese Christians attended Union in the twentieth century. Union students ascended the hills of Morningside Heights to arrive on a cosmopolitan campus in America's most important city. This uphill walk also brought them into the heart of American theological liberalism. Here they encountered a dense social network connected to some very important people, including the most famous pastor in the United States and the wealthiest family in the world. After explaining Union's history and four unique characteristics in this chapter, I explore the experiences of an international student at Union in the 1930s. The ever-intriguing Dietrich Bonhoeffer will offer important insight into the time period when many Chinese Christians studied there. The following chapter will then describe Union's connections with China.

1. Prentiss, *Union Theological Seminary*, 8.

## Union's Founding amidst Presbyterian Controversy 1830s

In the 1830s theological controversy swirled in the Presbyterian Church in the United States. The ecclesiastical tempest spread over theological, ecclesiological, and social issues. More precisely the conflict centered on the New Divinity, the heresy trials of Presbyterian clergy, and slavery. To the surprise of no one who knows Presbyterian history, the Old School-New School divide centered on the interpretation of the Westminster Confession of Faith, the doctrinal standards in the Presbyterian Church.[2] The Old School, with its strong Scottish and Scotch-Irish elements, advocated a stricter interpretation of Westminster, especially regarding original sin. Rooted in England, Wales, and New England, the New Side had been influenced by a Puritan emphasis on the "subjective" aspects of faith. They were more favorable to revivalism and held milder views on the doctrine of depravity. The Old School criticized the excesses of Charles Finney's "New Measures" in mass evangelism.[3] While the New School favored cooperation with the Congregationalists, the Old Schoolers perceived this as doctrinal laxity.

The controversy manifested itself in the courts of the Presbyterian Church. The outcome of heresy charges against George Duffield, Albert Barnes, and Lyman Beecher varied depending on which of the schools held power at the presbytery level. By 1837 the entire Presbyterian denomination across the US was split between the more conservative and confessional "Old Schoolers" and the more revivalistic and ecumenical "New Schoolers." This decade of conflict in the Presbyterian Church gave birth to Union Theological Seminary in New York City. "The character of an institution, like that of an individual, is apt to be determined in its origin and early years," wrote George Lewis Prentiss in his 1889 history of Union. "It has, indeed, grown and prospered far beyond the hopes of its founders; but it has grown and prospered largely along the lines they marked out, and in the spirit in which it was planned."[4] What were the "lines they marked out" in the founding of Union Seminary? The following section focuses on its location, its theology, and its mission.

2. Similar controversy enveloped the Presbyterian Church a century earlier (1741–58) in the form of the Old Side-New Side controversy.

3. For a more detailed explanation of the causes and outcomes of the controversy, see Handy, *History*, ch. 1; and Robert, *Occupy until I Come*, 7.

4. Prentiss, *Union Theological Seminary*, 5.

## Union's Distinct Characteristics: The "Lines" Marked Out by Its Founders

### Union's Urban Line

Union's founders placed the school in Manhattan to promote a moderate theological vision both in the United States and around the world. Touched by revival and eager for greater ecumenical cooperation, New School Presbyterians in the Northeast craved a seminary to match their theological leaning. On June 5, 1827, Rev. Dr. Holt Rice of Virginia, considered "one of the best and wisest men in the Presbyterian Church of that day," wrote: "And I do fully expect that there will be either a strong effort to bring Princeton under different management, or to build up a new seminary in the vicinity of New York, to counteract the influence of Princeton."[5] Established in 1836, Union sought to be a deterrent to the conservativism of the Old Schoolers at Princeton Theological Seminary. At a time when American seminaries were based in small towns, Union's founders located their school in the heart of New York City. They made their intent clear in establishing the school.

> It is the design of the founders to provide a Theological Seminary in the midst of the greatest and most growing community in America, around which all men of moderate views and feelings, who desire to live free from party strife, and to stand aloof from all extremes of doctrinal speculation, practical radicalism, and ecclesiastical domination, may cordially and affectionately rally.[6]

Union's founders gambled in placing the school in the greatest and fastest growing city in America. The wager paid off. New York City, in the last decades of the nineteenth century and well into the twentieth, stood tall as the center of American Protestantism. Within two years, ninety-two students enrolled at Union, making it the third largest seminary in the United States (behind Princeton and Andover).[7] By placing Union in America's largest city, the founders intentionally made their seminary cosmopolitan.

The world came to New York City so Union students encountered the world with all its diversity and problems. Divinity students in Oxford and Cambridge were shielded from London's grit and its diversity. Union's

5. Prentiss, *Union Theological Seminary*, 6.
6. Prentiss, *Union Theological Seminary*, 8.
7. Handy, *History*, 14.

students, however, were not forty miles away from New York City. The big city's problems and joys surrounded them. In a century transformed by the Industrial Revolution, Union's founders could have built a comfortable campus away from the City's billowing smokestacks. But they chose not to. In 1962 Union's acting president, John C. Bennett, welcomed new students to the school. In this address he described three characteristics of the school: its commitment to serve the broad church, its diverse and liberal theological outlook, and its location. The seminary, he said, is "very much in the world" and explained why: "The founders of the Seminary purposely put it in a city in order to keep theological students in close contact with the real world, with the church as it confronts the world under quite difficult conditions." Bennett's description of the school's theology reveals much of what the founders had intended in 1836:

> Union Seminary is committed as an institution and as a community to God as revealed in Jesus Christ and yet open to truth from all sources. It has always emphasized freedom of the mind in its search for truth. You will not be expected to conform in your theological thinking to any standards of orthodoxy or neo-orthodoxy. This combination of commitment and openness is difficult for an individual and it is difficult for an institution, and yet it is essential for our existence as a seminary. You will find that your professors differ from each other—as you move from one classroom to another you may sometimes wonder if you are hearing about the same gospel. This may not be quite as true as in some other decades. It will be an important part of your theological education to wrestle with the problems which this creates for your mind. We do not have any system of theology embodied in any professor.[8]

In the nineteenth century potential students were drawn to Union's distinguished faculty, to the fast-growing city of New York, and to the moderate theology espoused there.[9] As the nineteenth century passed into the twentieth, Union evolved from moderate Presbyterianism to the vanguard of theological liberalism. The heresy trial of Charles Augustus Briggs sealed Union's liberal reputation.

8. Bennett, "Address to Entering Students, 1962," John C. Bennett, ser. 1, box 1, folder 20, p. 6, Burke Library, Union Theological Seminary, NY.

9. Prominent faculty included Charles Hodge, Horace Bushnell, Edwards A. Park, John Nevin, Philip Schaff, and Henry Boynton Smith.

## Union's Liberal Line

In November 1890 Union appointed Charles Briggs to the Edward Robinson Chair of Biblical Theology. One year later the Presbytery of New York charged Briggs with violating the Westminster Standards. Though acquitted of heresy, the church courts appealed the decision the highest church court in the Presbyterian Church in the United States. In 1893 the General Assembly convicted Briggs in a vote of 383 to 116. The Presbyterian Church suspended Briggs from ministry and disavowed all responsibility for Union faculty. From this point forward Union shed any denominational affiliation. Briggs's trial was "not only a major turning point in the story of Union but also an important event in the history of Presbyterianism and of American Protestantism, " comments Handy.[10] Union emerged from these heresy trials as a place that prided itself in freedom of scholarship. Seven years later the Presbyterian General Assembly expressed their disapproval of Professor A. C. McGiffert's *A History of Christianity in the Apostolic Age* (1897). The assembly issued a warning: reform your views or withdraw from the Presbyterian church. McGiffert withdrew. Among American seminaries, Union defined itself as urban and liberal. The first two characteristics, or "lines," were planned and deliberate. Union's founders wanted it so. But the next two characteristics—important in understanding Union's influence in China, in the next chapter—are less clear. Because they are increasingly opaque, it will take longer to describe the school's global connections and its profound social network.

## Union's International Line

In the nineteenth century many professors at Union Seminary studied in Germany. German universities were the nation's pride and glory, exerting broad theological impact throughout the world. In 1857 Philip Schaff noted:

> The Universities of Germany are regarded by competent judges, as the first among the learned institutions of the world . . . The German theology of the last thirty or forty years, whatever be its errors and defects, its extravagances and fillies, which we would be among the last to deny, or to defend, is, upon the whole, the most learned, original, fertile, and progressive theology of the age, and

10. Handy, *History*, 63.

> no active branch of Protestantism can keep entirely aloof from its contact without injuring its own interests.[11]

This "original, fertile, and progressive theology," known as historical criticism, critiqued and reinterpreted historical Christianity.

Historical criticism asked what historical circumstances a text referred to and emerged from. It sought to employ the "scientific process of investigating a text's transmission, development, and origins."[12] German scholars distinguished between the traditional view of history (*Geschichte*) and a more scientific kind of history (*Historie*). Utilizing their newfound, scientific objectivity, they wanted to separate what the Bible claimed as happening from what actually occurred. They interrogated the Bible with skepticism, dismissing claims of the miraculous. At the University of Tübingen F. C. Baur (1792–1860) applied Hegel's dialectical approach to deny the Pauline authorship of most letters attributed to Paul. Baur's student, David F. Strauss, argued that the gospel's historical form was legend. Strauss's *The Life of Jesus Critically Examined* (1835) marked a "clear break with the orthodox and supernaturalist reading of Scripture."[13] The Tübingen School (1835–60) led the search for the "historical Jesus" which was followed in theology faculties across Germany. Eventually Christian beliefs that were inconsistent with modernity were abandoned or reinterpreted.[14] Union faculty would not permit American Protestantism to remain aloof from the historical-critical method.

The German influence on Union would continued for decades. This list of Union professors who studied or taught in Germany included: Roswell D. Hitchcock (1855–87, Berlin and Halle), Philip Schaff (1870–93, Tübingen, Halle and Berlin), George Lewis Prentiss (1871–97, Berlin and Halle), Charles Briggs (1874–1913, Berlin), Thomas S. Hastings (1881–1911), John H. Worcester Jr. (1891–93, Leipzig and Berlin), William Adams Brown (1892–1936, Berlin), Arthur Cushman McGiffert (1893–1927, Marburg), James E. Frame (1897–1938, Berlin and Göttingen), Julius Brewer (1904–45, Basel, Halle, and Berlin), William Walker Rockwell (1905–42, Marburg), John Baille (1930–34, Jena and Marburg), and Paul Tillich (1933–55, Tübingen, Halle, Berlin, Marburg, and Frankfurt).[15] The trend

11. Schaff, *Germany*, 8.

12. Burnett, "Historical Criticism," 290.

13. Yarbrough, "Tübingen School," 822.

14. McGrath, *Christian Theology*, 102.

15. The parenthesis indicated when they taught at Union and where they studied in

of Union professors studying in Germany started with Edward Robinson (1794–1863). Robinson taught biblical literature at Union from 1837 until his death. Known as the "Father of Biblical Geography" for his discoveries in Palestine, Robinson was one of Union's first hires and the first faculty member of international renown. He studied at Halle and Berlin from 1826 to 1830. In Germany Robinson developed the ability to engage with theology's growing technical specialization. His writing and teaching kept Union Seminary at the forefront of new developments in theological education.[16] But the professor who put Union on the theological map was Henry Boynton Smith (1815–77).

Smith taught at Union for twenty-seven years, beginning in 1850. Before arriving in Manhattan, he studied at Halle and Berlin (1837–40) under Friedrich A. G. Tholuck and August Neander.[17] Smith was "a mediator by temperament, conviction, and education" who believed "that neither the New Haven nor Princeton theologies would quite do, for the one overemphasized philosophy without faith, the other faith without philosophy."[18] He drew from the well of Edwardsean theology, Old School Calvinism, and the German theology of mediation. Smith helped American theologians distinguish evangelical theology from the rationalistic tendencies in German theology. Despite being taught otherwise in Germany, Smith endorsed the inerrancy and plenary inspiration of the Bible. He rejected the radical German views on the life of Jesus and embraced a biblical faith consistent with the Reformed tradition. Yet Smith admired German theologians, publicly testifying to his appreciation of Friedrich Schleiermacher (1768–1834). Smith introduced and interpreted Continental theology for the Union community. This industrious, frail professor infused American

Germany.

16. Handy, *History*, 14.

17. Tholuck (1799–1877), "one of the most fruitful and influential German theologians and authors during the second and third quarters of the nineteenth century, and better known in England and America than any other," taught Old and New Testament in Halle (1826–77). "He was original, fresh, brilliant, suggestive, eloquent, and full of poetry, wit, and humor. He cannot be classed with any school. He was influenced by Pietism, Moravianism, Schleiermacher, Neander, and even Hegel. His elastic mind was ever open to new light; and his heart was always right, and never shaken from faith and love to Christ." His works exerted great influence, yielding only "to that of Neander among his contemporaries." Schaff and Herzog, *New Schaff-Herzog Encyclopedia*, 9:420. Neander (1789–1950) studied under Schleiermacher at Halle and Plank at Göttingen before being appointed a professor in Berlin.

18. Handy, *History*, 29.

Protestantism with German theology, dominating the theological life of Union and New School Presbyterianism for twenty-five years. He was "the voice of the future at Union, especially in his mediating style, his longing for bringing divided Christians closer together, his Christocentric approach, and his knowledge of the continental theological scene."[19] He sought to unite Presbyterians following the Civil War. Union wanted its professors to engage with the world's most important theologians, and most happened to be German. But it also explicitly sought to impact the whole world.

## Union's Foreign Missions

From its founding Union desired to be an institution of international influence. The "Society of Inquiry Concerning Missions" was the first student society formed at Union. On December 9, 1837, a group of students appointed leaders of the society and resolved to devote one day a month to it.[20] From 4:00 to 5:00 p.m. on the first Monday of each month students participated in the "Society of Inquiry." In a sermon in the 1880s entitled "The Union Theological Seminary" George Lewis Prentiss commented:

> I have the clearest conviction that the Union Seminary is capable of doing a great work for Christ and the Church. It has already done much; not a few of the most useful ministers in the land, not a few of our best missionaries among the heathen, are its alumni. . . . But I trust it has a still nobler career in the future.[21]

During these decades the seminary encouraged students to consider seriously the call of foreign missions. Union established the first professorship of missions in American in 1873, installing George R. Prentiss as the Skinner and McAlpin Professor of Pastoral Theology, Church Policy and Missions. From 1838 to 1884 Union sent 146 alumni out to serve as overseas missionaries. The most common fields of service were Turkey (27), Syria (21), China (20), India (12), and Persia (9). A plaque next to the Van Dusen Gate at Union's entrance declares, "Through this gate let the world come to Union and Union go into the world." In the 1950s the official history of the school continued to boast of the missions-emphasis at Union. "From

19. Robert, *Occupy until I Come*, 37.

20. *Records of the Society of Inquiry of the New York Union Theological Seminary 1837–1854*. 5. UTS ser. 10, subser. B, box 2, Burke Library, Union Theological Seminary, NY.

21. Prentiss, *Union Theological Seminary*, 100.

its outset, Union Seminary had focused its eyes upon the entire globe as belonging to Christ and to be made His to its uttermost parts," wrote former President Henry Sloane Coffin in 1954. "In its first century ending 1936, one out of twelve of its alumni had gone to the foreign field."[22] Many Union-trained missionaries served in the Middle East in the nineteenth century. However, at the turn of the century, Union's eyes swung to China. Union not only sent many missionaries to China—and the number would grow significantly in the twentieth century—it sent these missionaries with a particular syncretistic vision of the Christian faith.

Union made changes in the first decades of the twentieth century to enhance its emphasis on overseas missions and the presence of international students. In 1914 the seminary hired Daniel J. Fleming, a Union graduate who had served as a missionary in India for eight years, to direct the newly formed Department of Foreign Service. An "intense, outgoing man" and a "prolific author on themes related to missions," Fleming taught at Union until his retirement in 1944.[23] Over the years various faculty had taught about foreign missions but there was no curricular organization around this field. Fleming reviewed the school's history and discovered that in its first fifty years, only two foreign nationals had enrolled at Union. Dissatisfied with these numbers, he set out to attract more international students. In 1924 the school created an annual Student Friendship Fund, which was funded by faculty and students for an outstanding international student to study at Union for one year. The low number of foreign scholars changed drastically over the next fifty years. Thirty years after the fund's creation, former Union President Henry Sloane Coffin boasted: "It has been Union's distinction to aid in the preparation of a number of the most influential leaders in the Churches of Asia, South America, Africa and the Pacific Islands."[24] Under Fleming's guidance the seminary community raised funds to allow Christian leaders from around the world to study there. The list of Chinese who came to Union reads like a Who's Who list of influential Chinese.[25] Chris-

22. Coffin, *Half-Century*, 207.

23. Handy, *History*, 136.

24. Coffin, *Half-Century*, 218.

25. The names are followed by the year they graduated from Union and their role in China: 1) Timothy Tingfang Lew, '18, professor and dean of the School of Religion in Yenching University and member of the Legislative Yuan of the Nationalist government in China; 2) William Hung, '20, faculty of Harvard University as director of the Harvard-Yenching Sinological Institute and professor at Yenching University; 3) Yu-Yue Tsu, '21, bishop in the Anglican Church in China and a professor in St John's University

tians from the world over studied at Union in the first half of the twentieth century. The next chapter centers on the school's impact in China; however, the remainder of this chapter explores the experience of an international student at Union in 1930. Dietrich Bonhoeffer (1906–45) offers unique insight into what Union was like in first half of the twentieth century, the time period it exerted a profound influence on Chinese Christianity.

## Dietrich Bonhoeffer's Experience at Union Seminary

Because he studied at Union, Bonhoeffer provides an inside view of the seminary.[26] His intellect and theological training gave him unique insight into what Union was like in the 1930s. Bonhoeffer's story is an extraordinary one that need not be rehearsed here, save in summary.[27] Born into a prominent academic family that was mildly Christian, by the age of fourteen Bonhoeffer had set his ambition on becoming a theologian.[28] Four years later he enrolled in a theology course at Berlin University, following a year of study at Tübingen. He commuted to classes from his family's home with his neighbor, Adolf von Harnack. Though Bonhoeffer admired the legendary Harnack, his theology became far more aligned to that of Karl Barth.[29] He earned a doctorate in theology at Berlin in 1927. In 1930 he won

in Shanghai; 4) Pao-chien Hsu, '24, professor in history and philosophy of religion at Yenching University until his death in 1944; and 5) Wallace Chun-Hsien Wang, '40, the first Chinese president of the West China Union Theological Seminary in Chengdu, China. Many of these men will be discussed in detail in following chapters.

26. Bonhoeffer's well-deserved popularity has allowed his academic and personal writings to be preserved and translated, available at any substantive library in the world.

27. See Bethge, *Dietrich Bonhoeffer*; Bosanquet, *Life and Death*; Metaxas, *Bonhoeffer*.

28. Bonhoeffer's father (Karl Bonhoeffer, 1899–1957) was the most distinguished psychiatrist in Germany in the 1920s/30s. His mother's grandfather (Karl August von Hase, 1800–1890) was a famous theologian and historian in the nineteenth century. His father was not a Christian but his mother was. "Though the Bonhoeffers could not be described as a church family, it would be entirely wrong to describe them as non-Christian. At all events, Dietrich's mother was the very opposite of a non-Christian. When she was young she had spent months at Herrnhut, and she had adopted the ideals of the Moravian Brethren with youthful enthusiasm. After her marriage, however, these things remained below the surface." Bethge, *Dietrich Bonhoeffer*, 21.

29. Bonhoeffer represented Harnack's former students in speaking at his memorial service on June 15, 1930. He praised Harnack as "a champion of the free expression of truth when it has been recognized, who continually revised his free judgment and plainly expressed it, notwithstanding the anxious restraint of many. . . . But, as we knew that with him we were in kindly and solicitous hands, we saw in him a bulwark against all

a Sloane Fellowship to study at Union. Prior to leaving Germany, a German friend who had attended seminary in America warned Bonhoeffer that he would have to enroll as an ordinary student. He would be subjected to the "credit system," accumulating points by attending lectures and submitting assignments. Eberhard Bethge, Bonhoeffer's closest friend and biographer, wrote:

> To prevent him from being excessively disappointed as a result of his German ideas of academic freedom, his informant advised him to imagine the atmosphere of a German secondary school. In his field of systematic theology there was of course nothing to learn. The only place that was worthwhile was Union Theological Seminary in New York, which had a great many other things to offer.[30]

As the *Colombus* steamed into New York the skyline of Manhattan overwhelmed Bonhoeffer: the silver-spired Chrysler Building had just become the tallest building in the world and the Empire State Building was under construction. But he was completely underwhelmed by the theology he encountered at Union.

On December 19, 1930, just months after arriving at Union, Bonhoeffer wrote Max Diestel, his church superintendent in Germany: "There is no theology here." He found Union's courses in systematic theology (dogmatics) and the philosophy of religion sorely lacking. Bonhoeffer viewed fellow seminarians as "completely clueless with respect to dogmatics" because they failed to ask basic questions and spoke much with little substance and no evidence of criteria. The Union community seemed "intoxicated with liberal and humanistic phrases" and "amused by the fundamentalists." He lamented the difference in German and American theological liberalism:

> In contrast to our own liberalism, which in its better representatives doubtless was a genuinely vigorous phenomena, here all that has been dreadfully sentimentalized, and with an almost naïve know-it-all attitude. It often just burns me up when people here deal with Christ and are then done with him, and laugh insolently if I present a citation from Luther on the consciousness of guilt. The Jamesean notion of the finite God is rooted deep within most of the theologians and pastors here. They find it to be profound

trivialization and destruction, all schematization of the life of the mind." Bethge, *Dietrich Bonhoeffer*, 102. Metaxas explains: "He did not agree with Harnack's liberal conclusions, but he appreciated and respected Harnack's respect for truth and for academic inquiry." Metaxas, *Bonhoeffer*, 103.

30. Bethge, *Dietrich Bonhoeffer*, 105.

> and modern and do not sense at all the impertinent frivolousness in all such talk.[31]

Bonhoeffer's condescending comments must be evaluated in light of his own background. He was the son of Germany's greatest psychiatrist, the great-grandson of an esteemed theologian, a neighbor with Harnack, close friends with Barth, and himself a brilliant theologian. Bonhoeffer offers a unique perspective into the atmosphere at Union in the 1930s.

At the conclusion of the Sloane Fellowship, Bonhoeffer submitted a report of his year in New York to the German Church Federation Office. He never intended his letter to Diestel, referenced above, for the public; however, this seventeen-page report was written for a broader audience. It contains a more reflective, though no less biting, analysis of Union.[32] Union Theological Seminary, he explained, was both notorious and venerated for its critique of theological conservatism and of the world's political, social, and economic circumstances. The school's radical and passionate openness had led to slow but steady decline. Bonhoeffer believed Union had replaced Christian theology with pragmatic philosophy. He commended Union as "a place of free expression between all members, which is made possible by the civil courage unique to Americans and by the lack of professional constraint in personal contacts."[33] He attributed the strong social environment—"the thousandfold 'hello' resonating through the halls" which "generates a strong spirit of camaraderie, of mutual readiness to help"—to the unique aspect of dormitory life. American students lived in dormitory setting for many years, giving them one "enormous advantage" over German students: they knew more about daily life.

Bonhoeffer went from observing communal life in American schools to explaining the effect he saw it having on the American psyche and approach to truth. "The unreserved nature of living together prompts one person to be open to another; and in the conflict between a resolve for truth with all its consequences and the will to community, the latter wins," he wrote. "Community is thus based less on truth than on a spirit of fairness."[34] Bonhoeffer observed that American theology students were not taught to work independently; professors treated students as "utter children."

31. Bonhoeffer, *Barcelona, Berlin, New York*, 265–67. Unless otherwise noted the preceding citations come from this letter.

32. Bonhoeffer, *Barcelona, Berlin, New York*, 305.

33. Bonhoeffer, *Barcelona, Berlin, New York*, 306.

34. Bonhoeffer, *Barcelona, Berlin, New York*, 306.

Professors and students fell into one of three categories: radical socialization (Harry Ward and Reinhold Niebuhr), philosophical secularization (Eugene Lyman and Harrison Sacket Elliot), and theological liberalism (John Baillie). The seminary's teaching of core Christian doctrines was in utter disarray. He concluded: "The theological spirit at Union Theological Seminary is accelerating the process of secularization of Christianity in America." Then he explained why:

> Its criticism is directed essentially at fundamentalism and to a certain extent also at the radical humanists in Chicago; such criticism is healthy and necessary. But the foundation on which one might rebuild after tearing down is not able to support the weight. The collapse destroys it as well. A seminary in which numerous students openly laugh during a public lecture because they find it amusing when a passage on sin and forgiveness from Luther's *de servo arbitrio* [On the bondage of the will] is cited has obviously, despite its many advantages, forgotten what Christian theology in its very essence stands for.[35]

To understand the theology of Union and "liberal enlightened Americans" Bonhoeffer knew he must understand the salient philosophical literature.

As a teacher and conversation partner, Bonhoeffer enlisted Professor Eugene Lyman. They met fortnightly for an afternoon. In between these meetings he carefully read the writings of William James, John Dewey, Bertrand Russell, and Alfred North Whitehead. In these philosophers, and especially in James, he found the key to the modern theological language. Bonhoeffer explained what he discovered about "truth":

> The destruction of philosophy as the question of truth, and its recasting as a positive individual discipline with practical goals—as most radically carried through by Dewey—alters the heart of the concept of scholarship, and truth as the absolute norm of all thinking is restricted by what proves to be "useful in the long run." Thinking is essentially teleological, aimed at serving life.[36]

Following his study with Lyman, he concluded that liberal Christians in America "are not only the purest Pelagians but also adherents of Protagoras." American Christians had made themselves the measure of all things, able to earn salvation with enough effort. This environment at Union sucked the air out of Christian message. Bonhoeffer recounted a time when

35. Bonhoeffer, *Barcelona, Berlin, New York*, 309.

36. Bonhoeffer, *Barcelona, Berlin, New York*, 310.

a leading Union professor admitted to him, to the applause of the gathered students, that justification by faith was unimportant, a trivial theological idea. Bonhoeffer's fellow students found his use of the apostle Paul to be inappropriate in modern times. He lamented: "In New York, they preach about virtually everything; only one thing is not addressed, or is addressed so rarely that I have as yet been unable to hear it, namely, the gospel of Jesus Christ, the cross, sin and forgiveness, death and life."[37] Rhetorically he wondered what stood in the place of the Christian gospel at Union? "An ethical and social idealism borne by a faith in progress that—who knows how—claims the right to call itself 'Christian.'" No wonder that John Baille, the Roosevelt Professor of Systematic Theology at Union, considered Bonhoeffer "the most convinced disciple of Dr. Barth that had appeared among us up to that time, and withal as stout an opponent of liberalism as had ever come my way."[38] Bonhoeffer's appraisal of Union is vital to my analysis because it offers the best extant description of what the seminary was like in the 1930s.

His critique offers valuable insight for understanding how Union impacted Chinese Protestantism. I will highlight relevant lessons from both Bonhoeffer's commendation and critique of Union. First, he repeatedly commended Union's robust social atmosphere. Bonhoeffer described seminary life as "quite stimulating and instructive as far as personal contacts are concerned."[39] Union provided its students with a robust social environment, a dense social network. This social web is not insignificant. It is, I believe, the primary contribution that Union offered to Chinese Protestantism. This network of influential, ambitious Chinese Christians became the leadership base in the SFPE and, after 1949, in the TSPM. Future historians would comment on the "budding ecumenism" Bonhoeffer developed at Union.[40] The school provided not only a philosophical base for ecumenical theology but also a network of social contacts around the globe.

Second, Bonhoeffer appreciated how Union students engaged with everyday life and the burning issues of the time. While German theology students sequestered themselves in lonely study, Union students immersed themselves in the social problems of Depression-struck New York. At

37. Bonhoeffer, *Barcelona, Berlin, New York*, 313.

38. Metaxas, *Bonhoeffer*, 106.

39. "Letter to Max Diestel, 19 December 1930," in Bonhoeffer, *Barcelona, Berlin, New York*, 266.

40. Godsey, "Dietrich Bonhoeffer," 1:51.

Union Bonhoeffer encountered something lacking in Berlin: "a burning concern to bring what they knew of Christianity into contact with daily life at every point."[41] Unimpressed with courses taught by the likes of Reinhold Niebuhr, James Moffatt, and Harry Emerson Fosdick, Bonhoeffer plunged into New York City life. Through his involvement with an African-American church in Harlem, the upper-class German academic learned to see things "from below," through the eyes of the oppressed.[42] Union emphasized the social gospel, which applied Christian ethics to social problems.[43] Chinese Christians and future missionaries to China were immersed in an environment that emphasized the Christians role in social justice or, as the Chinese called it, "national salvation." Bonhoeffer's criticisms of Union foreshadowed the criticism that many would later make of the Wu, Ting, and the TSPM.

Bonhoeffer lamented the absence of robust Christian theology at Union. Core Christian dogma was abandoned and replaced with pragmatic philosophy. He mourned that the theological training of the socially active students "is practically zero, and the self-confidence with which they gently smile at every specially theological query is both unjustified and naïve."[44] Union students, in Bonhoeffer's opinion, learned very little Christian theology. He describes the epistemology en vogue at Union:

> Truth is not "valid," but rather "works," and that is its criterion. Thinking and living takes place visibly here in very close proximity . . . Union Theological Seminary and the realm of enlightened Americans have greeted and parroted with extraordinary liveliness James's thesis of the "growing God."[45]

Consciously or not, future leaders in Chinese Protestantism breathed the air of Jamesean pragmatism.

41. Bosanquet, *Life and Death*, 83.

42. With its fiery, Bible-teaching pastor Adam Clayton Powell Sr., Abyssinian Baptist Church became the largest church in the United States in the 1930s, with over ten thousand members. Bonhoeffer called it the one place where one could hear genuine proclamation of truth. "This personal acquaintance with Negroes was one of the most important and gratifying events of my stay in America." Bonhoeffer, *Barcelona, Berlin, New York*, 315.

43. See Rauschenbusch, *Christianity and Social Crisis;* Rauschenbusch, *Theology for Social Gospel*; Matthews, *Jesus on Social Institutions*.

44. Bonhoeffer, *Barcelona, Berlin, New York*, 308.

45. Bonhoeffer, *Barcelona, Berlin, New York*, 311.

Lastly, Bonhoeffer provides a helpful taxonomy in analyzing the three types of professors at Union. Professors fell into three categories: radical socialization, philosophical secularization, or theological liberalism. Students tended to follow professors by identifying with one of these groups. The liveliest group was interested in socialization and deeply committed to addressing social problems. This group longed for a renewal of the gospel in the present age and gladly made theological concessions to do so. The second group gathered around Professor Lyman, whom Bonhoeffer admired, and focused on the philosophy of religion. They troubled Bonhoeffer with the carefree manner with which they spoke about God. The final group, in which "hardly anyone has a firm position," contained many missionaries. These three schools of thought at Union provided a tour de force that would exert tremendous influence on Chinese Protestantism. Many Protestant leaders in Republican China learned one or all of these lessons from someone trained at Union: be it through the YMCA, China's Christian college, the publications of Union professors, or actually attending the seminary. The ideas taught at Broadway and West 120th St. had far-ranging influence.

## Summary

I began this chapter by describing the history and key characteristic of Union Theological Seminary. Union's founders deliberately situated the school in the midst of the most important city in the United States. New York City's energy, diversity, and all its problems surrounded Union's students and faculty. This forced the seminary to address how a changing Christian faith should touch the world and its problems. Union's Presbyterian founders wanted it to be a place were "all men of moderate views and feelings" could "affectionately rally." The school welcomed and taught a diverse range of theological perspectives. Around the turn of the century, the heresy trials of two Union professors, Charles Briggs and A. C. McGiffert, confirmed the seminary as a place that defended academic freedom. Union evolved from moderate Presbyterianism to the vanguard of theological liberalism. Throughout the nineteenth century many Union professors studied in Germany. Men such as Edward Robinson and Henry Boynton Smith interpreted German theology for generations of American pastors, missionaries and theologians. The fast-growing seminary also wanted to shape Christianity around the world. Union's very first student organization, the Society of Inquiry concerning Missions, devoted one afternoon each month to discussing and praying for world missions. Even today a plaque next to the Van Dusen Gate at Union's entrance declares: "Through this gate let the world come to Union and Union go into the world." In 1914 Daniel Fleming formed the Department of Foreign Service. Fleming not only taught on world missions, he also worked hard to attract more international students. In 1930 Dietrich Bonhoeffer received a fellowship to study at Union. Bonhoeffer appreciated the seminary's robust social environment but mourned the lack of substantive, biblical theology. The Union of Bonhoeffer's experience mocked fundamentalism and celebrated modernism. And this is the Union that thirty-nine Chinese Christians and many missionaries to China experienced between 1911 and 1949. The following chapters moves into the heart of my argument: exploring how Union exported a dense social network to twentieth-century China.

# Part II

# Union Seminary Exports a Dense Social Network

# 4

# Union and China's Christian Colleges

Y. T. Wu

> I have heard of men using [the ways of our] great land to change barbarians, but I have not yet heard of any being changed by the barbarians.
>
> MENCIUS (372–289 BC)[1]

UNION SEMINARY EXPORTED ITS people and ideas to China. Its people included American graduates who served as missionaries in China, professors who visited China, and Chinese Christians who studied in Manhattan, then returned home. Union disseminated a progressive and ecumenical theology to China through its classrooms and the publications of professors and graduates. The school thus became a key agent in the traffic carrying liberal Protestantism between the United States and China. Undoubtedly, the road was busiest from New York to China but the influence was not one way. Union's greatest influence on Chinese Protestantism came via its dense alumni network. This chapter examines how the Union-trained missionaries influenced higher education in China. I will describe where the seminary's influence was greatest, the social network of Chinese Christians educated at Union, and discuss the role of Union graduates and professors in the modernist-fundamentalist controversy.

1. Cited in Xi, *Conversion of Missionaries*, 17.

## Numbers of Union Alumni in China

From 1838 to 1884, twenty Union graduates went to China as missionaries. These twenty missionaries included Chauncey Doorich, professor and dean of the North China Union Theological College; Leander Pilcher, president of Peking University; Gilbert Reid, founder of the International Institute in China; and John Newton Hayes, secretary of the Anti-Opium Society of China. These men tended to serve in educational and social arenas rather than evangelism and church planting.[2] The number of Union alumni going to China as missionaries swelled to 196 from 1911 to 1949.[3] Of these 196 missionaries, 114 people served over five years. The average size of Union's graduating class during this period was 97 students. Each year Union sent five graduates to serve in China; three of these would spend over five years there, many their whole careers. Every year for thirty-eight years, 5 percent of Union's student body ended up in China.

Young American Christians at the turn of the nineteenth century had an obvious outlet for their missionary zeal: the Student Volunteer Movement for Foreign Mission, which sent out 33,726 foreign missionaries between 1890 and 1920.[4] This flood of American missionaries came at a pivotal period in Chinese history. Social change rocked Republican China; because of this at times and despite it at others, Christian institutions flourished. More and more missionaries were going to China and they were building institutions and churches throughout the country. As Daniel Bays has noted, 1902–27 was the "golden age" for the SFPE.[5] By the 1920s there were over 8,000 foreign missionaries in China. During the hot summer

2. The distinction between these two fields of service for liberal and conservative missionaries becomes more pronounced in the 1910s and 20s, which I detail later in this chapter.

3. These figures are based on my study of *The Union Theological Seminary Alumni Directory, 1836–1958*. From 1838 to 1884, Union sent 146 alumni out to serve as overseas missionaries. The most common fields of service were Turkey (27), Syria (21), China (20), India (12), and Persia (9).

4. Described in ch. 2.

5. Bays, *New History of Christianity*, ch. 5. "Protestant growth between 1900 and 1915 was impressive by all indices. Foreign missionaries numbered about 3500 in 1905 and 5500 in 1915, well one the way toward their eventual high-water mark of more than 8000 in the 1920s. Chinese Protestants, about 100,000 in 1900, numbered almost 270,000 communicants (330,000 baptized) in 1915; this growth would also continue in the 1920s, reaching about 500,000 before the storms of nationalism hit" (94). Of particular interest for this study is the growth of the YMCA and the consolidation of the Christian colleges in China.

months, these missionaries gathered for conferences in the mountains or beaches across China. Not only was Union sending more and more missionaries to China but its professors traveled to China to speak at these conferences and elsewhere.

## The Chinese Roots of Fundamentalist-Modernist Controversy

Union Seminary made an acute contribution to the growing fundamentalist-modernist controversy when one of its most famous professors visited Kuling (庐山 *Lushan)* in 1921. Harry Emerson Fosdick, a pastor in New York and professor at Union, surfaces repeatedly as instigator of the controversy. In American church history, this theological controversy stands as a watershed event. Church historians usually circle May 21, 1922, as the start of the controversy.[6] On that day Fosdick preached a sermon from Acts 5:38–39 entitled "Shall the Fundamentalists Win?" at First Presbyterian Church in New York City. He bashed fundamentalists, urging American Christians to tolerance in the face of modern science and philosophy. Fosdick's sermon propelled conflict within American Protestantism; however, it did not initiate the controversy. Theological conflict had been growing in the Presbyterian Church. Fosdick's biographer, Robert Moats Miller, astutely comments: "The sermon was not a stone dropped into denominational waters that would otherwise have remained calm."[7] The conflict originated not in the United States but in a mountain resort in China.

Situated 4,836 feet above sea level in Jiangxi Province, Kuling provided an ideal resort for foreigners and wealthy Chinese to escape the stifling heat of south China's summers. Here and in the seaside resort of Peitaiho (北戴河 *Beidaihe*) Western missionaries gathered in the summer. Missionary conferences abounded in these summer resorts. Writing in 1922, Paul Hutchinson commented on the abundance of summer conferences: "It is probably possible, although I have never made a personal test to insure the truth of this statement, to go to a meeting of some kind every day of one's vacation."[8] He added that these conferences nurtured a conservative theological spirit in China. The Kuling summers of 1920 and 1921 featured two

6. Sandeen, *Roots of Fundamentalism*; Barr, *Fundamentalism;* Marsden, *Fundamentalism and American Culture*; Marsden, *Understanding Fundamentalism and Evangelicalism*; Carpenter, *Revive Us Again.*

7. R. Miller, *Harry Emerson Fosdick*, 116.

8. Hutchinson, "Conservative Reaction in China," 341.

men who would become leaders in their respective camps: W. H. Griffith Thomas and Fosdick. Each man had the financial backing of an oil-rich, Protestant millionaire: Lyman Stewart, of Union Oil, funded Thomas's trip; John D. Rockefeller, Jr., of Standard Oil fortune, backed Fosdick. Bays notes:

> In some ways the world-wide "Fundamentalist-Modernist Controversy" began in China in the summer of 1920, with acrimonious disputes over Biblical authority, higher criticism, evolution, and the like breaking out in some of the mountain summer retreats that provided relief from the summer heat for many missionaries. Some visiting theologians from the US were appalled by the prevalence of "modernist" views of the Bible which they encountered, and complained bitterly and publicly.[9]

Thomas's journey around China in 1920 confirmed the reports in the West. Missionaries in China were divided in two camps: one who favored "critical views" and another who were "strongly conservative."[10]

At Kuling in 1920 Thomas delivered a series of lectures on topics important to orthodox Christianity. He spoke about the life, death, and resurrection of Christ; the role of the Church; the authority of the Bible; the danger of evolution; and the end times. Thomas went from the Kuling conference to a similar one at Peitaiho. At this latter resort city, which is now the summer retreat for high officials of the CCP, missionaries from the YMCA opposed him. They were convinced that Thomas's presence would divide the missionary community. Throughout his China tour Thomas's fears were confirmed: modernity had infected the minds of many missionaries. In Beijing he discovered that Yenching University's Life Fellowship was publishing a journal that used science to interpret, critique, and correct theological questions. In Shanghai he saw the "inroads of Higher Criticism."[11]

Thomas spoke with a Methodist missionary who complained that in Guangzhou not a single missionary out of two hundred was engaged in evangelistic work. All the missionaries, Rev. Henry Anderson bemoaned, conducted institutional work. The task of evangelizing nearly two million people "is not being done as it should be done, and it will never be done at all, if it is left to these supposedly highly-trained men who are shaky in their theological convictions, and who hold loose views about

9. Bays, *New History of Christianity*, 106.

10. Thomas, "Modernism in China," 631.

11. Thomas, "Modernism in China," 639.

the authority and inspiration of the Bible."[12] Thomas identified, with great concern, the result of modernist theology filling missionary minds: evangelism has been abandoned for secular educational work because the modernist missionaries had no good news to preach. One missionary bemoaned the modernist influence in schools inside and outside China: "The seminaries are being filled with men who are New Theology men and who have no message to give. The students are filled with rubbish and then expected to preach, and what will they preach?"[13] Thomas lamented that the modernist views were not limited to Western missionaries. The poison had extended to Chinese Christians, especially those affiliated with the YMCA and the Christian colleges.

The worst offenders were Chinese who had studied in the West. Rev. Henry Anderson wrote: "The 'returned student,' the man who has been to America and obtained a degree there. He often returns home to China with views of the Bible and Christianity which are definitely critical."[14] One missionary told Thomas she would rather send her girls to a non-Christian school than one of the "so-called Christian schools in China." Another missionary gave him a paper prepared by a young lady volunteer in China which served "as a fair sample of the training the many volunteers in Union Theological Seminary, New York, are receiving during their preparation for foreign fields."[15] The instruction sheet, allegedly from Union, included two columns, Biblical and Modern. On the Biblical side the Earth is thought of as flat and as the center of the universe; on the Modern side, the Earth is thought of as spherical, revolving around the sun, and a part of a huge universe. Sickness, according to the Bible, is caused by spirits and demons but the modern view understands it as caused by germs. Significantly, among all Western theological schools, Thomas singled out only Union Seminary in New York as the source of this critical thought. Why not mention universities in Tübingen or Halle, the divinity schools at Harvard or Yale, or the seminaries at Lane or Andover? Thomas rightly perceived Union Seminary's key role in training Western missionaries and Chinese Christians in a modernist approach to the Christian faith. The New York seminary exerted a more profound impact on the fundamentalist-modernist controversy in China than any other theological school in the world. Upon returning to

12. Cited in Thomas, "Modernism in China," 641.

13. Thomas, "Modernism in China," 657.

14. Thomas, "Modernism in China," 644.

15. Thomas, "Modernism in China," 663.

the United States, Thomas summed up his China experience in a forty-two-page article in the *Princeton Theological Review* entitled "Modernism in China." Thomas stoked the theological controversy in the American Presbyterian Church but Fosdick made it explode with his 1922 sermon. But first he too visited the missionary retreat center in Kuling.

In 1921 missionaries in China invited Fosdick to address the annual gathering of missionary groups. Storm clouds of theological controversy billowed on the Chinese mission field following Thomas's Stewart-sponsored visit in the same year. Fearing the liberal distortion of the gospel message, fundamentalist missionaries organized the Bible Union of China in August 1920.[16] Back in the United States Thomas wrote and lectured about the threat of modernism in the Chinese church. At the same time a Baptist layman offered a gift of 100,000 shares of International Petroleum to the Baptist Home Mission Society, contingent on the missionaries agreeing to the fundamentalist distinctives. A growing theological tension pervaded the Sino-Foreign Protest Establishment in China at the time of Fosdick's visit. Fosdick agreed to go to the East, aware of this tension. He wrote Timothy Tingfang Lew, a former Union student and Yenching professor:

> Of course, I know all about the Bible Union Movement in China and we have had many conferences about it here. I am sincerely hoping that with the passage of time it may turn out that the bark of this animal is worse than its bite. I confess that it is with some trepidation I undertake the task of speaking to representatives of both theological camps at Kuling this summer. You can readily see that it is going to be a difficult task and if you should have any light that you can throw upon this matter I shall be delighted to receive it.[17]

At this point Fosdick held a unique position: both modernists and fundamentalists trusted him. The committee that invited him included both liberal and conservative missionaries. For eight days, Fosdick spoke twice each day at the Kuling conference to the audience of one thousand missionaries. Appeasing a deeply divided audience provided one of the greatest challenges he ever faced in his career. In his autobiography he reported that he felt like "walking a tightrope" because the tension between missionaries

16. "In most major works on fundamentalism, the formation of the Bible Union of China in 1920 was commonly considered to be the most significant indicator of the fundamentalist rallying against the liberal tendencies in the mission field." Yao, *Fundamentalist Movement*, 6.

17. R. Miller, *Harry Emerson Fosdick*, 106.

was "terrific." Fosdick confided with missionary leader Edwin Lobenstine that he hoped to win "peace with honor" for liberals at Kuling.[18] Did he succeed? Fosdick helped to make liberalism a more prominent feature of the SFPE but he did not introduce liberal ideas into Chinese Protestantism. Fosdick's 1921 lectures in China surfaced what already existed: conflict over how to relate the Christian message to an ancient culture.

China proved fertile ground for perplexing questions of how to relate the Christian message in a foreign context. Throughout its long history China had befuddled missionaries from the West. In 1707 Emperor Kangxi told troubled Jesuit missionaries: "If your king of the doctrine [the pope] . . . accuses you of having committed a fault toward the Master of Heaven through following Ricci's precepts, and orders you to return, I shall tell him that, having been so long in China, you have become completely acclimaticised and in no way different from Chinese, and consequently I shall not permit you to return."[19] The Jesuits encountered the enigma of contextualization in China in the seventeenth and eighteenth centuries and Protestants, in the nineteenth and twentieth centuries. Union's history of exporting liberal Christianity to China is demonstrated well in the case of Gilbert Reid (1857–1927).

Reid's forty-five year career in China began as a Presbyterian missionary in 1882, the year he graduated from Union. In 1890, at the Second General Missionary Conference in Shanghai, Reid read a paper written by W. A. P. Martin examining the veneration of ancestors (敬祖 *jingzu*). Horrified by the sympathetic treatment of ancestor worship, Hudson Taylor, founder of China Inland Mission, shouted "No! No!" and led delegates to stand in protest. Reid and Martin demonstrated an unusual generosity toward Chinese culture that challenged the predominating conservative views of missionaries. In 1894 he proposed the establishment of "the Mission among the Higher Classes in China." When the Presbyterian board refused this idea, he resigned and founded the International Institute of China in Shanghai. The institute sought to engage China's higher classes by cultivating interaction and synthesis among China's religions. By fusing the gods of the East and the Christian God of the West, Reid forced religious questions in new directions.[20] Reid's institute foreshadowed—and helped

18. R. Miller, *Harry Emerson Fosdick*, 108.

19. Xi, *Conversion of Missionaries*, 1.

20. The International Institute proved "too broad for most Christians and Reid plowed a solitary furrow until his death in 1927." Xi, *Conversion of Missionaries*, 173.

instigate—the controversy between conservative and liberal missionaries in the 1920s. Lian Xi comments: "By the late 1920s, two decades of the liberal movement in the China missions had expanded beyond the debates over biblical literalism, the social gospel, and the Sinicization of Christianity to include calls for spiritual alliance with all religions of the East."[21] Reid's interest in Chinese philosophy stemmed from his days at Union Seminary, where he became intrigued by Confucius's explanation of the unity between heaven and man. At many turns the school seems to be at the cutting edge of mitigating theological liberalism to China.

Union intended to influence the world through men like Gilbert Reid. Coffin, the seminary's president, praised Reid's "courage, vision and selflessness" that led to a "unique career in China."[22] In *The Conversion of Missionaries: Liberalism in American Protestant Missions in China, 1907–1932*, Lian Xi makes a convincing case that China's religious and cultural heritage unsettled American missionaries and helped cause the fundamentalist-modernist controversy. "The untraditional, often syncretic, religious and cultural ideas that emerged out of the missionaries' experience in the East—the eventual unmaking of many missionaries—precipitated a major crisis within the missionary enterprise in the late 1920s and early 1930s."[23] When American missionaries waded into the stream of Chinese cultural they did not all "wear waterproof rubber boots." Xi details three conservative missionaries who became modernists through their encounter with China: Edward Hume, the head of Yale-in-China, changed as he encountered Chinese traditional medicine; Frank Rawlinson, as he studied Confucianism; and Pearl Buck, as she interacted with Chinese peasants. While their friends in Europe and America wrestled with the science of Freud and Darwin and the theology of Schleiermacher and Ritschl, Western missionaries in China contended with the ancient philosophies of Confucius (孔子 *Kongzi*, 551–479 BC) and Mozi (墨子 *Mo Tzu*, 470–391 BC) and the contemporary teachings of Liang Qichao (梁启超 *Liang Ch'i-ch'ao*, 1873–1929) and Hu Shi. Modernism in China differed from that in the United States. Theological modernists in the United States wanted to reform Christianity in light of Darwin's theory of evolution and German higher criticism. But in China modernists sought to unify and reshape Christianity with Eastern

21. Xi, *Conversion of Missionaries*, 171.

22. Coffin, *Half-Century*, 211.

23. Xi, *Conversion of Missionaries*, xii.

philosophy. Modernism had been growing among missionaries since 1907. Eventually, in the 1920s, the conflict split the missionary community.

Missionary journals at the time noted the changing attitudes of new missionaries to China. In 1924 a missionary father in China wrote to his son:

> Of late years, the young people offering themselves for missionary service and commissioned by the Boards, coming, as many of them do from colleges and seminaries which teach only the modernist ideas, have brought modernism with them; so have found themselves out of sympathy,—in faith and often in policy and method,—with those of use how have established and for many years carried on the mission work. Sometimes rather impetuously, sometimes gradually, they have sought to change the old teachings and practices in the Missions, to bring them into line with what they have been taught are more "modern" and more "scientific" idea and ideals.[24]

Young missionaries landed in Shanghai, Tianjin, Guangzhou, and elsewhere with very different theological view from previous generations of missionaries. They arrived with a totally different perspective on what constituted the Christian message, what Christian missionaries ought to do, and how the Christian faith should interact with Chinese philosophy.

Not only did new Western missionaries arrive with modernist views, Western-educated Chinese Christians, who were theological liberals, rose to positions of prominence in the SFPE. In July 1922 Paul Hutchinson wrote in *The Journal of Religion*:

> One other source of gain to the liberal movement during recent years has been the coming to the fore of young Chinese leaders. Many of these have been educated abroad; some are the product of the mission colleges of China. The way in which they are assuming leadership is remarkable, and desperately frightening to the conservatives.[25]

Throughout the 1920s voices echoed this sentiment that profound social change would soon dawn on China's horizon. China's future no longer rested in the hands of eunuchs in Beijing but in a network of young, educated Chinese. The president of the University of Nanking, Dr. A. J. Bowen, noted in 1921:

24. Anonymous, "Puzzled," in Yao, *Fundamentalist Movement*, 44.

25. Hutchinson, "Conservative Reaction in China," 350.

> These men (students who have studied abroad), together with the most alert and volatile students in the universities and colleges of China, now form considerable of [*sic*] a group, united on a liberal program for China, covering all phases of thought and life. . . . A very searching and critical attitude pervades the movement. . . . China, through her younger scholars, is beginning to think as never before, and is thinking in terms of the twentieth century, and with an entirely forward looking attitude.[26]

Chinese students critically examined science, governance, and religion. Where would Chinese Christians turn for education and for answers to their modern questions? Union Theological Seminary. To the consternation of fundamentalist missionaries, Union educated more Western missionaries to China and more Chinese Christians than any other theological institution in the world. The reason for this is simple: many of these Union-educated missionaries went into higher education in China.

## Union and Higher Education: Yenching's Life Fellowship

Union influenced Chinese Christianity through its many alumni who became educators in China. While conservative missionaries, such as those with the China Inland Mission, tended to become evangelists and pastors in rural areas, missionaries from Union opted to teach at a school or work for the YMCA in the big cities In fact, thirty-nine Union alumni filled faculty positions in one of China's Christian colleges.[27] These missionaries taught in the reputable colleges that were part of the United Board of Christian Colleges in China, the coalition of thirteen Christian colleges that we examined in the second chapter. The two most famous Christian colleges were Yenching University in Beijing and St. John's University in Shanghai.[28] One particular faculty group at Yenching demonstrates the prevalence and influence of Union alumni. In 1919 a group of Christian faculty members

26. *Annual Report*, University of Nanking, 1921, in Hutchinson, "Conservative Reaction in China," 356.

27. The top six were: University of Nanking (8), Ginling College (1), Yenching University (8), Lingnan University (5), University of Shanghai (3), and St. John's University (3). See Appendix B for full list.

28. Yenching was formed between 1915 and 1920 from an amalgamation of four schools: the Methodist-run Peking University (1890), North China Union College (1903), North China Union College for Women (originally Bridgman Academy, 1907), and North China Educational Union (1907).

at Yenching University formed a group called the *Sheng-ming she* or Life Fellowship. The group met weekly with a stated purpose of demonstrating "the truth and merit of Christianity" in contemporary China.[29] It consisted of four Chinese and five Americans:

1. John Leighton Stuart (1876–1972), president from 1919 to 1945
2. Lucius Chapin Porter (1880–1958), dean of men and professor of philosophy
3. Howard Galt (1872–1948), professor of education
4. Luella Miner (1861–1935), dean of Yenching Women's College
5. John Stewart Burgess (1883–1949), leader of Yenching's social science program
6. T. T. Lew, "first distinguished Chinese returned student," Dept. of Religion and Chinese
7. P. C. Hsu (徐寶谦 *Xu Baoqian*, 1892–1944), professor of religion and founder of the group
8. T. C. Chao (赵紫宸 *Zhao Zichen*, 1888–1979), professor of theology and longtime dean of School of Religion
9. William Hung, dean of men and distinguished sinologist

Five of the nine members of the Life Fellowship—Burgess, Porter, Lew, Hung, and Hsu—attended Union.[30]

Significantly, three of the four *Chinese* leaders of the fellowship attended Union. All nine members had worked with the YMCA. They wanted to distance their group from conservative colleagues. West comments:

> In their search for an exportable Christianity missionary educators dissociated themselves from the narrow proselytizing of their fundamentalist colleagues. Before the founding of Yenching each had been involved in education or social work representing the more liberal side of the Protestant church. They were part of two trends, one within missions in China, which stressed good works

29. West, *Yenching University*, 17.

30. Burgess, Union 1909; Porter, Union 1908; T. T. Lew, BA/MA Columbia 1915/17, Union 1917, PhD Teachers College 1920; Hung, Union 1920; Hsu, Union 1924, PhD Columbia 1933. As an aside, in 1945 Yenching's board of trustees in New York included many people with Union connections: Mr. and Mrs. Charles H. Corbett, Rufus Jones, Henry Luce, Elizabeth Luce Moore, Henry P. Van Dusen.

> over evangelism, and the other within Protestantism, which emphasized the idea of Jesus as a social reformer, both a part of the broad movement known as the social gospel.[31]

In their quest to make Christianity relevant to modern China, the *Shengming she* eschewed the fundamentalist version of it. They embraced modern interpretations of their faith to meet the needs of modern China then exported these ideas. For eighteen years the group published a journal in Chinese.[32] Porter edited an English language issue of the journal in 1922, 1925, and 1927. The Life Fellowship serves as a prime example of how Union influenced Christianity in Republican China: through its people and ideas. The people included American and Chinese alumni; the ideas, both the spoken and written word. Most critical to our study however is the nature of the Life Fellowship. It represented a Sino-American nexus. Union exerted its greatest influence in Republican China through this social network that included the Christian colleges and the YMCA. American missionaries trained at Union played an important role in Chinese Protestantism; however, the greatest influence came not from American missionaries but from Chinese Christians.

## Chinese Christians at Union Theological Seminary

The greatest purveyors of Union-style theology in Republican and modern China were Chinese Christians who studied there. During the years of Republican China, Union accepted more Chinese students than any other divinity school or seminary in the United States. Timothy Tingfang Lew became Union's first Chinese student in 1914. Between then and 1949 thirty-eight more Chinese students and scholars studied at Union for a year or more.[33] Chinese Christians came to Union because of its reputation, because

31. West, *Yenching University*, 22.

32. For seven years the journal was called *Sheng Ming;* then it changed names to *Chen-li yu sheng-ming* (Truth and life).

33. These students and scholars were Wang Shanzhi (Lazarus Shan Chih Wang), Hou Xuecheng (Entang Hsuehcheng Hou), Hong Weilian (William Hung), Zhu Youyu (Yuyue Tsu), Jian Youwen (Timothy Yu-wen Jen), Bao Mingqian (Mingchien Joshua Bau), Cheng Jingyi (Ching-Yi Cheng), Cheng Zhiyi (Andrew Chih-Yi Cheng), Xu Baoqian (Pao-chien Hsu), Luo Shiqi (Shih Chi Lo), Xu Dishan (Ti Shang Kough Hsu), Zhou Tian (Tien Chow), Peng Jinzhang (Chin Chang Peng), Gao Chong (Chang Elijah Kao), Guo Qiongyao (Chwen-yaoGwoh), Wu Yaozong (Yao Tsung Wu), Lin Huacheng (George HiokChho Ling), Dai Huiqiong (Wai-king Taai), Wu Ruilin (Paul Yuey Len Wu), Xu

their professors in China recommended it, and because it was in New York City. Additionally, the seminary had joint programs with Columbia University and Teachers College, which were both right across Broadway from the seminary. Between 1854 and 1953 Columbia granted 1,834 degrees to Chinese international students, more than any other university in the United States.[34] During these one hundred years, 9,929 Chinese students were granted degrees from twenty-six American universities. Of these, 2,430 earned degrees from Columbia or New York University, representing 24.5 percent of the total. In comparison, 1,469 Chinese students graduated from schools in Boston (Massachusetts Institute of Technology, Harvard University, and Boston University) and 800 from schools in California (University of Southern California, University of California, Stanford University, and California Institute of Technology). Not only did Columbia attract more Chinese students than any other American university but Teachers College, which was affiliated with Union, also drew students. With the presence of distinguished philosopher John Dewey from 1904 to 1930, Teachers had a reputation for being the finest institution for training educators. The compact triangle in Morningside Heights of Columbia, Teachers, and Union provided outstanding educational opportunities in whatever a Chinese student might want to study.

During a pivotal period in Chinese history, New York City played an important role in educating China's future leaders. In 2004 Stacy Bieler published a study of the history of American-educated Chinese students. *"Patriots" or "Traitors": A History of American-Educated Chinese Students* explores the "significant but often unacknowledged role that American-trained students have played in building modern China" and concludes that these Chinese students "were sometimes exalted, but more often they were

Changling (Mencius Clifford Hsu), Shi Yufang (Peter Y. F. Shih), Wang Junxian (Wallace Chun Hsien Wang), Zheng Shaohuai (Sheffield Shao-Huai Cheng), Gong Pusheng (Pusheng Kung), Wei Yongqing (Yung-ching Wei), Lu Zhenzhong (Chenchung Lu), Cai Yongchun (Yung-ch'un Ts'ai), Yu Peiwen (Pei-wen Yu), Ding Guangxun (Kwang Hsun Ting), Yao Xianhui (Hsien-Hwei Yao), Jiang Wenhan (Wen Han Kiang), Liu Xinfang (Carl Hsin Fong Liu), Fang Kuangyu (David Kuang Yu Fang), Liu Yuchang (Yu-Tsang Liu), Liu Nianfeng (Nien-Feng Liu), Sheng Xuan'en (David Sheng), Zhang Lingzhen (Lydia Ling-chen Chang), and Hu Ren'an (Ronald Ren-An Hu). See Gillett, *Alumni Catalogue*; Tryon, *Union Theological Seminary*; and Alumni Office of Union Theological Seminary, *Union Theological Seminary*. List compiled by Y. Xu, "Union Theological Seminary," 15.

34. See Appendix D, "American Colleges and Universities Granting Degrees to Chinese Students, 1854–1953."

mistrusted, and even persecuted for being tainted by the West."[35] My research confirms Bieler's comment on the "significant but unacknowledged" impact of American-trained students in modern China. Even though these Union-trained Chinese Christians were "tainted" by a Western education, they rose to levels of prominence in the People's Republic of China. In Republican China an American education often served as an asset, but it became a liability in Communist China. Why would a Union-trained Chinese Christian have political advantages over a Harvard-trained financier or a MIT-trained engineer? Because, as I describe in the following chapters, Chinese graduates of Union had access to a powerful social network and a theology that could adapt to Communism. In 1906 the president of the University of Illinois, Edmund James, wrote a letter to President Roosevelt urging him to use the excess of the Boxer Indemnity Fund to support Chinese students in the United States:

> China is upon the verge of a revolution. . . . The nation which succeeds in educating the young Chinese of the present generation will be the nation which for a given expenditure of effort will reap the largest possible returns in *moral, intellectual, and commercial influence.* If the United States had succeeded thirty-five years ago, as it looked at one time it might, in turning the current of Chinese students to this country, and had succeeded in keeping that current large, we should to-day be controlling the development of China in that most *satisfactory and subtle* of all ways, through the *intellectual and spiritual domination* of its leaders.[36]

James's letter betrays a latent cultural imperialism; however, his point cannot be ignored. American universities exerted a profound influence on Republican China by training a generation of Chinese leaders. While this impact would be felt in the Republic of China (Taiwan) after 1949, it seemed to evaporate in every sphere of society in the People's Republic of China. But the realm of Chinese Christianity is an odd exception. As noted in the introduction, until now no scholar, apart from Xu Yihua, has noted the profound influence of Union on Chinese Christianity before and after 1949. Union Seminary provided a dense social network that manifested itself most clearly in the Christian colleges and in the YMCA. Faculty members in these Christian colleges and YMCA leaders identified the most outstanding students and helped them apply to study at the top schools in the United States.

35. Bieler, *"Patriots" or "Traitors,"* xi.

36. In Bieler, *"Patriots" or "Traitors,"* 43 (emphasis hers).

For those interested in studying theology, Union Theological Seminary was the obvious recommendation. It is where many American missionaries attended seminary, and later where the Chinese professors themselves studied. Y. T. Wu provides an excellent case study of a Chinese Christian who was involved in the YMCA, attended Union, and exerted a remarkable influence on Chinese Protestantism before and after 1949.

## Case Study of Y. T. Wu

Y. T. Wu became a Christian in 1918 after reading the Sermon on the Mount and attending a rally conducted by the famous YMCA evangelist Sherwood Eddy. Wu described an intense encounter he had with Jesus that changed him. In *Confucius and Christ: A Personal Experience*, Wu wrote that Jesus "captured me, and I was unable to escape."[37] Wu resigned from his job in the Customs Service to devote himself full-time to the Christian movement. He quickly rose up the ranks in the Chinese YMCA. In 1924 Wu applied to study at Union Seminary. Two of his three references came from members of Yenching's Life Fellowship who were Union graduates themselves: John Stewart Burgess and Timothy Tingfang Lew. Another member of the fellowship, P. C. Hsu, handwrote a letter to "My dear Prof. Fleming" to add his words of commendation. "What I want to add is that Mr. Wu is in all respects my superior and that there is great possibility in him. Anything you can make the Seminary do for him will be a real contribution to the whole Christian cause in China."[38] After studying at Union from 1924 to 1927, he served as national executive secretary of the Student Division of the YMCA and as editor-in-chief of the Associated Press of the YMCA. In this important position Wu decided what Christian materials would be published in China in the decades preceding the establishment of the People's Republic of China. The International Y identified Wu as one of the "top flight" secretaries in their Chinese branch, recognizing his "skill as a writer" that included translating and editing. Wu, in the words of the YMCA, "achieved a position as one of the leading Christian philosophers and interpreters of liberal Christian thought as applied to economics and

37. "Confucius and Christ: A Personal Experience," 81. Cited in L. Ng, "Christianity and Social Change," 176.

38. Hsu to Fleming, January 6, 1924. Series 10A: 4. Folder 10, Burke Library, Union Theological Seminary, NY.

politics."[39] In a key position in the Chinese Y, Wu influenced theological thinking across China in a direction that he favored.

Correspondence between Wu and D. Willard Lyon, founder of the Chinese YMCA in 1895, detail the interesting process of how the Y's Associated Press selected books for publication in China.[40] Lyon sent letters to Chinese and American Christians around the world to solicit their advice on potential Christian publication in China. Andrew Y. Y. Tsu at Yenching School of Religion, Ernest Hocking at Harvard University, and others would give their feedback on what books China most needed to be translated and published. A letter from Tsu to Lyon on May 6, 1933, reveals what Lyon had asked for: "The books believed best calculated, be turned into the Chinese language to be of service to the educated Chinese, as they grapple with emergent questions in the religious life, social and individual."[41] Writing in May 1933, Ernest Hocking wrote Lyon and identified the spread of humanism and anti-humanism to be the most significant religious trend in the US. He saw three "urgent unsolved problems" confronting American Christianity: Is there a God? Is language regarding Jesus literal or symbolic? What does Christianity say about wealth and the use of force?[42] On June 13, 1933, Lyon sent Wu a list of books that he consider for inclusion in the YMCA's three-year plan for translation and publication.[43] Wu took Lyon's list and consulted his colleagues in China to determine if they were the best books for publication in China. The Associated Press's first three-year plan (1934–36) called for fifty-two books to help young Chinese "think through the problems of religion, sex, social reconstruction and character-building

39. "Top Flight Secretaries of the Chinese YMCA Movement: Y. T. Wu." YMCA of the USA, Biographical Records, box 232, Y. T. Wu Folder, Kautz Family YMCA Archive, University of Minnesota.

40. This correspondence between Lyon and Wu is located in the D. Willard Lyon Papers in the Missionary Research Library Archives (MRL) housed at Union Theological Seminary in New York. John Mott founded the MRL in 1914 following the 1910 World Missionary Conference in Edinburgh. Housed in the Brown Memorial Tower at Union Theological Seminary in New York since 1929, the library came under the care of the Burke Library at Union in 1967.

41. Tsu to Lyon, May 6, 1933. MRL 6: David Willard Lyon Papers, ser. 3, box 1, folder 8, Burke Library, Union Theological Seminary, NY.

42. Hocking to Lyon, May 12, 1933. MRL 6: David Willard Lyon Papers, ser. 3, box 1, folder 8, Burke Library, Union Theological Seminary, NY.

43. Lyon to Wu, June 13, 1933. MRL 6: David Willard Lyon Papers, ser. 3, box 1, folder 8, Burke Library, Union Theological Seminary, NY.

in a period of great social, intellectual, and spiritual upheaval."[44] Wu continued to use Lyon to solicit advice from Christian leaders around the world. On May 2, 1936, Wu wrote Lyon to update him on their progress of a second three-year plan (1937–39).

Wu explained that Lyon's recommendations were too "religious" and not general enough for the constituency of those reading Y publications.[45] While the second three-year plan sought a deeper understanding of Christianity's historical setting, Wu was more interested in relating Christianity to pressing social needs in China. I detect in Wu's leadership of Y publications, a desire to circulate books to China's educated elite that would provide a critique of capitalism *(Social Salvation* by John C. Bennett, *Christianity and Economics* by A. D. Lindsay, *The Story of Social Christianity* by F. H. Stead, *Christianity and the Modern State* by Christopher Dawson, *Nature of the Capitalist Crisis* by John Strachet) and exploration of communism (*Fascism and Social Revolution* by R. P. Dutt, *Stalin* by Herni Barbusse, *Lenin* by Ralph Fox, *Introduction to Dialectical Materialism* by August Thalheimer). Y. T. Wu used his position to disseminate information that would make Chinese Christians more open to Communism. Wu's theological views seem to confirm this suspicion.

In the 1920s Wu and other modern thinkers saw the vital role Christianity could play in establishing a new China. The Christian message offered an ethical power supply to rebuild China and, in doing, establish God's kingdom on the earth. Wu did not see God sitting in heaven, judging humanity according to his laws. He viewed God as an absolute like the laws of the universe, the *dao*. Wu drank deeply from the theology prevalent in the Ys, in China's Christian colleges, and at Union Seminary. This modernist theology emphasized the fatherhood of God, brotherhood of man, value of the human person, Jesus as model of the perfectly God-conscious man, and the kingdom of God. In Wu's thinking Jesus provided the foundation of his faith: not because he was divine but because of the kind of human he was.[46] Jesus stood for real peace built on justice. Consequently, Jesus was

44. "The Second Three-Year Plan of Literature Production, National Committee of Y.M.C.A. 1937–1939." MRL 6: David Willard Lyon Papers, ser. 3, box 1, folder 8, Burke Library, Union Theological Seminary, NY.

45. Wu to Lyon, May 2, 1936. MRL 6: David Willard Lyon Papers, ser. 3, box 1, folder 8, Burke Library, Union Theological Seminary, NY.

46. "The foundation of my faith is only this one Jesus, and all the rest is secondary. I rely on Jesus, not because he is 'God', but because he is a 'man', a man just like ourselves." Wu, "My Personal Religious Experience," 3. Cited in L. Ng, "Christianity and Social

"most uncompromising toward the social evils of His time and toward their perpetrators, and that was a social struggle."[47] Christian renewal depended on identifying with the common people. This identification, Wu reasoned, must be the purpose of the church.[48] He skillfully intermeshed religious and political ideas. Taking his cue from Albrecht Ritschl—knowingly or not—Wu emphasized the kingdom of God. God's kingdom was not a spiritual or ethical idea but a real society: a place where humanity was liberated from material wants, political oppression, and social injustices.

One cannot understand Y. T. Wu's theological views apart from his political views or his political choices apart from his religious perspective. After becoming a Christian, a British Quaker influenced Wu to become a pacifist. But the Japanese aggression against China unsettled his pacifist ideas. The Nationalists, in his mind, had failed China. Wu concluded in 1933 that China needed not "piece-meal improvements, but basic reforms" which should take the form of a "new global economic and political system."[49] With rhetoric rich in Christian language, Wu turned to Communism to fulfill his vision of the kingdom of God. In 1950 he wrote: "The old dead Christianity must doff its shroud and come forth arrayed in new garments. It must learn that it is no longer the sole distributer of the panacea for the pains of the world. On the contrary, God has taken the key to the salvation of mankind from its hand and given it to another."[50] Wu believed God had taken the keys to salvation from the Christian church and given them to the Communist Party. Through his work as chairman of the Chinese Fellowship of Reconciliation, Wu worked closely with the CCP. In the 1930s he served as a middleman between Communism and Christianity. He helped to "meet and interpret" the Communist criticism of

Change," 188.

47. Wu, "Christianity and China's Reconstruction." Cited in L. Ng, "Christianity and Social Change," 213.

48. "New life will not come to the Church and its members until all have felt the strong power of a passion to identify themselves with the needs of the common people, not in an accidental way and as a means to an end, but as the very end in itself." Y. T. Wu, "How One Christian Looks at the Five Year Movement," 147–48. Cited in L. Ng, "Christianity and Social Change," 195.

49. Wu, "Meaning of the Social Gospel," 20; and Wu, "The Price of Peace," 99. Cited in L. Ng, "Christianity and Social Change," 204.

50. Wu, "Reformation of Christianity," in Jones and Merwin, *Documents of Three-Self Movement*, 14.

Christianity. It should come as no surprise that Zhou Enlai, Mao Zedong's right-hand man, called on Wu after the Communists came to power.

Many Christians consider Wu a traitor to the Christian faith, a heretic, or an anti-Christ. He did in fact conflate Christianity and communism; however, in Wu's mind, no tension existed between the two. The latter represented the fulfillment of Jesus's ideas of justice and freedom from oppression. The Chinese Communist Party embodied the kingdom of God. Wu deserves his reputation as one of the most controversial Chinese Christian leaders in the twentieth-century. He is also, perhaps, the least understood. To those in the TSPM he is a hero, a humble and devoted Christian prophet. I believe the fairest critique of Wu came four decades ago in Lee Ming Ng's 1971 thesis at Princeton:

> All this does not mean that serious questions may not be raised regarding Wu's position. Although his cooperation with the Communist government did not seem to represent any compromise on his part, one cannot help but wonder if identifying himself with the government and in viewing the government almost as the perpetrator of God's will—"the key to salvation"—Wu had not in fact given up the "prophetic" role of the church.[51]

Whatever label one affixes to Wu, "complex" is probably the most accurate one.

I am intrigued with how Wu subverted the typical process of indigenization in the Sino-Foreign Protestant Establishment. As Daniel Bays explains, Chinese Christians went from being participants, to subordinate partners to owners of the Chinese church.[52] But Wu turned the tables of control in the realm of Y publication. In many cases, tokenism prevailed. Although a Chinese Christian might be appointed to a position of authority, the real power remained in a board of directors in London or New York City.[53] Not so when it came to YMCA publishing in China: Wu controlled what was published. He excelled at playing the political game. He maintained close communication with Lyon and, through Lyon, the international YMCA. Y publications in China relied on funding from the international headquarters in Manhattan. Wu seemed to beat the American missionaries at their own game, maintaining an allusion of seeking their advice but publishing whatever he thought best. And what he believed most helpful to

51. L. Ng, "Christianity and Social Change," 245.

52. Bays, *New History of Christianity*, 1.

53. See J. Liu, "Same Bed, Different Dreams."

China in the 1930s was less theology and more books on economics and culture. I suspect that Wu used his control over Y publications to push his growing pro-Communist views.

Union Seminary played a vital role in equipping Wu with an adaptive Christianity that could blend in with Communism. Wu studied at Union from 1924 to 1927 and again from 1937 to 1938. On August 27, 1936, Wu wrote to Professor Fleming to explain why he wanted to return to Union to study. His letter captures Union's impact on the SFPE:

> Ten years' work in turbulent China among youth, especially in my present capacity, makes me feel very strongly the need for a period of intellectual and spiritual regeneration. This makes me immediately think of Union which really opened my eyes to the meaning and truth of religion in those years when I was initiated into Christian work. I am thinking therefore of applying for a missionary fellowship of the Union Seminary for the year 1937–38, which will enable me to come into contact again with the prominent minds and spirits which Union so helpfully offers.[54]

Wu's experience of using his social network in China to gain admission and funding to attend Union was not an isolated example, as I describe in upcoming chapters. In Republican China, Union Seminary played an instrumental part in the development and continuation of a dense social network of Chinese Christians. The seminary recruited Chinese students, granted them full scholarships, and, in the process, deepened their social network with prominent leaders of the SFPE.

## Summary

Earlier in this chapter I suggested that the modernist-fundamentalist controversy began not in New York City in 1922 but in missionary resorts in China in 1920/21. At the summer Bible conferences in Kuling and Peitaiho, the conflict between various missionaries metastasized. Missionaries struggled with how to respond to scientific, philosophical, and theological trends from the West. How should they relate the Bible to Darwin's science, Hegel's philosophy, and Schleiermacher's theology? The confusion magnified in China as missionaries also encountered Confucianism, Daoism, and Buddhism. How did the Christian message relate to the Chinese

54. Letter from Wu to Fleming, August 27, 1936. Series 10A: 4. Folder 10, Burke Library, Union Theological Seminary, NY.

worldview? Philosophical questions from the West and cultural questions from the East unsettled many American and European missionaries in China. Like the Jesuits centuries before, Protestant missionaries struggled to answer these fundamental questions. The man credited with igniting the controversy, both in New York City in 1922 and in Kuling in 1921, is Harry Emerson Fosdick, himself a Union graduate and key figure in the next chapter. Fosdick and Union played a key role in the modernist-fundamentalist controversy in the East and West. Fosdick's 1921 talks deepened the rift between conservative and liberal missionaries that exploded in the United States in the form of the modernist-fundamentalist controversy one year later. Union had a distinct theological voice that became unmistakable, especially in China.

Between 1911 and 1949 the seminary sent 196 missionaries to China, more than any other seminary or divinity school in the world. Alumni came from and were sent to China's Christian colleges and the Chinese YMCA. Christian leaders in the YMCA/Christian college/Union network had key roles in the SPFE before 1949 and the TSPM after 1949. For example, of the nine founders of Life Fellowship at Yenching University, five were Union graduates. The seminary trained thirty-nine Chinese Christians, more than any other school outside of China. Men like Y. T. Wu, T. T. Lew, and William Hung studied in New York and returned to China to places of prominence. In the late 1920s and early 1930s, Wu controlled the publication arm of the YMCA and decided what books were important to meet China's pressing social needs. American and Chinese graduates of Union pop up time and time again in the story of the Chinese Christianity in the last century. Yet, despite Union's important role, only one Xu Yihua has noticed and written about this trend. Union's role has been virtually ignored because it is difficult to piece together. In the next chapter I will use James Davison Hunter's framework of a "dense social network" to connect the dots. I cannot offer a simple, linear correlation between the TSPM and Union Seminary; however, my research demonstrates a complex, multilayered connection. Union was at the center of a matrix of influential leaders in China. This network included wealthy, liberal Protestants in New York, such as the Rockefeller and Luce families.

# 5

# Union and New York's Elite

## John D. Rockefeller, Jr., and Henry R. Luce

As the Middle Kingdom transformed in the twentieth century, Union students, faculty, and graduates were eager to get involved. In the preceding chapter I explained the various ways Union engaged China: by sending missionaries, by Union faculty visiting China, by publishing works of Union faculty and alumni, and, most importantly, by training Chinese Christians. This chapter posits how these factors bore significant impact on Chinese Protestantism before and after 1949. One does not produce a cake by pouring miscellaneous ingredients in a bowl and hoping for the best. There are particular ingredients that must be combined in the proper amount and baked a certain way. The ingredients were in place for Union to have an impact—its people and ideas were spread throughout the country. But I rely on a theory presented by James Davison Hunter to explain how these ingredients were "baked" to have significant impact on China. This baking can be summarized in three words—dense social network. Before describing Hunter's theory, I offer an example from Union in the 1890s.

Preceding China's cataclysmic social changes, a trio of Yale graduates, Sherwood Eddy, Henry W. Luce, and Horace T. Pitkin, enrolled at Union. From 1892 to 1894 this "small but intense group of students devoted themselves to the cause of foreign missions."[1] The trio shared rooms in a Union dormitory and gave their free time to serving the Student Volunteer Movement for Foreign Mission (SVM). Pitkin arrived in Tianjin in 1897. He would experience the social cataclysm of the first decade of the twentieth century in the most profound way. In July 1900 Chinese Boxers beheaded Pitkin during the Boxer Uprising. Eddy served as a leader in the SVM and then with the International Committee of the YMCA from 1896 to 1931. Luce served in Christian higher education in China from 1897 to 1928.

1. Handy, *History*, 101.

From 1897 to 1917 he helped establish and manage Shantung Christian University (*Cheeloo University*) and from 1921 to 1925 he did fund-raising for Yenching University. Eddy, Luce, and Pitkin became a dense social network while at Union. They exerted more impact on China collectively than they would have individually. Eddy and Luce's careers in China forecast where Union exerted its most profound impact on Chinese Christianity: the YMCA and Christian higher education. Over time a dense network was established through the Y and the Christian colleges. In the decades preceding the establishment of the Republic of China in 1911, this network consisted primarily of Americans in China and the United States. But more Chinese Christians joined the network in the decades following 1911. By the 1940s the network of liberal Protestants connected with Union Seminary was vast, deep, and influential. The extent of its influence would be felt most acutely in the establishment of the Three-Self Patriotic Movement. In the following chapters I will describe the key figures in this web of Union alumni. But I begin with detailing Hunter's theory and applying it to an influential network of Americans connected with Union.

## James Davison Hunter's Theory of "Dense Social Network"

I introduced James Davison Hunter's ideas in the introductory chapter, but will now explain the concepts in greater detail and apply them to Union. In *To Change the World: The Irony, Tragedy, and Possibility of Christianity in the Late Modern World*, Hunter seeks to understand what culture is, how it changes, and the role of Christianity in culture change.[2] The goal in this chapter is not to offer a comprehensive analysis on Christian engagement with culture, to do so would go beyond the scope of my research. I will neither probe nor survey what Kuyper, Niebuhr, Wolsterstorff, or Hauerwas have written on culture and culture change.[3] My fundamental questions are not: What is culture? Or, how do cultures change? My questions are: Did Union influence Chinese Christianity in a significant way? If so, how? Hunter's theory helps answer this how question. I use his assessment of culture change because it explains, better than anything else I have found, why a particular group of Union graduates exerted a

2. For an insightful review of Hunter's book see Smith, "How (Not) to Change," and Crouch, "How Not to Change."

3. Kuyper, *Lectures on Calvinism;* Niebuhr, *Christ and Culture;* Wolsterstorff, *Until Justice and Peace*; Hauerwas and Willimon, *Resident Aliens.*

profound influence on twentieth-century Chinese Christianity. Hunter's ideas allow the impact of Union to come into clear focus. This book does not intend to advocate Hunter's perspective as an all-encompassing theory of culture and culture change. I will simply borrow aspects of Hunter's theory to explain Union's impact.

Hunter challenges the idealism of Johann Gottfried Herder and Georg W. F. Hegel. These men and others believed that ideas change cultures. Culture is reduced to mental constructs of beliefs and ideas or, as many contemporary American Evangelicals put it, "worldview." Idealism undervalues the role of historical forces surrounding ideas and fails to appreciate *how* ideas change culture. When it comes to culture change, idealism ignores the institutional nature of culture and disregards how culture is embedded in power.[4] Culture is more than a set of propositions. If ideas do not change cultures, then it must be individual people who do so. The nineteenth-century Scottish historian Thomas Carlyle (1795–1881) adapted Hegel's concepts to suggest just this: world history is the biography of great men with great ideas (or "Thoughts"). In a series of 1840 lectures on leadership, Carlyle argues that world history, which he called "Universal History," is "at bottom the History of Great Men." These great men:

> were the leaders of men, these great ones; the modelers, patterns, and in a wide sense creators, of whatsoever the general mass of men contrived to do or attain; all things that we see standing accomplished in the world are properly the outer material result, the practical realization and embodiment, of Thoughts that dwelt in the Great men sent into the world: the soul the while world's history, it may justly be considered, were the history of these.[5]

Hunter rejects Carlyle's "great man" view of history primarily for its incomplete understanding of the social networks between these great individuals.

> The only problem with [Carlyle's] perspective is that it is mostly wrong. Against this great-man view of history and culture, I would argue (with many others) that *the key actor in history is not individual genius but rather the network* and the new institutions that are created out of these networks. And the more "dense" the network—that is, the more active and interactive the network—the more influential it could be.[6]

4. J. Hunter, *To Change the World*, 27.
5. Lecture 1, "The Hero as Divinity," in Carlyle, *On Heroes, Hero Worship*.
6. J. Hunter, *To Change the World*, 38 (emphasis his).

The key factor in culture change is not individual genius but social networks.

Cultures are not changed simply by ideas or great individuals but by a social nexus, a dense network of influential people. The denser the network, the more active and interactive it is, the more influential it will become. Hunter offers seven propositions on culture.[7] From these propositions, he argues that culture change is top down, initiated by elites who are outside the inner circle of power, and most concentrated when networks of elites overlap. With this view of culture and culture change, Hunter concludes: "Cultural change at its most profound level occurs through dense networks of elites operating in common purpose within institutions at the high-prestige centers of cultural production."[8] Change on a broad scale is instigated and maintained by a network of "cultural gatekeepers." Hunter offers the church fathers as an example. These theologians and church leaders, with very few exceptions, were born into prosperous or well-educated families that had high social status. This social standing enabled them to be well versed in Greek, Latin, and rhetoric. They met and engaged one another in the urban centers of the Mediterranean, especially in Rome. In this example, and in the case of Chinese Protestantism, centers of learning were "exceptionally important." Cultures are shaped by social elites who are networked around institutions of education in key cities and who work toward a common purpose. In the case of the Sino-Foreign Protestant Establishment in Republican China, the Christian colleges not only provided a liberal education but also of a network of elite Chinese Christians. Hunter adapts Richard Weaver's 1948 adage that "ideas have consequences" to "*under specific conditions and circumstances* ideas can have consequences."[9] Ideas move nations but only when they are propagated in the context of an influential social network. As I will demonstrate, in the case of Union Seminary and Chinese Christianity, Hunter's theory works well.

7. Culture is: 1) a system of truth claims and moral obligations, 2) a product of history, 3) intrinsically dialectical, 4) a form of power, 5) stratified in a rigid structure of "center" and "periphery," 6) generated within networks, and 7) neither autonomous or fully coherent. J. Hunter, *To Change the World*, ch. 4.

8. "The potential for word-changing is greatest when networks of elites in overlapping fields of culture and overlapping spheres of social life come tighter with their varied resources and act in common purpose." J. Hunter, *To Change the World*, 274.

9. J. Hunter, *To Change the World*, 41.

## Support of Hunter's Ideas: Elite Theory

Hunter's ideas tie well into elite theory. Elite theory attempts to explain how power is held and exerted in contemporary states. It contends that a small group of people holds the keys of that nation's economic and political power, all outside the democratic process. These power elite transcend the "ordinary environments of ordinary men and women," putting them in "positions to make decisions having major consequents."[10] Particular institutions catapult people into a privileged and influential social network. Association with these institutions enables people to establish and develop interpersonal ties. Though elite theory lends support to Hunter's idea of the power of a dense social network, other theories question this emphasis on top-down cultural change.

## Alternative Perspectives on Social Change: Gramsci and Piven

The theory of culture change derived from Antonio Gramsci (1891–1937) challenges Hunter's perspective.[11] From the premise that "all human beings are intellectuals," Gramsci rejects the simplistic Marxist distinction between workers and intellectuals and proposes categories based on social status (organic versus traditional intellectuals) and origin (urban versus rural intellectuals).[12] Contra Hunter, he argues that cultures change from the bottom up: from journalists and other opinion makers. In her 2007 presidential address to the American Sociological Society, Frances Fox Piven asked a related question: "Can Power from Below Change the World?"

Piven argued for an expanded view of power. She suggested that there is a kind of "interdependent power" that is not based on resources but on "social and cooperative relations in which people are enmeshed by virtue of

10. Mills, *Power Elite*. First published in 1956, other authors who follow Mills's tradition include Domhoff, *Higher Circles;* Schwartz and Mintz, *Power Structure*. Classical elite theory was first developed in Italy by Vilfredo Pareto (1848–1923) and Gaetana Mosca (1858–1941) in opposition to Marxist theory.

11. See Gramsci, *Antonio Gramsci Reader*.

12. Gramsci, *Selections from Prison Notebooks*, 9. Organic intellectuals represent common people; traditional intellectuals are part of the aristocracy and represent the old class structure of society. In Italy's history, rural intellectuals tended to be traditional, whereas urban intellectuals, schoolteachers, doctors, journalists, and lawyers, tended to be organic. For a brief history of Gramsci see Bondanell, "Antonio Gramsci." For a summary of Gramsci's concepts, see Custers, "Introducing Gramscian Concepts."

group life."[13] Globalization creates new avenues to organize and deploy interdependent power from below. Protests from the bottom levels of society can and do produce change. While Piven looks at change from the bottom up, in the same journal volume D. Michael Lindsay examines top-down social power for one subgroup: American Evangelicalism. Lindsay interviewed 360 "elite" American Christians to determine what mechanisms they use to advance Evangelicalism.[14] He concluded that their religious identity and cohesive networks play a key role in expanding their movement. Institutional inertia and internal factions have limited the actual impact of these evangelical elites; however, the creation of overlapping networks across social sectors elicits tremendous potential for social change. Some theories emphasize change from the top down, and others, from the bottom up; however, there seems to be agreement on the impact of social networks. But how do these social networks function? What makes dense social networks strong?

## Explaining How Social Networks Function: The Strength of Weak Ties

In 1973 Mark Granovetter wrote an influential paper for *The American Journal of Sociology* that helps answer these questions.[15] One way social networks change culture is in how they strengthen relational ties. The strength of interpersonal ties varies from strong to weak. Ties strengthen with time, emotional intensity, intimacy, and mutual service. Stronger ties lead to a greater overlap in the circle of mutual friends. Our acquaintances (weak ties) are less likely to be socially connected to each other than our close friends (strong ties). While a set of a person's acquaintances constitutes a low-density network, a set of someone's close friends makes a densely knit network. The strength of weak ties, Granovetter argues, lies in their role as a "crucial bridge" linking "two densely knit clumps of close friends." Weak ties allow disparate groups of people to connect; therefore, "individuals with few weak ties will be deprived of information from distant parts of the social system and will be confined to the provincial news and views of their close friends."[16] Weak ties facilitate the sharing of relationships,

13. Piven, "Can Power from Below," 5.
14. Lindsay, "Evangelicals in Power Elite."
15. Granovetter, "Strength of Weak Ties" (1973).
16. Granovetter, "Strength of Weak Ties" (1983), 202.

and thus power, between previously unconnected groups. Individuals with few weak ties are difficult to integrate into broader social or political movements, which rely on recruiting by friends and acquaintances. Social systems lacking weak ties tend toward fragmentation and incoherence.

By layering Granovetter's concept of the strength of weak ties with Hunter's thoughts on dense social networks, Union's hidden influence on Chinese Christianity comes to the surface. Per Hunter's theory, the recipe for culture shaping and world changing is in place if powerful networks overlap. In using Hunter and Granovetter, I am not suggesting that I am a sociologist or an expert in their theories. However, I borrow and combine their ideas to help explain Union's role in Chinese Christianity. Union Seminary happened to be the place where influential American and Chinese leaders connected. They would shape and mold the SFPE in a particular direction, especially after 1949. The seminary connected international Christian leaders to a powerful network of American Christians. A dinner banquet at the Ritz Carlton hotel in New York City in 1949 illustrates well the power of Union's network.

## Union Seminary's Dense Social Network of American Leaders

On March 25, 1949, Henry R. Luce hosted a dinner banquet for Winston Churchill at New York City's Ritz Carlton.[17] The guest list included leaders in politics, military, and business. Over 222 men and women listened as Churchill explained why the Soviet Union built up an Iron Curtain. The seventy-four-year-old former prime minister believed the Soviets "deliberately united the free world against them" because they "feared the friendship of the West more than they do its hostility."[18] With a chance to hear one of the greatest orators of the twentieth century while eating next to a senator, a general, a former presidential candidate, the "Father of the Atom Bomb" or, even better, a Rockefeller, I imagine tickets to the event were highly coveted. The table list represented those in the highest echelon of American society, a gathering of the wealthiest and most powerful people in the nation. Included on the list were Henry Pitney Van Dusen, president of Union Seminary; Reinhold Niebuhr, professor of Union Seminary; and Eugene Barnett, a Union alumnus and executive director of the YMCA. At

17. Eugene E. Barnett Collection, box 14 (1948–49), folder 1949, Rare Book and Manuscript Library, Columbia University, NY. See Appendix E for table list.

18. Internatonal Churchill Society, "Never Despair."

the head table with Churchill, Luce, and the most important dignitaries sat George Buttrick, pastor of Madison Avenue Presbyterian Church and guest professor at Union. The presence of Christian leaders was not a token invitation, offered out of altruistic pity. Union leaders lived in the same social strata as others on the invitation list. They were, in short, part of the New York establishment. The deep social ties between Union and New York's aristocracy meant that Union students were connected with some of the most powerful Christians in America. To explain this social network, I will explore the lives and Union connections of four men, in this order: Henry R. Luce; John D. Rockefeller, Jr.; Harry Emerson Fosdick; and Henry Pitney Van Dusen.

## Henry R. Luce: Missionary Child and Publisher

In 1922 Henry R. Luce and Briton Hadden quit their jobs at *The Baltimore News* to pursue a dream of starting a new kind of publication: a weekly news magazine.[19] The pair had met in secondary school in Connecticut and started their literary partnership at *The Yale Daily News*. Just two years out of Yale, they launched *Time* magazine, which Luce called "the gamble of our lives on which everything depends."[20] Launched in March 1923, the new magazine gave mainstream America access to world news. The growing publishing empire was left in Luce's hands alone when Hadden died in 1929. As head of Time Inc., he launched *Fortune* in 1930, *Life* in 1934, *House & Home* in 1952, and *Sports Illustrated* in 1954. Time Inc. became one of the largest news empires in the world, reaching over twenty million people every week. As Luce's publishing empire grew, so did his wealth and influence. Luce's acumen lay not only in building a business empire but also in his insight into global affairs. He seemed to both anticipate and turn public opinion.[21] He urged the United States to assist China, to intervene in the Second World War, and to escalate the Cold War before such issues were popular. One biographer called him "the most influential private citizen in the America of his day."[22] It is no surprise that the wealthy, influential, and PR-savvy Luce would invite Winston Churchill to speak at the Ritz Carlton

19. Brinkley, *Publisher;* Herzstein, *Henry R. Luce;* Kobler, *Luce;* and Swanberg, *Luce and His Empire.*

20. Brinkley, "Henry Luce."

21. Lambert, "Luce, Henry (1898–1967)."

22. Herzstein, *Henry R. Luce*, 1.

in 1949. What might surprise some, though, is Luce's deep connection to China and to Union.

Luce was born in Shandong Province in China in 1898. His parents, Henry Winters Luce and Elizabeth Middleton, were Presbyterian missionaries devoted to higher education in China. Before going to China, H. W. Luce attended Union Seminary with his Yale classmates Sherwood Eddy and Horace T. Pitkin. In 1897 the Luces arrived in Tungchow (now Penglai City, 蓬莱市) to help establish Shantung Christian University (*Cheeloo University*). In his first letter home after arriving, Luce described Tungchow as a "walled city of some eighty thousand people about the size of Scranton [PA]." He urged his family to put aside "every fear for our Physical well being" and instead be concerned that "the pressure of heathenism will tell on us spiritually."[23] The Luce family remained in Shandong Province until 1917. All four of their children were born there. In the 1920s he raised funds for Yenching University in Beijing. The careers of Eddy and Luce forecasted the spheres in which Union Seminary would have the most profound impact in China: the YMCA and the thirteen Christian colleges. The wealthy, influential Henry R. Luce happened to be a liberal Protestant with connections to Union Seminary and a deep commitment to China. Similar characteristics applied to the wealthiest family in New York City and the world: the Rockefellers.

## John D. Rockefeller, Jr.: Philanthropist and Ecumenist

In 1913 the $900 million net worth of John D. Rockefeller, Sr. ("Senior"), exceeded the United States national budget by $185 million.[24] His wealth reached $1 billion by 1916. Frederick T. Gates, Rockefeller's closest advisor, thundered a warning to the elder Rockefeller: "Your fortune is rolling up, rolling up like an avalanche! You must distribute it faster than it grows! If you do not it will crush you and your children and your children's children!"[25] Rockefeller focused on expanding Standard Oil; Gates, on using this colossal wealth for the wellbeing of humanity. In 1913 Senior established the Rockefeller Foundation to promote human welfare around

23. Letter from H. W. Luce, dated October 29, 1897. Special Collections, Yale Divinity School Library, New Haven, CT (hereafter YDSL), H. W. Luce Family Papers, RG 203, box 1, folder 1.

24. Bullock, *Oil Prince's Legacy*, 15.

25. Fosdick, *John D. Rockefeller, Jr.*, 110.

the world. Within two years Rockefeller had endowed his foundation with $100 million. The foundation's board elected John D. Rockefeller, Jr. ("Junior"), as president at their first trustee meeting.[26] In 1910 Junior had served as the foreman of the "White Slave" Grand Jury. This special grand jury investigated charges of an organized prostitution ring and systematic protection by Tammany Hall Democrats. The jury had sat for a staggering six months and returned with fifty-four indictments, winning Rockefeller widespread public praise. After the trial, Junior resigned his positions with Standard Oil and U. S. Steel. He devoted himself to a new cause: philanthropy.[27] Senior Rockefeller devoted his life to acquiring wealth; Junior, to giving it away.

Wealth ran deep in the Rockefeller family, as did religious conviction. The Rockefellers attended Fifth Avenue Baptist Church (which became Park Avenue Baptist Church in 1922) on Sixty-Fourth Street, close to their home. Every Sunday Junior taught the men's Bible class. Three nights a week he prepared his Sunday talk. "No single activity during young Rockefeller's early years absorbed so large a proportion of his time or was followed with such genuine preoccupation," observed his friend, employee, and biographer Raymond Fosdick.[28] Between 1919 and 1933 he annually contributed between 5.8% and 12.6% of the total budget of the Northern Baptist Convention.[29] Junior's religious views centered on the practical application of Christian principles to life rather than doctrine or denominational loyalty. Miller describes his faith as "sincere and sanguine, idealistic and practical, undogmatic and experiential."[30] On December 11, 1917, he spoke at a dinner of the Baptist Social Union on "The Christian Church—What of Its Future?" Rockefeller highlighted his growing ecumenical perspective. His talk was printed in the *Saturday Evening Post* later that year. He urged interdenominational cooperation and stressed the establishment of the kingdom of God on the earth. What should characterize this kingdom?

26. See Harr and Johnson, *Rockefeller Century*, 87.

27. "For Junior, however, the public critique and pressures of being a Rockefeller had a huge effect: Behind his lifelong embrace of the Rockefeller philanthropic tradition was a desire to redeem the Rockefeller reputation." Harr and Johnson, *Rockefeller Century*, 87. Cited in Bullock, *Oil Prince's Legacy*, 19.

28. Fosdick, *John D. Rockefeller, Jr.*, 125.

29. Thomas T. Shields called Rockefeller's contributions "the most gigantic corruption fund that ever cursed the Christian world." R. Miller, *Harry Emerson Fosdick*, 153.

30. R. Miller, *Harry Emerson Fosdick*, 152.

> It would pronounce ordinance, ritual, creed, all non-essential for admission into the Kingdom of God or His Church. A life, not a creed would be its test; what a man does, not what he professes; what he is, not what he has. . . . I see all denominational emphasis set aside. I see co-operation, not competition.[31]

While his father gave to specific Baptist institutions, such as the University of Chicago and Southern Baptist Theological Seminary, Junior preferred an ecumenical approach. Just as Senior preferred consolidation to competition in the business world, Junior followed the same approach in church matters.[32]

Rockefeller not only wanted ecumenism, he wanted ecumenism on a global scale. After the end of the Great War, the Board of Foreign Missions of the Presbyterian Church launched the Interchurch World Movement (IWM). Rockefeller became a major advocate and the financier of the IWM in 1919. His grand ambitions for the IWM stemmed from his belief that an organized and international religious movement could restore class harmony. The movement represented his hopes for Christianity. But the IWM did not have the nationwide appeal that Rockefeller had longed for. Christians across the United States gave generously to postwar solicitations from the thirty-one denominations involved ($176 million) but sparingly to the IWM ($3 million). Liquidation became inevitable for the IWM. Rockefeller turned to Raymond Fosdick, who served as a kind of receiver in bankruptcy, to clean up the mess. Interestingly, Charles Harvey has demonstrated the way Fosdick concealed the depth of Rockefeller's involvement in the IWM.[33] The virtual "conspiracy of silence" surrounding Rockefeller's crucial role in the IWM "too long has been obscured, to the detriment of a better understanding of the issues involved and of their relationship to the other dimensions of the historical process."[34] Rockefeller's ecumenical commitment would later be manifest in erecting the Interchurch Building next to Union Seminary to house the national Council of Churches (1959), the Ecumenical Institute in Geneva (1946), and Riverside Church in New York (1930). Rockefeller constructed Riverside as a national showcase for his friend and America's best-known preacher: Harry Emerson Fosdick.

31. Fosdick, *John D. Rockefeller, Jr.*, 206.

32. G. Miller, *Piety and Profession*, 307.

33. C. Harvey, "John D. Rockefeller, Jr." Harvey contends that the standard history is "based primarily upon an elaborate falsification of the historical record" (198).

34. C. Harvey, "John D. Rockefeller, Jr.," 209.

The Union-China connection manifested itself in the friendship between Rockefeller and Fosdick.

## Harry Emerson Fosdick: Rebel against Creedal Sectarianism

Harry Emerson Fosdick arrived at Union for graduate studies in 1901. New York City unsettled Fosdick's psychological wellbeing. The academic pressure at Union and the social misfortune in New York's Bowery led to a mental breakdown and admission in the Gleason Sanitarium.[35] Fosdick recovered from his reactive depression and went on to study with Arthur Cushman McGiffert, George William Knox, and others. In Knox's class on the philosophy of religion, Schleiermacher and Ritschl came to life for Fosdick. McGiffert taught Fosdick what he considered the most characteristic religious doctrine of the nineteenth century: the immanence of God. Divine immanence became central to Fosdick's developing position and to the New Theology. Following Adolf von Harnack, McGiffert stressed Christian morals over Christian dogma, the infinite value of the human soul, and universal fatherhood of God. Fifty years after graduating from Union, Fosdick said:

> This seminary made my ministry possible. Over 50 years ago, I came here a confused and hungry student, wishing above all else to teach and preach the Christian gospel, but wondering how I could do it with intellectual integrity and self-respect. And here the doors were opened.[36]

Union Seminary transformed Fosdick's theology and destiny. Miller minces no words in assessing Union's impact on Fosdick: "In all of Fosdick's ninety-one years, there were none more decisive that the three following his journey to New York in the summer of 1901 to enter Union Theological Seminary."[37] After graduating from Union in 1904, Fosdick was ordained as a Baptist pastor.

Despite Baptist ordination, theological particulars were not too important to him, he preached to standing-room only crowds at New York's First

35. Interestingly, a prominent Chinese Christian also had a mental breakdown at Union. While Fosdick went to become a leading spokesman of liberal Protestantism, John Sung became a famous evangelist in China, vehemently denouncing Union's liberalism. See ch. 9.3.

36. R. Miller, *Harry Emerson Fosdick*, 53.

37. R. Miller, *Harry Emerson Fosdick*, 43.

Presbyterian Church for seven years. In 1918 three historic Presbyterian churches—Madison Square, University Place, and First—consolidated to form one church, taking the name and site of the oldest: First Presbyterian. Fosdick's explosive 1922 sermon "Shall the Fundamentalists Win?" called Christians to tolerance as Christianity wrestled with modern issues of science and philosophy. Printed as "The New Knowledge and the Christian Faith," Ivy Lee, Rockefeller's public relations guru, sent the sermon to every pastor in the United States. Rockefeller suggested the new title and funded the nationwide distribution. Fosdick attacked the conservatives in the Presbyterian church. In 1910 the General Assembly of the Presbyterian Church in the USA approved the "Doctrinal Deliverance." The assembly agreed on five core and essential teachings of the Christian faith, the nonnegotiables: the inspiration and inerrancy of Scripture, the virgin birth, penal substitutionary atonement, Christ's bodily resurrection, and the historical reality of miracles. These five "fundamentals" became the theological battleground of the modernist-fundamentalist controversy. Further stoking the fire, brothers Lyman and Milton Stewart financed the publication and nationwide distribution of "The Fundamentals: A Testimony to the Truth." Fosdick disagreed with the fundamentalists. He wanted Christianity to be open to modernity and believed it was possible to be a Christian in the twentieth century "without throwing one's mind away." Miller summarizes Fosdick's life as a "rebellion against creedal sectarianism."[38] Despite the General Assembly's warning, the New York Presbytery refused to punish Fosdick after he preached his inflammatory sermon in 1922. Clarence Macartney, pastor of Arch Street Presbyterian Church in Philadelphia, volleyed back with an article in *The Presbyterian* entitled "Shall Unbelief Win?" J. Gresham Machen, of Princeton Theological Seminary, questioned if Fosdick's theology was Christian at all in *Christianity and Liberalism*. Eventually, Fosdick surrendered his pulpit at First Presbyterian Church. The methodical, shrewd Rockefeller pounced on the opportunity.[39]

Park Avenue Baptist Church hired Fosdick immediately. Concerned about the connections to Rockefeller wealth, Fosdick told Junior that he did not wish to be known as the pastor of the richest man in the country. Rockefeller responded: "I like your frankness but do you think that more people

38. R. Miller, *Harry Emerson Fosdick*, 9.

39. "In assessing John D. Rockefeller, Jr., most historians have emphasized his painful conscientiousness, methodical tenacity, calculating shrewdness, cold reserve, and severe repression of self." R. Miller, *Harry Emerson Fosdick*, 154.

will criticize you on account of my wealth, than will criticize me on account of your theology?"[40] Knowing Fosdick's reticence in accepting the offer at Park Avenue Baptist, Rockefeller offered to build a new church for Fosdick. In 1930 Park Avenue Baptist Church became Riverside Church. The tallest church in the United States, Riverside is situated in Morningside Heights, directly next to Union Theological Seminary. New York City's foremost fundamentalist pastor, John Roach Straton of Calvary Baptist Church, ridiculed Fosdick as a Baptist bootlegger and a Presbyterian outlaw: the Jesse James of the theological world. Straton suggested that Riverside Church should have an enormous electric sign rather than a cross, which was incompatible with Fosdick's cross-rejecting modernity. The sign, Straton advised, should read "SOCONY" for the Standard Oil Church of New York.[41]

Rockefeller and Fosdick's close friendship is evident in their frequent correspondence. In letters to Fosdick, Rockefeller apologized for missing church (September 6, 1926), discussed the name of the new church (August 12, 1927), and disputed comments made in a sermon (December 19, 1927).[42] The warmth and honesty in their correspondence only grew over time. Rockefeller wrote to Fosdick on February 13, 1941: "I was never prouder of my partnership with you in this great enterprise than last night when I faced that magnificent audience in our beautiful building."[43] In 1913 Rockefeller hired Fosdick's younger brother, an attorney who was working for the city of New York. Raymond Fosdick helped develop what Rockefeller called "the difficult art of giving."[44] Between 1901 and 1923 Rockefeller created five philanthropic trusts, to which he gave gifts of almost half a billion dollars. By 1953 grants from the five foundations totaled over $800 million. Raymond Fosdick served as trustee on the boards of all five trusts and as president of the Rockefeller Foundation from 1936 to 1948. During a critical period in China's history, one Fosdick led Rockefeller's church and another, his philanthropic empire. The founding trustees agreed that the Rockefeller Foundation ought to confine itself to important projects that were too large or too unlikely to be undertaken by other agencies. One of

40. Fosdick, *John D. Rockefeller, Jr.*, 221. See also R. Miller, *Harry Emerson Fosdick*, 162.

41. R. Miller, *Harry Emerson Fosdick*, 165.

42. Fosdick-Rockefeller Correspondence, UTS1: Harry Emerson Fosdick Collection, ser. 2, subser. A, box A, folder 20, Burke Library, Union Theological Seminary, NY.

43. Harry Emerson Fosdick Collection, ser. 2, subser. A, box A, folder 21, Burke Library, Union Theological Seminary, NY.

44. Gant, review of *Story of Rockefeller Foundation*, by Raymond B. Fosdick.

these large and unlikely projects proved to be the United Board of Christian Colleges in China. Fosdick served on the faculty at Union Seminary from 1906 to 1944. One of his students became a professor at Union and, eventually, the seminary's president in 1945. His name was Henry Pitney Van Dusen (1897–1975). Like Fosdick, he faced the heat of the Presbyterian Church. And he too rejected orthodox Christian teaching.

## Henry Pitney Van Dusen: Union Professor and President

Henry Pitney Van Dusen came from a long and storied family in New York City. Abraham Pieterszen, known as "Abraham the miller," landed on the island of "Manatus" around 1626.[45] He was one of the first 300 European settlers in New Amsterdam. His family picked up the surname Van Dusen from the Dutch town of Duersen. By 1880 there were 3,000 heads of households descended from Abraham. By the twenty-first century there were 200,000 descendants spread over fifteen generations. His progeny included American presidents Martin Van Buren and Franklin Delano Roosevelt; Eliza Kortright (wife of President James Monroe); and the president of Union Theological Seminary, Henry Pitney Van Dusen. On April 19, 1954, the cover of *Time* magazine featured Henry Pitney Van Dusen. In a year when *Time*'s covers featured Joseph McCarthy, Willie Mays, Jonas Salk, Humphrey Bogart, Ho Chi Minh, Billy Graham, Ernest Hemmingway, Richard Nixon, and Walt Disney, what was the president of Union Seminary doing there? The article heralded this tenth-generation Van Dusen as the "Protestant Architect."

Henry Pitney Van Dusen followed his father, maternal grandfather, and three uncles to Princeton University. Nicknamed "Pit," Van Dusen led any society he joined at Princeton: the undergraduate council, the student Christian association (the Philadelphian society), and the university's debating team.[46] Unsurprisingly for this overachiever from a prominent family, he graduated as valedictorian in 1919. His classmates voted him most likely to succeed. His valedictory address warned of the "humdrum of peacetime materialism" and the peril of losing interest in public service following World War I.[47] Rather than follow his father into law, he proceeded to theology studies: first at New College, Edinburgh, and then at Union

45. Cowan, "Van Dusens."

46. Leitch, "Henry Pitney Van Dusen."

47. Cotey, "Generations."

Seminary. When he returned to Scotland for PhD studies, he married Elizabeth Bartholomew, daughter of the king's cartographer. Van Dusen was very much a part of the northeast establishment. He had deep social connections in New York City and was destined to become a leader in any career he chose. After graduating from Union in 1924, Van Dusen came up for Presbyterian ordination. The New York Presbytery ordained him—influenced, perhaps, by a letter of support from John Foster Dulles—despite his refusal to affirm the virgin birth. Van Dusen began teaching at Union in 1926 and became dean of students six years later and professor of systematic theology ten years later. In 1945, he became Union's tenth president.

Van Dusen made a distinct contribution as head of the seminary. In a postwar world he envisioned Union growing in size and in influence as a leader of the ecumenical movement. He did little to hide his commitment to institutionalized Christian unity. At his inaugural address on November 15, 1945, at Riverside Church, he said: "Unity is laid as an inescapable obligation upon the Protestant Churches because none of their greatest problems can be adequately met, none of their most clamant tasks can be effectively discharged, by individual churches or separate Communions, but only by the total resources of the whole Church of Christ." After quoting this section of Van Dusen's speech, Handy wryly notes: "Perceptive listeners could hear undertones of a longing for a new version of the nineteenth-century dream of an American Protestant Christendom in ecumenical guise."[48] Van Dusen wanted Union to be at the center of the local, national, and global ecumenical movement. He sought to double the number of foreign students, from the twenty-five enrolled in the mid-1940s, and provide special fellowships for these students. In 1948 he told the board of directors:

> The same factors which have lifted the United States to a dominating role in world politics, and are drawing all eyes to New York City as the world capital, apply in the realm of theological education . . . here should be found through the next decades, the greatest center of theological learning and teaching in the world.[49]

Van Dusen retired as Union's president in 1963. Praise from the faculty and board of directors was unrestrained. The faculty declared Van Dusen's presidency as the "high-water mark of its achievement" in the school's long history. He "expanded not only the personal and physical resources of the

48. Handy, *History*, 213.
49. Handy, *History*, 214.

Seminary, but above all, its spirit and outreach."[50] Van Dusen had the financial backing of the New York Protestant establishment as he fashioned Union into the capital of the worldwide ecumenical movement. An intriguing and little known aspect of the ecumenical movement was its impact in China. Before detailing Union's influence in Republican China, the subject of our next chapter, I will briefly describe how the social network of Luce, Rockefeller, Fosdick, Van Dusen and others made a significant financial contribution to China.

## The Chinese Connections of Luce, Rockefeller, Fosdick, and Van Dusen

Vast amounts of money flowed from New York to China, partly due to the influence of Union Seminary. In 1936 Luce established the Luce Foundation as a lasting tribute to his parents. Since then the Foundation has made over $600 million in grants.[51] Many of these grants have gone to educational purposes in and for Asia. In 1945 Van Dusen secured an endowment from the Luce Foundation, in memory of Henry W. Luce, to bring a prominent Christian leader from another country to New York. The first Luce scholar was Francis Wei, president of Huazhong University, one of the thirteen Christian colleges in China. Van Dusen's ties to Christian colleges in China went deep: in 1947 he served as president of the board.[52] He leveraged his influence in advocating for China's Christian colleges to raise funds among his wealthy friends.

Even though Luce was born in China, the Rockefellers had an even longer history there. In the midst of the American Civil War, Rockefeller, Sr., sold his first kerosene to China. In the same year, 1863, he made a $10 donation to China missions. Rockefeller profits in the Middle Kingdom skyrocketed over the upcoming decades. By 1914 half of all American exports to China were Standard Oil products. When Junior and his wife, Abby, visited China in 1921, they dined in Guangzhou with Sun Yat-sen and his wife, Soong Ching-ling. But Rockefeller's giving reached a breaking point after World War II. After World War II many of the China's Christian colleges returned to their home campuses. As fighting between the

50. Leitch, "Henry Pitney Van Dusen."

51. Henry Luce Foundation, "History."

52. Special Collections, YDSL, United Board of Christian Higher Education in Asia, ser. 2, box 64, folder 1692.

Nationalists and Communists continued, the schools faced an uncertain future. The United Board repeatedly appealed to the Rockefeller Foundation and to John D. Rockefeller personally. The foundation continued to give. When they did not, Rockefeller gave personally.

At the end of 1947 the United Board solicited a donation of $50,000 from the Rockefeller Foundation. The Christian Colleges were in dire financial straits in postwar China. In response to a giving appeal, Thomas Appleget of the Rockefeller Foundation wrote to C. A. Evans of the United Board on January 6, 1948. Appleget rejected Evans's request but added a reminder of all the money they had already given:

> I know that I need not remind you that the Foundation has had a long interest in China and the Christian Colleges. Early in 1947, the Foundation contributed $10,000,000 to the Peiping Union Medical College, an enterprise in which it has already invested over $30,000,000. In 1946, the Foundation contributed $500,000 to the Associated Boards for Christian Colleges in China. Previous contributions from the Foundation for this purpose total $425,000. All in all, the Foundation has given well over $50,000,000 to China. This total represents the largest contribution on the part of the Foundation to any country outside the United States.[53]

Despite giving $50,000,00 to China, the United Board decided to appeal directly to Rockefeller. Who would make the appeal? The man most connected with Rockefeller and the board: Van Dusen. Rockefeller's reply to Van Dusen on February 9, 1949 reveals the depth of their friendship:

> Because of my appreciation of the important contribution that the Christian Colleges have made to China and because of your interest and Henry Luce's in them, I am glad to make a further contribution as you suggest. I do so, I will have to admit, with some reservations because I have real question as to how effectively or how long the colleges in the communist area can operate.[54]

Despite serious misgiving, Rockefeller gave again. Between 1913 and 2008 Rockefeller philanthropy in China totaled $246,519,386.[55] "The Rockefeller name is not often associated with China—Asian art and Japan perhaps, but

53. Special Collections, YDSL, United Board of Christian Higher Education in Asia, ser. 2, box 64, folder 1700.

54. Special Collections, YDSL, United Board of Christian Higher Education in Asia, ser. 2, box 64, folder 1705.

55. Bullock, *Oil Prince's Legacy*, 215.

not China," observes Mary Brown Bullock in her thorough study of Rockefeller philanthropy in China. "And yet, during the first half of the twentieth century, China was the primary foreign beneficiary of Rockefeller philanthropy, and Standard Oil was the most successful American company in China."[56] Bullock's study examines Rockefeller's nongovernmental yet significant role in Sino-American relations but her research avoids what most interests me: his role in Chinese Christianity and connections to Union Seminary. Luce and Rockefeller were part of a network of wealthy men in New York who shared a liberal Protestant faith and an interest in China. As the invitation to the 1949 banquet with Winston Churchill illustrates, these men were often connected with Union.

## Summary

In the previous chapter I explained Union Seminary's intentional engagement with the world. The school emphasized foreign missions in their curriculum, encouraged the establishment of the Inquiry into Foreign Missions, established a school for foreign missions and appointed Daniel J. Fleming to head the school, provided funding for foreign scholars to study in Manhattan, and sent professors around the world. These activities meant that Union sent more missionaries overseas than any other seminary or divinity school in the United States. A social tsunami hit China at the turn of the century. The ancient, proud, and isolated Middle Kingdom opened up like never before. With each passing decade, more foreign missionaries poured into China. More than any other institution, Union graduates and faculty helped instigate the theological conflict in China that erupted into the modernist-fundamentalist controversy in the United States. Over these years a Sino-American highway of people and ideas flowed between the two countries and concentrated in Shanghai and New York City. The highway carried theological liberalism through the lanes of the Chinese Christian colleges and the YMCA. Union Seminary served as a control center, directing the traffic in both directions. The seminary influenced China because of its intentional location in Manhattan and its access to the power therein. Luce, Rockefeller, Fosdick, and Van Dusen are four of the many people who constituted this dense social network. By layering the theories of Hunter and Granovetter, Union's influence in China becomes clearer.

56. Bullock, *Oil Prince's Legacy*, 1.

Union impacted China through a dense and influential social network and the institutions created by that network.

Between 1911 and 1949 Morningside Heights in general and Union Theological Seminary in particular became the de facto hub where Chinese Christians in America established or strengthened ties with each other and with American Christians. In turn, these American Christians provided weak ties that linked Chinese Christians to an elite network of Americans, as I describe in the upcoming chapters. Union shortened the social distance between Chinese Christians and the power elite in America. These Chinese Christians then became an elite network of their own in China, with deep ties that extended far beyond religious affairs into politics, education, and business. The funeral service of Sun Yat-sen, the Father of Republican China, serves as one example. Two prominent Chinese Christians officiated the private service on March 19, 1925: Timothy Tingfang Lew and Andrew Y. Y. Tsu.[57] Both Lew and Tsu studied at Union Seminary. The service occurred in the chapel of Peking Union Medical College, a campus built largely with donations from the Rockefeller foundation. The following chapter continues to explore the nexus of Chinese Christians connected with Union.

57. Dr. Sun Yat-sen funeral service sheet. MRL 6: Timothy Tingfang Lew Papers, ser. 3, box 2, folder 5, Burke Library, Union Theological Seminary, NY.

# 6

# Union and the Student Christian Movement

K. H. Ting

THE PURPOSE OF THIS chapter is to examine a key figure in Union's dense social network in China: Bishop K. H. Ting. The evaluations of Bishop Ting and his role in Chinese Protestantism range from glowing praise to deep disdain. Both sides however recognize Ting's prominence. From 1979 until his death in 2012, he was the undisputed leader of the official Protestant church in China. In the textbook on Protestantism in contemporary China, Alan Hunter and Kim-Kwong Chan note: "The outstanding leader of the official church in the 1980s, and indeed since about 1960, has been K. H. Ting."[1] He yielded remarkable theological and political influence as head of the China Christian Council and the TSPM. In 1961 Leslie Lyall wrote a history of Christianity in China to correct, in his view, the pro-Communist slant in reports of Christianity in China. The former missionary with the China Inland Mission believed that the Chinese Communist Party "deliberately adopted the policy of using the Christian Church as a political tool and for political propaganda."[2] The Three-Self movement became a tool of the Communist government, betraying the Christian church and message. Many Christians around the world, both Chinese and non-Chinese, agree with Lyall's assessment. K. H. Ting lies, in their view, at the heart of this betrayal. Li Xinyuan recounts an interview Ting had in 1979 and concludes: "Quite clearly, as a young man [T]ing had jettisoned orthodox, evangelical Christianity and personal salvation."[3] For many people, Ting's collusion with the CCP demonstrates

1. A. Hunter and Chan, *Protestantism in Contemporary China*, 87.

2. Lyall, *Come Wind, Come Weather*, 6.

3. Li, *Theological Construction—or Destruction?*, 13.

his abandonment of orthodox Christian conviction. Opinion is polarized regarding Ting and his role in Chinese Christianity.

While many Chinese house church leaders criticize Bishop Ting's theology and role in the TSPM, some scholars acknowledge his role as an advocate for freedom of religion in China. Hunter and Chan believe "he has probably done as much as any person to promote freedom of religion in China and has argued far more vigorously for the rights of house churches than any of his colleagues."[4] Ting deserves his reputation as one of the most important Chinese religious leader of the past century. Effusive in praise for Ting, Miikaa Ruokanen writes:

> [Ting] has been since the 1950s the leading figure of both the Chinese Protestant church and of Chinese theological thinking. His role as the most outstanding representative of Chinese Protestant Christianity from the early 1950s to the present is incomparable in the history of nearly any church of our times.[5]

Ruokanen seems to overreach in his assessment, but not by much. Ting is a key figure in understanding Union's influence on Christianity in twentieth-century China. Two incidents in 1957 help demonstrate why Ting befuddles those who study him and why he is the source of such controversy.

In November a delegation of Chinese Christian leaders flew to Hungary where the Communist regime had quelled a recent democratic uprising. Ting, a member of the delegation, recorded his thoughts as the plane descended.

> As we looked down on Budapest from the air, we could not help but think of the dark days a year ago, when the imperialists were carrying on their counterrevolutionary activities. In those days, as we Chinese read in the papers, our hearts were very sad, and we asked ourselves, "Can it be true that Hungary is leaving the Communist family of nations?" But then when the workers' and farmers' revolutionary government was re-established, and Hungary with the help of Soviet Russia was able to suppress so quickly this counterrevolutionary revolt, our hearts were made peaceful again. Looking down from the air, I could not help but think of Luke 15, "This your brother was dead, and is alive; he was lost, and is found; therefore let us make merry and be glad."[6]

4. A. Hunter and Chan, *Protestantism in Contemporary China*, 91.
5. Ruokanen, "K. H. Ting's Contribution," 107.
6. Jones, *Church in Communist China*, 127.

Five months before this flight (June 12, 1957) Ting had defended Christianity in a speech at China's leading seminary:

> We know that the various atheistic theories are wrong, but we must also know wherein they are wrong, and still more, what the right view is. We must think deeper and strengthen our faith so that when we go out to preach the truth of the gospel our words may carry weight because of their reasonableness. . . . Communists divide all systems of thought into materialism (which they approve) and idealism (which they condemn). But Christianity does not correspond with materialism or idealism. In itself it is not the fruit of history, and the gospel is not an ideology. The gospel comes from the free revelation of God. This gospel is Christ himself, through whom all things were made.[7]

Ting rejected the Marxist notion that Christianity was an opiate of the masses. He encouraged Christians to welcome Communism but admitted that a change of social system could not solve the problem of sin. Sin could be healed only by salvation and grace.[8] It is difficult to reconcile the Ting journaling in the descending plane with the one delivering the speech. One celebrates the Communist victory in Budapest; the other defends Christianity against Marxism. How can one person believe these seemingly contradictory sentiments? Ting beguiled both critics and supporters. Yet for the first five decades of the People's Republic of China, Ting and Y. T. Wu dominated the Three-Self Patriotic Movement theologically and politically. Both men were primary figures in creating an organization loyal to Communism and committed to Christianity. Wu founded the Three-Self movement in 1951 with the support of Zhou Enlai, China's premier for twenty-seven years. Following Wu's death in 1979, Ting, who had been the president of Nanjing Union Theological Seminary, became the chairperson of the TSPM Committee and president of the China Christian Council. How did two graduates of Union Seminary so dominate China's official Protestant church? Part of the answer lies in the dense social network of American and Chinese Christians connected with Union. The following chapters examine other key figures in this network. For now, I sketch Ting's life and ministry.

7. K. Ting, "Christian Theism." Cited in Jones, *Church in Communist China*, 139.

8. K. Ting, "Christian Theism." Cited in Jones, *Church in Communist China*, 142.

## K. H. Ting's Early Years

K. H. Ting's father, Ding Chufan (丁楚范 *Chu Van Ding*, 1884–1963), moved to Shanghai from Zhejiang Province at the end of the nineteenth century. His mother, Li Jinglan (李静栏 *Li Lizi*, 1886–1986), grew up in Shanghai where her father K. C. Li (李嘉青 *Li Jiaqing*) was one of the first clergyman in the Episcopal church in China (中华圣公会 *Zhonghua Sheng Gong Hui*, hereafter Sheng Gong Hui). Sheng Gong Hui ordained Li as a deacon in 1884 and a priest in 1907. Li Jinglan's warm heart and deep faith profoundly influenced her third and favorite son, whom she called *Bao Bao* (precious). Li took responsibility for the spiritual formation of her children. Every evening she led family Bible studies in their home. Each child read a verse from the Bible followed by singing a hymn. If they grew fidgety, she would refocus them by reading the twenty-six verses of Ps 136. "Li Jinglan's piety was of an orderly and embracing Anglican character, neither high church nor evangelical, never to extremes of enthusiasm but still satisfying on both emotional and intellectual levels," explains Wickeri.[9] The Tings attended the church where their maternal grandfather had been ordained: St. Peter's Church.

Started as a mission outpost in 1857 and consecrated in 1899, St. Peter's served middle-class and educated Chinese who lived in the International Settlement. The parishioners gave generously. By 1914 St. Peter's declared itself to be self-supporting. Equally unusual for missions' churches, the church also installed its first Chinese rector in the same year. Like a prophetic omen in Chinese Protestant history, the self-governance and self-support of Ting's family church occurred one year before he was born. But like so much of the SFPE in Republican China, the Episcopal bishop responsible for Shanghai was an American. Frederick Rogers Graves (1858–1940) was consecrated as a missionary bishop of Shanghai in New York City in 1893. In 1930 Bishop Graves confirmed Ting at St. Peter's and later approved his request for theological studies. The clergyman that Ting remembered best was Dong Jianwu (董健吾 H. C. Tung). Dong led youth activities during a formative time in Ting's spiritual formation. Wickeri reveals a startling fact about the popular priest: "Unbeknownst to his parishioners, he secretly joined the Communist Party in 1928, while he was still rector."[10] In 1936 Dong led the American journalist Edgar Snow to meet

9. Wickeri, *Reconstructing Christianity in China*, 22.

10. Wickeri, *Reconstructing Christianity in China*, 25.

the Communist leadership in Yanan. In *Red Star over China*, Snow conceals Dong's true identity, calling him Pastor Wang. Another priest at St. Peter's, Pu Huaren (浦化人 Paul H. J. Poo), also joined the Communist Party. Pu went on to prominent positions in the CCP. Interestingly, Wickeri's description of Dong—"complex and fascinating, flamboyant and secretive, Christian priest and Communist cadre all in one"—could perhaps also be applied to Pu and, later, to K. H. Ting.[11] Ting's mother and church shaped his Christian faith but his social setting formed his view of the world.

The Ting family lived on Cunningham Road in the Northern District of the International Settlement, near the old railway station. Later in life Ting recounted the hordes of people who came to Shanghai in times of famine, especially from the Yangzhou area of Jiangsu Province. Rickshaw pullers worked barefoot in all weather conditions, housemaids offered to work only for food to eat, and everywhere, people begged. In wintertime walks to school, Ting and his siblings would see dead bodies: beggars frozen to death despite their attempts to stay warm in sheets of advertising paper.[12] Life in cosmopolitan Shanghai fomented with social inequities. This city shaped and confused the young Ting. In a country known for its fierce isolation, *Shanghairen* lived on the cutting edge of where China met the world. They loved and loathed the foreigners in their midst. The May Thirtieth Incident reminded Chinese that the fingers of the foreigners were always, literally and figuratively, on the trigger.

On May 30, 1925, Shanghai Municipal Police officers opened fire on Chinese students protesting in the city's International Settlement. The students were protesting on Nanjing Road against a Japanese-owned textile mill whose Japanese guards had killed a striking Chinese worker. The May Thirtieth Incident (五卅运动 *Wusa Yun Dong)* incited anti-foreign outrage throughout China, with massive strikes in Shanghai, Guangzhou and Hong Kong. A palpable anti-foreign and anti-imperialism fury filled the hearts and minds of Chinese youth, especially those in major cities. No longer did Confucianism bind these youth to an imperial exam or to loyalty to the Son of Heaven. Spence characterizes the rage across China as "immense," noting that the KMT and CCP were now prepared to "channel the rage and

11. Wickeri, *Reconstructing Christianity in China*, 25. Nowhere does Wickeri acknowledge that K. H. Ting was a Communist Party member. But I believe he was. I cannot substantiate this claim but I believe Wickeri can but does not want to, given the intimacy of his friendship with Ting.

12. Wickeri, *Reconstructing Christianity in China*, 20.

frustration of Chinese into their own party organizations."[13] Chinese intellectuals, young and old, wondered where to place their allegiance, what to believe in, and how to give China a hopeful future. It was into this China and this Shanghai that K. H. Ting was born and raised. Shanghai is also the city were the Chinese Communist Party was established in 1921.[14]

In his teens Ting would benefit from a special education in this strange international bubble. Ting attended primary and middle school in the International Settlement in schools attached to Christian colleges: Soochow University and St. John's University.[15] The Christian colleges accounted for 15 percent of total college enrollments in China. But the colleges' importance lay not in size but in the particular cultural space they occupied in the Sino-Foreign world in China. Students and teachers in the Christian schools lived in a "unique bicultural atmosphere" at a time when relations with the West were of critical importance.[16] Graduates of the Christian colleges would go on to have significant influence on Sino-American relations and on Protestantism in China. Union influenced China through the Christian colleges and the network of Chinese Christians in these colleges. After matriculating from the Senior Middle School of St. John's University in 1933, Ting entered St. John's University.

## K. H. Ting's University Years

Two American missionaries loom large in the history of St. John's. The vision for the school came from Samuel Schereschewsky (1831–1906), the bishop of the Sheng Gong Hui, but it was F. L. Hawks Pott, president of St. John's for fifty-two years, who made the school great. The cornerstone of the first buildings was laid on April 14, 1879, in a peninsula of land surrounded by the Suzhou Creek. St. John's and Yenching University in Beijing were the two finest Christian colleges in Republican China. Both schools were led by long serving, visionary, domineering, and unrelenting presidents: Pott at St.

13. Spence, *Search for Modern China*, 341.

14. In 1921 the Communist International—the Comintern—sent an agent, Hans Sneevliet, to Shanghai for a secret meeting with alleged Communists. In July the Chinese Communist Party was established. Chen Duxiu, who had advocated science and democracy as the cure for China's maladies, was appointed as the party secretary.

15. Number Two Junior Middle School attached to Soochow University in 1930 and the Senior Middle School of St. John's University in 1933.

16. Bays and Widmer, "Introduction," xvi.

John's and J. Leighton Stuart at Yenching. Pott came to China expecting to do evangelical work but changed his mind after being converted to the importance of educational work. Theologically, Potts favored the modernist approach. He disliked religious obscurantism such as the verbal inspiration or the infallibility of the Bible. In 1937 Dr. M. H. Troop wrote a sonnet in *The Johannean* to celebrate Pott's fifty years at St. John's.

> You, captain bod, have conned the ship aright;
> The wished-for haven now looms in sight.
> Oh highway builder for the mind of man,
> The nation is now thronging where you ran
> A lonely race. Behold, your narrow Field
> A golden harvest for the world will yield.[17]

The celebration of Pott makes no mention of any Christian influence, other than the label "Rev." in the sonnet's title.

The contribution Pott and St. John's made to China was an emphasis on science and a liberal education. Xu Yihua asks if St. John's fulfilled its original goal as an agent of Christian evangelism. He easily concludes no. "St. John's had never been very successful in converting its students to the Christian religion, despite claims of authorities that 'the mode of thinking of the students is basically Christian.'"[18] The average student at St. John's seemed to be more a "spectator than a rigorous supporter" of Christianity. The educational goals of the school eclipsed any religious objective, regardless of the paraphernalia used to garner financial support in the United States. Ting joined 440 undergraduate students enrolled at St. John's in 1933. In his freshman year he received the mark of A in religion and ethics, English and mathematics; B in physics and engineering; and C in Chinese and physical education.[19] It is not unique to Ting that he excelled in English but did poorly in Chinese.

Ryan Dunch argues that the Christian colleges sought to have balanced curricula between Chinese and Western. They wanted to strike a balance between three areas: Western classical, Chinese classical, and science. They intended "not to supplant but to supplement and round out, in

17. From M. H. Throop, "Sonnet to The Rev. F. L. Hawks Pott" in vol. 23 of *The 1937 Johannean*. Shanghai Municipal Archives (*Shanghai shidangan guan*), Y8-1-259-51.

18. Y. Xu, "St John's University," 33. Prof. Xu Yihua (Fudan University) comes from four generations of St. John's alumni and has devoted his career to studying the school.

19. St. John's University Grade Report for Ting K. H. Shanghai Municipal Archives (*Shanghai shidangan guan*), Q243-41-1109-273.

its secular subjects as in its Christian content, a standard Chinese classical education."[20] Despite a hope to supplement a classical Chinese education, the Christian college operated differently than their Chinese equivalents. They de-emphasized Chinese classics,[21] encouraged the use of English, and transitioned away from a unitary curriculum to one with electives and majors. St. John's unique selling point, in many ways, was teaching in English. From 1887 Pott had insisted that all instruction outside the Chinese department be in English. Xu Yihua credits St John's growth from an "insignificant training school for native evangelists" to a "distinguished institution of higher learning nicknamed the 'cradle of Chinese diplomats'" to the use of English throughout the curriculum.[22] The school gained a reputation for producing excellent English speakers, creating a demand for St. John's graduates in foreign companies, banks, and Chinese customs. In the weekly English newspaper, *St. John's Dial*, a student wrote on November 22, 1929: "What distinguished *Johanneans* most from others is their good knowledge of English. Yes, that is why the University has gained in fame; that is what the people admire St. John's for."[23] While students at St. John's excelled in English, their poor grasp of Chinese literature and culture became a cause for reproach. Graduates of the Christian colleges gained a unique foothold in the transnational parts of Chinese society but they often alienated themselves culturally and linguistically from traditional China. If Ting had gone to the government-run Jiaotong University, as his father desired, his college experience and life-trajectory would have been far different. A young K. H. entered a hybrid university campus dominated by the English language where the campus culture felt very Western.

After a year of studying civil engineering, he switched to theology, much to his father's dismay. Ting realized that engineering could provide a better income, his father's argument, but he was troubled by China's social problems. "I came into contact with the darker aspect of society and its problems, which made me think that engineering was of no help," Ting reflected in a 1990 interview about his decision to change courses. "I felt that I would be doing something much more meaningful if I served the

20. Dunch, "Science, Religion, and Classics," 63.

21. "In a sense, then, the Christian colleges prefigured the dethroning of the classics." Dunch, "Science, Religion, and Classics," 81.

22. E. Xu, "Liberal Arts Education," 107.

23. Anonymous, "The Mother-Tongue," in E. Xu, "Liberal Arts Education," 111.

church."[24] The decision of nineteen-year-old Ting so upset his father that he cut off all financial support, creating a break that never healed. Ting went to President Pott to seek financial assistance. With fewer than ten students in the theology department, Pott was pleased to have a new Chinese candidate for priesthood. He offered Ting a full scholarship. M. H. Throop, professor of Old Testament and dean of the School of Theology, described his department as "very small" but "very important" because they were "training men to meet the most vital need of today."[25] Ting excelled in theology: by his junior and senior years he was a straight-A student.[26] While not in the classroom or library, Ting immersed himself in the student Christian societies. While K. H. Ting's early life was shaped by his childhood in Shanghai, the Christian influence of his mother, a broad Anglican formation in St. Peter's Church, and a bicultural university experience at St. John's, student Christian organizations helped shape his future.

In his senior year at St. John's, the University Christian Fellowship elected Ting as their president. The fellowship, which sought to "show Christian spirit through fellowship as well as to develop cooperation among students," wanted to engage Christian and non-Christian students at the school.[27] Ting represented St. John's at the first meeting of the citywide Union of Shanghai Christian Student Organizations (*Shanghai xuelian*, hereafter, Shanghai Lien). The Shanghai Lien brought together the student Christian organizations across Shanghai and sought to share experiences and coordinate programs. But, interestingly, a young Ting explained in a letter to President Pott that the more "conspicuous part" of the Lien's work was not "religious work, which is really the centre of the Student Christian Movement."[28] Early on Ting's interpersonal skills and political acumen led him into a position of coordinating Christian groups—though not necessarily to religious ends—and communicating with others, like Pott, in positions of authority. Leaders of the YMCA noticed Ting's leadership skills.

24. Ting, interview with Wickeri, Nanjing, China, October 31, 1990, in Wickeri, *Reconstructing Christianity in China*, 28.

25. M. H. Throop, 1937 Course Catalogue for St. John's School of Theology. Shanghai Municipal Archives (*Shanghai shidangan guan*), Y8–1–261–34.

26. St. John's University Grade Report for Ting K. H. Shanghai Municipal Archives (*Shanghai shidangan guan*), Q243–41–1115–337 and 358.

27. *The St. John's Daily* 17 (1936) 1, in Wickeri, *Reconstructing Christianity in China*, 29.

28. Letter from Ting to Pott, December 4, 1939. Shanghai Municipal Archives, Q243–41–36.

In a time of robust nationalism and soul-searching following the May Fourth Movement, the Ys were one of the few places where the collegiate population could have freedom of expression. Daniel Bays sees the crucial role the YMCA/YWCAs played in supplying "a group of intellectuals and students who were liberal and leftist in politics, somewhat sympathetic to the Communist side in the civil war, loosely identified as Christian, but not organized as a church."[29] Ding Yenren, son of K. H. Ting and professor at the University of Nanjing, goes one step further in suggesting that the "Communist Party sent many young people to [the] Y then [the] Y sent many to the CCP."[30] He clarified that the Ys did not promote Communism; they promoted liberalism and this led them to have associations with the CCP in the 1930s and 1940s. Ding Yenren concluded: "The contribution of the Y to the revolution is not talked about." Between 1911 and 1949 the Chinese YMCA became the nation's largest importer of American culture. The KMT even attempted to subsume the Ys under its auspices.[31] Infected with a Western liberalism, Chinese students opened their minds to new ideas for national salvation. In so doing, the Ys played a key role in providing future leaders for the TSPM and the CCP.

Pu Huaren, the St. Peter's priest turned Communist agent, returned to Shanghai in the 1930s. Pu urged students like Ting to consider questions of national salvation. In his first published essay, a twenty-one-year-old Ting explored religion's role in a changing Chinese society. "Young people like the here and now, but religion is forever making extravagant claims about some far off heaven and hell which are hardly believable."[32] The core of Christianity should depend not on Bible study or church attendance but on its daily effect on life. Chinese youth wanted a church with answers to pressing social issues, "an extremely concrete path." The young Ting craved answers to hard social questions because he lived in a "complex society with progressive thinking."[33] Wickeri argues that Ting's mounting political and social concern, seen clearly in this 1936 essay, "resulted in his increasing dissatisfaction with institutionalized Christianity and the church."[34] In the

29. Bays, *New History of Christianity*, 148.

30. Ding, interview with the author in Nanjing, People's Republic of China, April 16, 2012.

31. X. Xu, "Institutional Transformation."

32. K. Ting, "Youth and Religion," 7.

33. K. Ting, "Youth and Religion," 7.

34. Wickeri, *Reconstructing Christianity in China*, 31.

final paragraph of the essay, Ting congratulates St. Peter's priests because they "have not overlooked young people's lives, but have striven to promote the youth fellowship as a manifestation that Jesus is indeed the salvation for twentieth century youth, that he can fully understand the difficulties we meet."[35] Chinese priests at St. Peter's encouraged students to strive for China's salvation. In an era when Western missionaries ran most churches, St. Peter's indigenous leadership is striking.

Chinese youth lamented their nation's social conditions and longed for change. Shanghai had boiled with social tension since 1932. One year earlier Japan had invaded Manchuria (the Mukden Incident). After five months of fighting, the Japanese military had established the puppet-state of Manchukuo and installed Puyi, the last emperor of China, as puppet ruler. From January 28 to March 3, 1932, Japanese and Chinese forces fought in and around Shanghai. The January 28 Incident ended with the League of Nations demanding a cease-fire.[36] The ensuing agreement made Shanghai a demilitarized zone, forbidding Chinese troops but allowing Japan to retain a small military presence in the city. Like changes in atmospheric pressure following a major storm, students in Shanghai in 1936, Ting's senior year at St. John's, felt the growing possibility of further Japanese military action against China. At a meeting of the Shanghai YMCA in May 1936, sixty National Salvation Unions from across China established the All China Federation of National Salvation Unions.[37] Salvation means rescue from danger. There had been plenty that China needed salvation from since 1910: ineffective Qing rule, archaic Confucianism, self-cannibalizing warlordism, and aggressive imperialism. In the 1930s the threat increasingly became the Japanese. Students in Shanghai and across China resented the Japanese military presence on their soil. On July 7, 1937, tension between China and Japan reached a turning point.

Shooting broke out on an ancient eleven-arch granite bridge straddling the Yongding River southwest of Beijing. The Lugou Bridge had been praised by Marco Polo in the thirteenth century and restored by the Kangxi Emperor in 1698.[38] From the KMT's military headquarters in Lushan, Chi-

35. K. Ting, "Youth and Religion," 7–8.

36. Western sources often call this the Shanghai War of 1932 but the Chinese call it 一二八松虎 (*yierbasonghu*, the January 28 Incident.).

37. Stranahan, *Underground*, 197.

38. "Over this river there is a very fine stone bridge, so fine indeed, that it has very few equals in the world." Polo, *Travels of Marco Polo*, 2:3.

ang Kai-shek (蔣中正 *Jiang Zhong Cheng* 1887–1975) declared the Republic of China's commitment to resist Japan. "If we allow one more inch of our territory to be lost," declared the generalissimo in military field gear, "we shall be guilty of an unpardonable crime against our race."[39] Prince Takamatsu, the emperor's brother, retorted: "We're really going to smash China so that it will be ten years before it can stand straight again."[40] Over the ensuing weeks, fighting erupted in and around Beijing. Japanese forces attacked the Summer Palace on July 27. A Japanese mechanized force with fifty tanks rolled into China's former capital. By August 8 the Japanese Imperial Army occupied Beijing. Soon, Tianjin fell. The Chinese War of Resistance had begun.[41]

Within a year the Japanese military had devoured east China. China's capital experienced especially horrific carnage. After capturing Nanjing on December 13, 1937, Japanese soldiers massacred at least 100,000 Chinese there.[42] Chiang Kai-shek had vowed that his capital would never fall but he unwisely trusted the city's defense to an opium-addicted politician and former warlord, Tang Shengzhi. Tang, in a November press conference, vowed to live or die with Nanjing. But in the teeth of Japan's naval, ground, and air superiority, General Tang abandoned the city on December 12. Chinese civilians and soldiers were buried in holes up to their necks to be savaged by dogs, used for bayonet or samurai-sword practice, nailed to boards and run over by vehicles, sprayed with acid, hung up by their tongues, and raped. Japanese soldiers believed that raping a virgin would give them prowess in battle. Fetuses were ripped out of the bodies of pregnant women. Some Japanese soldiers photographed their Nanjing exploits and sent the film to Shanghai to be developed. The Chinese who developed the pictures in

39. Crowley, *Japan's Quest for Autonomy*, 445.

40. Fenby, *Penguin History*, 275.

41. Called the Second Sino-Japanese War by many, Chinese refer to this war as 抗战, War of Resistance. I will use the Chinese designation throughout.

42. The figure of 300,000 has been accepted throughout China and repeated in most accounts; however, the historian David Askew argues that there were only 250,000 left in Nanjing when the Japanese arrived. The International Military Tribunal of the Far East (1948) estimated 200,000 casualties. More contemporary accounts suggest a number under 100,000. John Rabe, the "Good Nazi of Nanjing," who helped to set up a Safety Zone, put the death toll at 50,000–60,000 civilians and soldiers. For an excellent summary of recent research, see Askew, "Nanjing Incident." While appreciating Askew's work, I disagree with his decision to label what happened in Nanjing the "Nanjing Incident" rather than the "Nanjing Massacre." Scholars can debate the scale of the massacre but a massacre certainly occurred in Nanjing in 1937/1938.

Shanghai showed the images to foreign journalists, who alerted the world to the atrocities. Spence comments that the Nanjing Massacre must "rank among the worst in the history of modern warfare."[43] The well-equipped and well-trained Japanese war machine marched east, taking the city of Wuhan. Chiang moved the government to Chongqing. After the Chinese won victories in Changsha and Guangxi, the war stalemated. With a common enemy, the Nationalists and Communist worked as a united front in the first years of the war. The Nanjing Massacre deepened China's humiliation and spurred its fury.

This brutalized, raped, and humiliated China is the country that K. H. Ting lived in as a young man in the 1930s. The postgraduation years are formative in any person's life and future and more so for Ting, given the Japanese occupation. Wickeri explains that these years "left a distinctive imprint on [Ting's] approach to nation, church, and society, one that has informed his understanding ever since."[44] The Japanese occupation deepened the peculiarity of cosmopolitan Shanghai. While the invaders imposed limitations throughout the city, the International Settlement and French Concession remained free from direct Japanese rule. With Westerners administering these districts, they became islands of freedom and resistance until Japan attacked Pearl Harbor in December 1941.

Protestant churches such as St. Peter's were one of the few safe places to gather and discuss what the Chinese response ought to be. Intellectuals in Shanghai had three options: do nothing, resist Japan, or aid Japan. Poshek Fu explains that these options of passivity, resistance, or collaboration correspond with the traditional responses of Chinese literati in times of social change: eremitism, loyalism, and cooption.[45] Discussions about China's national salvation among students became more than talk. As noted before, the Ys attracted Chinese students not for evangelistic engagement but to engage pressing social issues. Y. T. Wu, one of these YMCA leaders, would have a profound influence on Ting and his peers in occupied Shanghai. Among the Chinese Christians that Ting associated with, Wickeri notes that the "dynamic and inspiring" Wu had "by far the greatest influence."[46] K. H. Ting cannot be fully understood apart from Y. T. Wu.[47]

43. Spence, *Search for Modern China*, 448.

44. Wickeri, *Reconstructing Christianity in China*, 35.

45. Fu, *Passivity, Resistance and Collaboration.*

46. Wickeri, *Reconstructing Christianity in China*, 36.

47. See ch. 4.

## K. H. Ting in Toronto

On August 15, 1945, Japanese forces in China formally surrendered. Nationalist planes swooped into Shanghai, eager to assert GMD authority over the pivotal city. As missionaries returned from internment camps, a US navy chaplain succeeded Ting as pastor of Community Church. Y. T. Wu appointed Ting as the director of the "Chinese Christian Democratic Research Society" that autumn. But several months later Ting decided to accept a role as the missionary secretary of the Student Christian Movement (SCM) in Canada. T. Z. Koo, Ting's Chinese predecessor at the Community Church and well-known Chinese Christian speaker, had made quite an impression on Canadian students in a speaking tour in 1945. With Koo priming the pump, Canadian Christians, especially progressive ones in the SCM, were eager to understand China and deepen ecumenical contacts in the "younger churches" around the world. The executive committee invited Ting as proof of their commitment to and solidarity with the world church. After twenty-eight days on a cargo ship from Hong Kong to Vancouver and two days on a train across Canada, Ting and his wife arrived in Toronto.

In December 1946 the SCM newsletter announced the arrival of Ting and Kuo in Toronto and explained the purpose for their visit. Ting would provide unique insight into the mission enterprise of the Christian church and speak authoritatively about China's urgent needs. The newsletter added:

> Mr. and Mrs. Ting speak of themselves as "symbols" of the reality of the Word Church, and possibly their most important contribution to the life of the Canadian Movement will be made simply as a result of their being here in that capacity. Through them, students will be helped to feel their kinship in a wider family, which is the Church Universal.[48]

Throughout 1947 Ting and Kuo traveled across Canada, meeting Christian groups wherever they went. They spoke to university chapters of the SCM, preached in churches, and joined YMCA meetings.[49] They had no interest in recruiting missionaries for China, at least not the old type of missionaries. Like other leaders in the SCM, they criticized the missionary enterprise and its relationship with colonialism. Demonstrating her command of English and commitment to the ecumenism of her husband, Siu-may Kuo

48. University of Toronto Archives, SCM, B1979-059/007 (Archives 1946–47).

49. See Wickeri, *Reconstructing Christianity in China*, 60–70, for a description of Ting's time in Canada.

offers her opinion of the missionary movement in the monthly publication of the SCM, *The Canadian Student*. She criticizes the time when "missionaries were sent out with patronizing, paternal attitudes and charity-giving, condescending manners" and suggests that new missionary efforts should be a "cross fertilization that enriches and re-enforces not only the receiving side, but the sending side, too."[50] Kuo argues that there can be no "such thing as being a Christian without being a missionary" because true Christianity requires wholehearted acceptance to the extent that it becomes "an obsession, dominating and directing every conscious, sub-conscious and semi-conscious act in relation to others."[51] With the spoken and written word, both K. H. Ting and Siu-may Kuo advocated a particular vision of Christian faith.

With his typewriter, K. H. Ting demonstrated rhetorical skill that combined Christian ideas and a trenchant political analysis. He lamented not original sin but the sin of imperialism, political indifference, and Western support of Chiang Kai-shek and the Nationalists. He advocated not a personal salvation from sin but national salvation from China's social upheaval. In his earliest essay published in English, Ting explained that while Western churches continued their missionary work in China, Chinese Christians wondered "how so many missionaries can honestly preach the gospel of peace and reconciliation, supposedly representing the goodwill of the West towards China, while at the same time giving unquestioned support to the hostile policy of the American government."[52] One month later, in *The Canadian Student*, he addressed the dilemma that students ought to face in their university education: To what end am I receiving this training? He tells the story from a novel of a doctor in Nazi Germany who looked after the well-being of twelve attractive young women.[53] The physician's job—keeping these women healthy and free from sexually transmitted diseases, an honorable thing—went to a dishonorable end, protecting the Nazi officials who frequented the brothel-house. Ting uses this story to argue

50. S. Ting, "World Begins Now," 48. The Tings became regular contributors to *The Canadian Student*. See also Ting's articles: "The Dilemma of the Sincere Student," *Canadian Student* 25 (1947), "The Simplicity of the Gospel," *Canadian Student* 26 (1947), and "The Simplicity of the Gospel–II," *Canadian Student* 26 (1948).

51. Wickeri notes: "Siu-may always seemed to know that she was going to change the world, and she put all her energy into this task. " Wickeri, *Reconstructing Christianity in China*, 67.

52. K. Ting, *No Longer Strangers*, 112.

53. Maltz, *Cross and the Arrow.*

that learning to cure diseases or build bridges is not enough. Each student must ask to what end they develop these skills and how those skills fit into the broader life of the nation.

> If an education merely imparts or transmits certain information and data and skills, it is like merely sharpening a knife without seeing to the sanity of the one holding it, or like training ourselves to shoot arrows without pointing them at any target. We must define the ends for which we live and concern ourselves, with our systems of values and our philosophies of life, so that we will dedicate our knowledge and skills to only the right cause.[54]

This applied to ministers as much as it did to engineers, scientists, and physicians. "There is the minister who considers his job to preach the gospel of peace and love, but there are so many other forces, political, economic and military, undoing on a much larger scale the very things he tried to do."[55] Ting closed his article by praising the SCM in its efforts to move university students to an abundant life in the family of the eternal Father by relating their individual life purpose to the all of humanity as a world community. To the individualistic mindset of North American students, this message must have been a welcome challenge.

The Tings succeeded in moving the thinking of the Canadian SCM in opposition to the Nationalists and in favor of the Communists. Through their personal relationships with Christian leaders, their itinerant work across Canada, and their writing, Canadian Christians felt the influence of K. H. Ting and Siu-may Kuo. In April 1948, less than a year after the Tings left Toronto for New York City, the editors of the SCM *Bulletin* addressed "The China Question Again."[56] They admitted that the international issue receiving the most attention in the Canadian SCM that year was the question of Christian responsibility in China. The issue centered not on Christian evangelism or Christian education but on the political crisis in China. The editors quoted Professor Bruce Collier, former United Church missionary at West China University:

> The most acute issue in China today as it concerns us in the relationship of the Church to the government and to the political crisis. . . . The so-called political issues in China are also moral issues, and therefore the Church must be concerned. . . . To "keep

54. K. Ting, "Dilemma of Sincere Student," 81.

55. K. Ting, "Dilemma of Sincere Student," 92.

56. University of Toronto Archives, SCM, B1979–059/007 (Archives 1947–48).

> out of politics" when it involves moral principles surely cannot be justified in the light of the history of the Hebrew prophets and of the Christian church. As informed people everywhere are now well acquainted with the corrupt, reactionary, and oppressive nature of the present Koumintang regime, it is puzzling that many missionaries still support the regime and claim that its leaders are good Christians.[57]

As K. H. Ting sat somewhere on Union's campus in New York, a smile must have broken across his face when he read the next section. The SCM lamented: "Since we apparently have no message for these millions of oppressed peasants who are struggling to free themselves from the crushing burden of rents and taxes, can we blame the peasants for turning to the Communists, or can we blame the Communists for stepping in with a solution to this great problem?" The Canadian SCM condemned their government's cooperation with the Americans in supplying munitions for a "reactionary, corrupt and oppressive regime which has thwarted the aspirations of the Chinese people for a better life." They understood China's growing anti-foreign and anti-Christian sentiment, concluding that if the Christian church was driven out of China, they would have no one to blame but themselves. Before Ting arrived in Canada, the SCM already leaned in the direction espoused in this editorial. However, he gave the movement a healthy shove in this pro-Communist direction. Ever the shrewd politician, Ting shrouded any political agenda in a Christian guise.

K. H. Ting showed his colors most clearly in an anonymous article written in 1948.[58] He assessed the traditional system of land-tenure in China, describing the current Civil War between the Nationalists and Communists as a "war of liberation." In this war, the Nationalists stood against the peasants and against democracy. Though not unfamiliar language within the SCM, the essay must have shocked many North American Christians. Readers probably assumed the author was a Communist Party member, or at least a CCP sympathizer, because the rhetoric echoed Maoist propaganda. From his Union residence hall in Manhattan, Ting wrote: "Washington war-mongers and American finance-imperialist adventurers

57. University of Toronto Archives, SCM, B1979–059/007 (Archives 1947–48).

58. The *Bulletin of the Society of the Catholic Commonwealth* describes the unnamed author of "The Sociological Foundation of the Democratic Movement in China" as "a Priest of the Holy Catholic Church in China, intimately familiar with the current Chinese scene." Wickeri believes this could only have been Ting. Wickeri, *Reconstructing Christianity in China*, 38.

are still stubbornly credulous of the possibly of successful intervention on the side of the reactionary forces on China." The reactionary forces were a "fascist-minded class of land-lords and wealthy industrialists, in union with their sycophant hangers-on among army officers and government bureaucrats."[59] With one hand Ting gladly accepted a fellowship funded by wealthy industrialists and, with the other, typed inflammatory words against the same class of people. He chose to live in the world's wealthiest city, one built on the capitalistic machine that he abhorred. How could he hold together the tension, the irony, of writing one way and living another? If nothing else, this article provides insight into Ting's bewildering complexity and aggravating genius.

Ting's friends from Toronto painted a picture of their Chinese friend that unravels some of his mystery.[60] One of the radical SCM leaders at McGill University in Montreal in 1946, Vince Goring, saw Ting as "a person who really didn't let his right hand know what his left had was doing." Ting supported the Marxist position of the SCC, but not openly. When the Society caused a split in the Canadian SCM, both those for and against metacosmesis claimed Ting for their side.[61] Another friend from the Toronto days, Cyril Powles, described Ting as a man of "tempered steel, but well covered." At a camp in August 1947, Ting engaged in a "gentlemanly debate" with Philippe Maury regarding a Christian's role in society. Ting made a comment that resonated in people's minds at the camp and long

59. Wickeri, *Reconstructing Christianity in China*, 63.

60. Based on a tape transcript of "Conversations about K. H. Ting in Canada in the 1940s," Toronto, February 3, 1992. The people who gathered got to know Ting in the 1940s and shared their memories. In Wickeri, *Reconstructing Christianity in China*, 63, from which I cite throughout this paragraph.

61. The Society of the Catholic Commonwealth (SCC) was an Anglican society of priests and laypeople based in Cambridge, Massachusetts, that combined high church liturgical theology with Marxism. The founder, F. Hastings Smyth, called it "dialectical sacramentalism" or "metacosmesis." Wickeri notes that Smyth's ideas "enjoyed certain influence" in the Canadian SCM in the 1940s and 1950s and helped form their understanding of social justice and global affairs. Ting visited Smyth in Cambridge in 1946 and 1947 and corresponded with him (*Reconstructing Christianity in China*, 64). For more on dialectical sacramentalism see Brown, "Metacosmesis." Brown concludes that "Smyth and the SCC had little dramatic impact on the church, particularly in the US, Smyth was marginalized in the church and the Society virtually unknown. Yet, on the positive side, Smyth attracted a group of people who were both intelligent and deeply committed to social justice. They had and continue to have an individual and corporate impact on the church, particularly in Canada and Japan" (380). China should also be included in this note: Smyth impacted China through Ting.

afterward. He told the group that God might disown the church and work through other organizations if those groups more effectively carried out God's will. No doubt, Y. T. Wu planted this idea in Ting's mind. Three years after Ting's debate in Canada, Wu articulated the same vision publicly.[62] Ever the friend and supporter, Wickeri put a positive spin on Ting's acumen in masking his thoughts and in speaking differently depending on the audience: "he respected the fact that the language of the church was different from the language of politics." Ting had the chameleonlike skill in turning on the Christian and Communist colors, depending on his environment. Wickeri summarizes that Ting's "tempered but well-covered" style reflected his "personal reserve" and "political judgment" and aided in making him an "unusually effective communicator to many different audiences." What a friend calls "political judgment," a critic might call "Machiavellian." Yet it would be unfair to characterize Ting as an opportunistic hypocrite. He wholeheartedly believed in a recast Christian message, just like Wu and his professors at St. John's and at Union. He saw the Chinese Communist Party doing what the Christian church failed to do, providing national salvation. Though Ting's psychology deserves further study, I am more interested in his theological complexity, which I explore in chapter 9. I now turn to his time at Union.

## K. H. Ting in New York City

Ting applied to study at Union when he was still in Toronto. He wrote Union's president, Henry Pitney Van Dusen: "My wife hopes to work for her MA in education and I shall like to get a master's degree either in education or in some field of theology. In the latter my interest is in ecumenism and Christian social ethics."[63] After World War II, Van Dusen had traveled throughout China to visit the Christian Colleges. In his letter Ting reminded Van Dusen that they had met in Shanghai. "I was the pastor of the Community Church of Shanghai when you visited that city early last summer," wrote Ting. "I can still remember very vividly your sermon and the interesting meeting you had

62. Wu, "Reformation of Christianity," in Jones and Merwin, *Documents of Three-Self Movement*. See ch. 4.

63. Union Theological Seminary administrative alumni records, K. H. Ting (1948). Staff at Union kindly created a memorandum for me, summarizing the contents of Ting's alumni records. Unless otherwise noted, all citations in this paragraph originate in that memorandum.

in our home with some Chinese students the same afternoon." Ting closed by asking Van Dusen for advice regarding scholarships and accommodation. That same week one of Kuo's former professors also wrote to President Van Dusen. On January 22, 1947, Alice H. Gregg offered her support of "my young friends." Gregg's friendship with the Tings went back to 1938–41 when Ting served as a student secretary in the Shanghai YMCA. Gregg's letter gushes with admiration of Siu-may Kuo, her student at St. John's in the 1940s: "She was possessed of brilliant mind and an ardent spirit—as she still is. . . . She will be a leader in her own right. I could wish she would get interested in preparing courses for Young People into which she would pour her social ardour." Gregg concluded: "K. H. did not ask for a chance to study. . . . However, I think he would jump at a chance to study. He is the student type. T. Z. Koo calls him 'one of the coming men in China.' Union would always be proud of both of them—I am sure of that."[64] In response to Ting and Gregg's letters, Van Dusen noted on an internal memorandum on January 29, 1947, that Ting was "one of the most promising leaders in the Christian Church in China." Within a few weeks the seminary wrote Ting to let him know that they could offer him a Missionary Fellowship and housing. None of this would have happened apart from Ting's participation and engagement in the dense social network, the *guanxi*, that connected Union so deeply with the SFPE. Ting also received the Hazen Fellowship.[65] With this fellowship, he could have studied anywhere in the United States. But he chose Union and New York City.

Ting chose Union for a variety of reasons. First, the city of New York itself held tremendous appeal.[66] The city bristled with energy and it had a sizeable Chinese population, making it attractive to the cosmopolitan Tings. Second, Union had partnerships with Teachers College and Columbia University, which were both situated across the street. Union students were allowed to co-enroll at Teachers and Columbia. Despite the abolition of the Chinese imperial exams in 1905, academic credentials carried tremendous weight in China. A joint degree from Union and Teachers or Union and

64. Gregg's prophecy, that Union would always be proud of the Tings, came true. In 1994, Union's Board of Trustees awarded Ting the Union Medal, the school's highest honor, for his "faithful and visionary ministry in China." Rosen, "Union Medal," 14.

65. Letter from Siu May Ting to Hilda Benson, March 17, 1949. Special Collections, YDSL, SVM group 42, ser. 6, box 491, folder 5877A.

66. In 1940 and 1941, amateur photographer Charles W. Cushman captured New York life as the Tings would have experienced it. To view these images see Angelova, "Vintage Photos."

Columbia appealed to ambitious Chinese Christians. In the first half of the twentieth century, more Chinese students attended Columbia than any other university in the United States.[67] Between 1910 and 1925, one thousand Chinese students made use of scholarships from the Boxer indemnity funds. With John Dewey (1859–1952) anchoring the faculty, Teachers College became the most important institution exporting education theory to China. Chinese international students at Teachers in the 1920s and 1930s returned home eager to apply their newly learned pedagogical ideas. And, as Jessie Lutz rightly notes, some intellectuals in the floundering Chinese republic turned to education as panacea.[68] Another reason Union appealed to the Tings: the seminary boasted of one of the best teaching faculties in the world.

In the 1940s the staff at Union included Paul Tillich, Reinhold Niebuhr, John Bennett, and John T. McNeill. William E. Hordern, a Union student in the 1940s, reminisced that during his time at Union he "had been exposed to one of the greatest galaxies of theological stars ever gathered into one faculty in this country."[69] Union's president, Henry Pitney Van Dusen, liked to brag about his school, calling it the "great theological college of the world, with a place of absolute preeminence." He often repeated a compliment paid by William Temple, the archbishop of Canterbury, who called Union "the foremost theological college in the world."[70] Van Dusen committed to double the number of international students to fifty per year. When qualified Christian leaders from outside North America applied to Union, the seminary offered fellowships to lure them there. K. H. Ting benefitted from both Van Dusen's vision and the school's generosity. It is no historical accident that the Tings moved to New York City. Union gathered a remarkable faculty in the world's most important city and recruited Christians from around the world. As the theological vanguard for progressive and ecumenical theology, the seminary eagerly exported their ideas globally.

The flexibility of Union's joint MA program allowed the Tings to take classes at Columbia and Teachers. Ting took three courses in theology and ethics. For all his elective courses, he chose education: three at Union and five at Teachers. He sought classes in fields that had interested him since

67. See Appendix D. Based on Bieler, *"Patriots" or "Traitors,"* 382.

68. Lutz, *China and Christian Colleges*, 162.

69. Lutz, *China and Christian Colleges*, 162.

70. Handy, *History*, 216.

his undergraduate days at St. John's, namely education and psychology. He burned with a desire to apply these fields to help supply answers to China's social issues. Ting took two classes from Union's leading figure in Christian Education: Harrison Sacket Elliot (1882–1951). After graduation from Ohio Wesleyan University in 1905, Elliot served as the personal secretary for James W. Bashford, the bishop of China for the Methodist Episcopal Church. While working for Bishop Bashford for three years in China, he also served as correspondent for the Associated Press in Shanghai. China left an indelible mark in Elliot's professional career. Ronald Cram, in the *Biography of Christian Educators*, explains: "Elliot's lifelong interest in international affairs, what we might today call globalization in theological education, began as the result of his time in China."[71] After returning to the United States, Elliot worked for the YMCA. He would remain connected to the YMCA for the next forty years. In 1915 Elliot enrolled in graduate school at Union and at Teachers College.

Three years later he published a book that applied psychology and scientific analysis to society. *The Leadership of the Red Triangle Groups* reflected clearly the influence of John Dewey, then the education maestro at Teachers. His next book, *How Jesus Met Life Questions*, creatively blended progressive educational theory and progressive theological thought. Jesus wrestled with real and contemporary social issues. According to Elliot, a twentieth-century Jesus would favor a social gospel. Elliot caught the eye of Union faculty. In 1923 the seminary appointed him the Skinner and McAlpin Professor of Practical Theology. Two years later he became head of the Department of Education and Psychology. Elliot's best-known book, *Can Religious Education Be Christian?*, summarized his life work. One year later Shelton Smith, a prominent Christian educator at Duke University, attacked Elliot's work and the liberalism behind it. He contested Elliot's denial of the sovereignty of God, rejected Elliot's view that God evolves as result of social evolution, and questioned Elliot's perspective on the infinite value of human personality. Smith's liberal assumptions had been assaulted by the grotesque realities of World War II; his views transformed by the neoorthodoxy of Karl Barth. In *Faith and Nurture*, Smith wrote:

> Liberal Christianity has also had a part in obscuring the principle of the sovereignty of God in His Kingdom. This is reflected, for example, in the liberal's emphasis on divine immanence. If religious

71. Cram, "Harrison S. Elliot."

> orthodoxy sometimes tended to deny all continuity between God and man, liberalism has tended to overemphasize continuity.[72]

Smith contested Elliot's liberalism that was rooted in the immanence of God and goodness of humanity. But what did K. H. Ting think of Elliot and his theology?

The answer is unclear. The archives offer little help to this question. Given his lifelong interest in China and his YMCA affiliation, I imagine that the sixty-six-year-old Elliot took a keen interest in Ting. After all, here was an intelligent, articulate Chinese student with an impressive background and a wide-open future before him. Elliot stressed that Christian education should serve the current political and economic needs of society. This message would resonate deeply with Ting his entire life. But it resonated with Ting before he ever came to Union. In a 1991 interview with Wickeri, Ting recounts a Teachers College course by Goodwin Watson (1899–1976) on psychology and social change.[73] Memories from this class resonated in Ting for forty-three years. Could the same be said for other courses at Union? Ting never singled out Elliot or his courses. The evidence suggests that Ting chose courses at Union that reinforced what he already thought on these topics. Ting arrived in New York not as a twenty-two-year-old tabula rasa, eager to have his theological views formed but as an experienced and, literally, war-hardened thirty-three-year-old ready to have his theological views confirmed. Union influenced Ting before he arrived at the seminary. The school influenced him through its social network in China's Christian colleges and the YMCA. K. H. Ting is but one example of how Union provided social capital—*guanxi*—like no other seminary in world.

## Summary

In this chapter I examined K. H. Ting's life and his connection to Union Seminary. I devoted many words to Ting's early life to give a clear picture of the man and his world. This picture relies on the excellent work of Philip Wickeri, whose biography of Ting I use extensively in this chapter. Wickeri argues that Ting's Anglican formation, his involvement in the Student Christian Movement, and his social setting "mitigated against the

72. Smith, *Faith and Nurture*, 53. Cited in Cram, "Harrison S. Elliot.

73. Wickeri, *Reconstructing Christianity in China*, 72.

theological outlook that Union had to offer."[74] I believe Wickeri underestimates the impact of Union on Ting. The later K. H. Ting cannot be understood apart from a study of his life in China before he went to North America. Union played a crucial role in making K. H. Ting who he was. Union's primary influence on Ting came not via the classroom but through the dense social network connected to Union. Union impacted Ting and other Chinese Christians through its ideas and its *guanxi* (social capital). Yet K. H. Ting and Y. T. Wu were just two Chinese Christians whose lives were changed through the social network in and around Union. I now turn to explore two prominent networks of Chinese Christians in the United States: the Cross and Sword secret society and the Chinese Students' Christian Association. These organizations and their leaders, Timothy Ting-fang Lew, William Hung, Andrew Y. Y. Tsu, and Siu-may Kuo, help us understand the density of Union's social network and why this network exerted such profound influence on China before and after 1949.

74. Wickeri, *Reconstructing Christianity in China*, 72.

# 7

# Union and the Cross and Sword Secret Society

## Timothy Tingfang Lew and William Hung

UNION THEOLOGICAL SEMINARY EXERTED a significant, though largely unnoticed, influence on Protestantism in twentieth-century China. The New York school wielded its influence through several means: disseminating publications by Union alumni and professors throughout China, educating American missionaries to China, and recruiting and training Chinese Christians. Union impacted Chinese Christianity through a dense social network of Chinese and American Christians. This network permeated the leadership of both the Chinese Christian colleges and the YMCA/YWCA. In previous chapters I explained the importance of Wu and Ting to Chinese Christianity. Two Chinese leaders, however, do not make a network.

In the next two chapters I will elaborate the density and interconnectedness of the Union network in the Sino-Foreign Protestant Establishment in Republican China. This chapter will explore a secret society formed by Chinese Christians in New York in 1917, Cross and Sword (Cands), and two Chinese Christians who founded Cands, Timothy Tingfang Lew and William Hung. The following chapter explores another nexus of Chinese Christians: the Chinese Students' Christian Association (CSCA). In both chapters I will contend that Wu and Ting are not isolated instances of the influence of Union on Chinese Christianity. To the contrary, an elite network of Chinese Christians swirled around Union Seminary and institutions under Union's influence. At times Union's influence was clear. Other times, though, Union's sway was hidden below the surface.

## Cross and Sword Secret Society

In the summer of 1916, the International Committee of the YMCA hosted a conference in New York. At this conference Chinese students from across the nation met each other, men such as William Hung from Ohio Wesleyan University and Timothy Tingfang Lew from Columbia University. Hung, Lew, and their Chinese friends were smart, devoted, and ambitious. They were convinced that the hope for China's future lay in Christianity and that they would play an important role in that future. Susan Egan aptly describes the attitude of this generation of Chinese students in the US:

> China perhaps will never again produce a group of young men and women—predominantly men—as idealistic, patriotic, and as sure of themselves as the some two thousand Chinese students in the United States in the 1910s. They knew that they were going to be the leaders of a new China. A whole country of crumbling institutions awaited their return. . . . Regardless of their individual ambitions, to the youthful group there assembled [at a conference], the victory of their generation was all but certain. Little did they know that for much of the rest of their lives, they would be battling not doddering old men, but fiery young ones whose heroes were Marx and Lenin, and by whom men of their liberal persuasion would be ultimately crushed.[1]

Union Seminary helped develop a network of Chinese and American Christians. These Chinese Christians in turn formed and led organizations. James Davison Hunter's argues that the key actor in history is not individual genius but rather a network of people and *the new institutions generated from those networks.*[2] During their time at both Columbia and Union, Lew, Hung, and other ambitious Chinese Christians strengthened ties with each other and formed weak ties with leading American Christians. These men and women became an elite network of Chinese Christians who would establish and lead institutions in China. Lew and Hung demonstrated this tendency in their creation of Cands.

On June 24, 1917, seven Chinese Christians formed a secret fraternity for Chinese students who were devout Christians and excellent students. They named their society *Cands*, for Cross and Sword. The founding members, which included Timothy Tingfang Lew and William Hung, pledged

1. Egan, *Latterday Confucian*, 58.
2. J. Hunter, *To Change the World*, 38 (emphasis mine).

to secrecy and the motto: "We Unite for the Uplift of China."[3] Modeling themselves after the Society of Jesus, Cands members committed to take up the cross in emulating Jesus and the figurative sword in the zeal of the Crusaders. Hung took seriously the fraternity's vows to secrecy. When a member at Princeton University died of pneumonia, Hung immediately traveled to New Jersey. He posed as a close family friend to gain access to the deceased man's dormitory room and diary. The diary contained Cands' secrets. Hung tore the diary and burned it. As the fraternity grew, its ranks included ambitious Chinese Christians who would have important roles in Republican China. These men would become leaders in government, education, and business.[4] In 1918 at a meeting in Brooklyn, Wang Chengting divulged to the group the existence of another secret fraternity of Chinese Christian students in the US.

David and Jonathan (D&J) had formed in 1907 with the same motto: "We Unite for the Uplift of China." Lew pushed for the two fraternities to unite, noting that such a union would benefit their future careers. Hung publicly opposed the union on the same grounds, believing the fraternity should not be used primarily for personal advancement. Lew's argument won the day. The amalgamation of Cands and D&J became the Association for Accomplishing Ideals (*Cheng Zhi Hui* or CCH). By 1936 the association had 270 members. These members rose to prominence in Republican China, creating a dense social network in which members helped advance one another's careers. In his study of Chinese students in the United States between 1900 and 1927, Weili Ye notes:

> Many CCH members held preeminent positions in republican China, in the areas of politics, education, banking, diplomacy, business, engineering, and Christian church organizations. CCH held an interesting place in modern Chinese history that has not been fully understood and recognized, partly because the fraternity

3. See Egan, *Latterday Confucian*, ch. 7. Founding members also included Chen Huqin (future professor in Shanghai) and Tu Yuqing (future general-secretary of the Shanghai YMCA).

4. They included: Jiang Tingfu (head of Qinghua University's History Department and the Republic of China's ambassador to the USSR, USA, and UN), Zhang Boling (founder and longtime president of Nankai University), Zhou Yiqun (president of Qinghua University), Nie Qiqie (founder of the Great China Spinning and Weaving Company), Wang Chengting (vice-speaker of China's Senate in the 1910s and member of the Chinese delegation to Paris Peace Conference), and Eugene Yuren Chen (protégé of Sun Yat-sen and China's minister of foreign affairs from 1926 to 1927).

remained secretive throughout its history and few members have candidly recorded their experiences.[5]

This powerful social network included Wang Chonghui (chairman of the Law Codification Committee, chief justice of the Supreme Court, acting premier in 1922, and minister of foreign affairs from 1937 to 1941) and H. H. Kung (one of the wealthiest men in China, minister of industry, minister of finance, governor of the Central Bank of China, and premier of the KMT from 1938 to 1939).

The creation and existence of these two secret societies provide clues to the ambition and interconnectedness of Chinese Christians in the United States. Intentionally and unintentionally, members of the CCH strengthened interpersonal ties. Absent ties became weak ones and weak ties grew strong. Even the weak ties connected society members to prominent social networks in China and the United States. While these secret societies might testify to the density of the social network of Chinese Christians in America, the role of Union therein must be demonstrated. To do so, I turn to examine the life, American experiences, and careers of Timothy Tingfang Lew and William Hung.

## Timothy Tingfang Lew (1892–1947)

Timothy Tingfang Lew was born in Wenzhou, Zhejiang, in 1892.[6] Unusual for nineteenth-century China, he was born into a Protestant family that was third generation on his father's side and fourth on his mother's. Lew's paternal grandmother dedicated her grandson to be a Christian minister. Trained as a physician by the China Inland Mission (CIM), Lew's father moved his family to Zhejiang to open a CIM hospital there. He died in November 1902. The elder Liu left behind his wife, Li Ruyu, and six children. To provide for her family, Li became headmistress of the CIM women's school (a role long held by her mother-in-law). Growing up in a school suited Lew's gifts well. Barwick describes him as "an unusually intelligent child, quick to learn and possessing a remarkable memory."[7] He wrote his first poem by the time he

5. Ye, *Seeking Modernity*, 46–47.

6. I follow Barwick's conclusion that the evidence favors 1892. Barwick, "Protestant Quest for Modernity," 187. Barwick devotes ch. 4 of his unpublished dissertation to examining Lew's life and influence in China. For the fullest examination of Lew, see Wu, "Idea and Practice."

7. Barwick, "Protestant Quest," 190.

was seven years old. By nine, he could recite from memory the forty-nine chapters of the Book of Rites (礼记 *Liji*). Lew proceeded to secondary school at Wenzhou College and to university at St. John's University in Shanghai. The role of Christian schools in China, where Union exerted great influence, played a significant role in Lew's life and in the lives of other Chinese Christians examined in these chapters. Lew came from a Christian college and he would return to a Christian college after his time abroad.

Lew's writings were first published in missionary newspapers when he was fifteen years old.[8] As a university student he continued to submit articles to various missionary publications. Lew's articles demonstrate the qualities that characterized his career: "an earnest Christian, a fervent patriot, a gifted writer, an independent thinker, and a fearless critic."[9] In one article Lew argued for missionary educators to respect Chinese culture. This idea resonated with a John Leighton Stuart, an American missionary and professor at Nanjing Seminary. Stuart would loom large over the SFPE.[10] Born to missionary parents in China in 1876, Stuart later served as president of Yenching University (1919–46) and as the US Ambassador to the Republic of China (1946–52). In assessing Stuart's impact in China, Shaw concludes:

> Stuart was the embodiment of the social-gospel wing of the Christian missionary movement, and was perhaps the most successful missionary of that faction in China. His major concern was not merely for saving souls but also for the social welfare of the people. . . . As a Christocentric liberal, Stuart believed that all religions or spiritual systems derived from the same supreme source; therefore, Chinese religion and philosophy has intrinsic value and power. Furthermore, Stuart believed that Chinese religious sentiments and cultural traditions could complement and reinforce Christian teachings, and vice versa. In this regard, his position echoes that of his contemporaries, such as the liberal Chinese theologian Chao Tzu-ch'en, and of his forerunners, such as Matteo Ricci.[11]

8. Liu Tingfang's essay "A Tearful Proclamation to my Compatriots Regarding the Zhejiang Railway Affair" was published as "An Appraisal of the Issue of Chinese Christian Patriotism, *Zhongguo Jidutu aiguo wenti de pingyi*" in the *Christian Intelligencer* (*Tongwenbao* 通问报).

9. Barwick, "Protestant Quest for Modernity," 192.

10. He had the unique misfortune of being singled out and vilified by Mao. Mao called Stuart "a loyal agent of US cultural aggression in China." Mao, "Farewell, Leighton Stuart!"

11. Shaw, *American Missionary in China*, 294. See also Stuart, *Fifty Years in China*.

Stuart wrote the newspaper's editor to learn more about the articulate, opinionated author. Then, he contacted Lew. So began a lifelong friendship that would play prominently in Lew's future.

Lew eventually grew frustrated with St. John's educational policies and left the school before graduating. Stuart came to his rescue. He arranged for Lew to study in the United States and obtained the necessary funds.[12] Lew traveled to Tennessee in 1911. A semester at a Presbyterian preparatory school was followed by two years at the University of Georgia. Lew transferred to Columbia University to finish his undergraduate studies. He spent the years of the Great War in New York City piling up various degrees (Columbia University BA, 1915; MA, 1915; Teachers College cert. education, 1916; PhD, 1920). Lew studied at Union for two years (1915–17) but transferred to Yale Divinity School as a Fogg Scholar. According to Lew's friend, William Hung, he transferred to avoid an oral exam in Hebrew, which was needed for graduation from Union.[13] He graduated with a BD in 1918. Lew's doctoral dissertation from Teachers College examined the psychology of learning Chinese characters.[14] In 1920 the Congregational Church of Manhattan ordained Lew. Despite incessant physical maladies, Lew remained a flurry of activity.[15]

In addition to his studies and church involvement, Lew also played important roles in Chinese student associations in New York City. In 1915 he began serving as associate editor of the *Chinese Students' Monthly* (the official publication of the Chinese Students' Association) and editor of the *Chinese Students' Christian Journal (Liu Mei Tsing Nien*, the monthly journal of the Chinese Students' Christian Association [CSCA]). One year later he became executive director of the CSCA, which I describe in the following chapter. In his message as the new leader, Lew argued for the need to establish a stable republican government in the wake of Yuan Shikai's death:

> This should help us to realize more concretely than ever the urgent need of genuine leadership with irreproachable character as it is represented in the life of Jesus Christ. Whether or not we shall be able to stand up as the worthy followers of Christ and cooperate

12. West, *Yenching University*, 60–61.

13. See Barwick, "Protestant Quest for Modernity," 195.

14. Lew, "Psychology of Learning Chinese."

15. Less than five feet tall, Lew struggled with respiratory problems and headaches his whole life. Stuart observed that if he ever took an often-advised vacation "his brain would spin like a ship's propeller out of water." West, *Yenching University*, 59–60.

> with each other for the creation of a New China, will depend largely on how well we are developing our Christian character while we are students in this country.[16]

As noted earlier, Lew helped form Cross and Sword secret society in 1917. When the group merged with David and Jonathan, he continued to lead the combined society, CCH. In the midst of all these activities, Lew surrounded himself with other Chinese students who would also play prominent roles in China's future, men such as T. V. Soong (宋子文 *Song Ziwen*, 1891–1971). Soong hailed from the most prominent family in Republican China and had been a classmate with Lew at St. John's.[17]

Lew was the prototype of the type of Chinese students who would come to Union for the ensuing thirty-five years. These Union-educated Chinese Christians tended to be brilliant, bicultural people who attended Christian schools in China and had strong ties with one another. These leaders blended a commitment to Christianity and love for China. Their robust patriotism saw great hope for China in and through the Christianity. In both Republican and Communist China, Union influenced Protestantism through this social nexus. Members of this Union-saturated network held roles in churches and universities throughout China. Before returning to China Lew taught religious education at Union. Lew's lectures outlined five components of "the ideal training for the fullest expression of the Chinese Christian experience": 1) Chinese scholarship, 2) able expression in the best Chinese style, 3) religious experience firsthand, 4) knowledge of foreign languages, and 5) Western theological training.[18] In another lecture Lew asks: "Will China Become Red?"[19] This was the 1920s, in the heart of Republican China, long before most people were asking this question. His teaching notes from the 1920s—outlines handwritten in English

16. Liu, "President's Message." Cited in Barwick, "Protestant Quest," 197.

17. See Seagrave, *Soong Dynasty*. Charlie Soong did not have much success as a Methodist missionary in China but experienced tremendous success in publishing. With his growing wealth came greater social power. His daughter Ai-ling married one of China's wealthiest men, H. H. Kung; Ching-ling married Sun Yat-sen, Father of Republican China; May-ling married Chiang Kai-shek, Sun's successor as leader of Republican China; and T. V. Soong served as finance minister, foreign minister, and premier in the KMT.

18. 1927–28 lecture notes. MRL 6: Timothy Tingfang Lew Papers, ser. 3, box 1, folder 3, Burke Library, Union Theological Seminary, NY.

19. 1920 lecture notes. MRL 6: Timothy Tingfang Lew Papers, ser. 3, box 1, folder 3, Burke Library, Union Theological Seminary, NY.

cursive—demonstrate his clarity of thought, deep patriotism, and prophetic voice. After Lew completed his doctorate, and his wife, her master's degree in education from Teachers College, several job options were available.

Lew could have worked for the government or a state university, but he opted for a Christian college. He had planned on reuniting with J. Leighton Stuart at Nanjing Seminary. But in 1919 Stuart assumed the presidency of Yenching University. A year later President Stuart invited Lew to join his faculty in Beijing.[20] Loyal to Stuart and excited about Yenching's vision of education, Lew accepted his friend's offer. Stuart envisioned Yenching as a university that blended the East and West, emphasized Christianity and modernity, and combined Chinese and Western staff. Lew became the first Chinese staff member with a doctorate. He began teaching psychology, his specialty, in the School of Religion. A man of profound energy and a deep capacity, Lew also served as dean at the graduate school of education at Peking Normal University and professor of psychology of Peking University. Within a year at Yenching, Stuart promoted Lew to assistant to the chancellor and dean of the School of Religion.

Stuart did not hide his admiration for his Chinese colleague. In a letter to a friend, Stuart praises Lew's "remarkable intuition" and "incisive appreciation of the larger movements and their significance." Stuart describes that he repeatedly turns to Lew to "form judgments in these baffling perplexities."[21] In a letter to Lew, Stuart marvels at Lew's work in the midst of poor health:

> [Your] letter shows an amazing amount of work even for a man in robust health. How you can accomplish so much with your physical ailments is a reproach to all the rest of us. Even more do I marvel at your uncomplaining acceptance of the pain and the constant drain upon your vitality and patience.[22]

Lew's role as Stuart's right-hand man gave him a significant voice in determining Yenching's direction and in hiring Chinese faculty. He turned, naturally, to the dense social network of Chinese Christians in Morningside Heights. The dense social network between Columbia-Union-Teachers

20. Stuart, *Fifty Years in China*, 77. Stuart claims he did not pressure Lew to join him at Yenching.

21. Correspondence, Stuart to North, April 13, 1927. Cited in West, *Yenching University*, 61.

22. MRL 6: Timothy Tingfang Lew Papers, ser. 2, box 1, folder 17, Burke Library, Union Theological Seminary, NY.

and Yenching included Yenching faculty and trustees. In 1945 the school's trustees had significant links to Union: Mr. and Mrs. Charles H. Corbett, Rufus Jones, Henry Luce, Elizabeth Luce Moore, and Henry P. Van Dusen. Eventually over one-quarter of Yenching's faculty attended Columbia, Union, or Teachers.[23] In addition, many of these faculty members had ties to the YMCA. Lew urged Stuart to raise Yenching's academic standards by ousting those with inadequate qualifications, which did not endear Lew to other Yenching faculty. The animosity of some faculty toward Lew caused no small measure of strain in the already fragile Lew. Lew's flurry of activity was not limited to university campuses in Beijing. He served a vital role in church and other academic roles throughout China.

In Chinese academia Lew made significant contributions in the field of education and educational psychology. He co-founded and co-directed the Psychological Association in China. In 1923 the Chinese Christian Education Association appointed him the chairman of the Committee of Standardized Tests. Lew also served as executive secretary of the National Association for the Advancement of Education. From 1924 to 1927 he became the first Chinese to be elected as president of the China Christian Educational Association and from 1930 to 1935 served as chairman of the China National Committee on Christian Higher Education. Lew founded and edited several journals in China: *The Truth and Life Journal*, *The Amethyst Quarterly*, and *Education for Tomorrow*. He had ample opportunity to utilize his gifts in writing, translating, and editing. Lew's contribution in China extended into the church. He supervised the creation of *Hymns of Universal Praise*, a Chinese union hymnal. He helped organize the National Christian Council of China in 1922 and remained involved for the next nineteen years. In 1932 Lew led a newly formed joint commission of six missionary societies. Throughout the 1920s and 1930s Lew served on the committee of the World Student Christian Federation, the Peking YMCA, and the YMCA's publication branch.[24] He became a member of the Legislative Yuan in 1936, extending his influence to the state. Not only did

23. "In 1930 twenty-six of the ninety-eight full time and part time Chinese faculty and thirteen of some forty full time and part time Western faculty had studied at Columbia University. Another common connection among the Chinese faculty, which Liu symbolized, was the YMCA. In 1930 twelve of the senior Chinese faculty had served as YMCA officers or secretaries, while many more than that had been long-time participants in YMCA activities." West, *Yenching University*, 118.

24. MRL 6: Timothy Tingfang Lew Papers, ser. 1, box 1, folder 1, Burke Library, Union Theological Seminary, NY.

Lew make profound contributions within China, he represented Chinese Christianity to the West.

In the 1920s and 30s, Lew served as an important voice for China and Chinese Christianity in the West. In 1927 he was invited by several Christian entities, including the Anglican bishop of Victoria and the British Student Movement, to preach throughout Great Britain. Lew spoke before the Royal Society of International Affairs and at Eton College. Throughout the years of Republican China, Lew served as China's delegate to the Ecumenical Conference in Lausanne, 1927; Oxford, 1937; Edinburgh, 1937; and Madras, 1939. In the United States between 1926 and 1928, he served as visiting professor at Boston University, Yale University, Columbia University, Union Theological Seminary, and Hartford Theological Seminary. He gave a series of lectures at nine colleges on the West Coast,[25] the Alden Tuthill Lectures at Chicago Theological Seminary in 1927, and the Enoch Pound lectures at Bangor Theological Seminary in 1928. Professors at the University of Oregon wrote Stuart on November 18, 1927, to thank him for Lew's lectures and to offer their impressions. Professor William Maddox wrote:

> Dr. Lew's lectures have given us a keener insight into Chinese intellectual and social life than many of us have previously possessed, they have illuminated for us the dim and obscure, they have offered us the impressions of a sensitive mind and the crystallisations of a searching judgment—all in a manner so simple, so direct, and so shot through with "humanness" that we have wondered at the strange powers of the man. He has done more in a week to help us to a true understanding of China than most lecturers could do in a year.[26]

Lew's intellectual and rhetorical prowess exerted a significant influence in both academy and church throughout the world. During Lew's two years outside China (1926–28), he did not suffer from want of invitations to speak.

Union Seminary and other institutions connected with the school eagerly promoted Lew. Daniel Fleming, head of Union's Department of Foreign Service, asked Lew to give a course for two hours per week in the fall semester of 1926 and the spring of 1927 on "Some Aspects of the

25. Washington State College, Reed College, University of Oregon, Oregon State College, Mills College, Stanford University, Occidental College, and Pomona College.

26. MRL 6: Timothy Tingfang Lew Papers, ser. 1, box 1, folder 3, Burke Library, Union Theological Seminary, NY.

Development of Christianity in China."[27] Harry Emerson Fosdick wrote to "My dear Lew" on June 1, 1927, asking him to take the pulpit in three evening services at his church, Park Avenue Baptist Church. Fosdick asked Lew to address "Christianity in China" and explained: "I feel sure that this will give you an opportunity to reach many influential people who ought to know what you have to say."[28] Undoubtedly, one of the "influential people" Fosdick was referring to was John D. Rockefeller, Jr. The familiarity of Fosdick's letter suggests that the pair had become well acquainted during Lew's years at Union (1916–20). Both Lew and Fosdick had served on Union's faculty in 1920. Union Seminary influenced Chinese Christianity through a dense social network of Chinese and Americans. The seminary strengthened ties among American and Chinese Christians. It is highly unlikely that Timothy Tingfang Lew would have come into contact with Harry Emerson Fosdick, John D Rockefeller, Jr., or Daniel Fleming without Union Seminary. The school provided significant *guanxi* (social networks) for a particular set of Chinese and American Christians. Many of these Christians had a profound role in twentieth-century China. Another leader in this Union-saturated network was William Hung.

## William Hung (1893–1980)

William Hung's life story resembles that of Timothy Tingfang Lew in several ways.[29] Both men did undergraduate studies in a Chinese Christian colleges and graduate studies at Union Seminary. After graduating from Union, both taught at Yenching University and exerted significant influence on Chinese Protestantism in Republican China. Unlike Lew, though, Hung grew up in a non-Christian family. His father was a magistrate in Fuzhou, where he was born on October 27, 1893. Hung received a traditional Chinese education, preparing him for the civil service examination. Like other pupils across the Middle Kingdom, Confucian rigor and memorization marked his education. His first day of school, around four years of age, began with kowtowing three times to a plaque inscribed with "The Place

27. Letter dated June 1, 1926. MRL 6: Timothy Tingfang Lew Papers, ser. 2, box 2, folder 5, Burke Library, Union Theological Seminary, NY.

28. MRL 6: Timothy Tingfang Lew Papers, ser. 2, box 2, folder 5, Burke Library, Union Theological Seminary, NY.

29. See Egan, *Latterday Confucian*.

of the Perfect Great Master Confucius."[30] The young Hung attended school seven days a week from seven in the morning to seven in the evening. Each year they had only two weeks off for Chinese New Year and occasional days off for Chinese holidays.[31] Students learned by memorization: each day the teacher would read and explain a Confucian text. Then, Hung and his five classmates would read the passage over and over until memorized. Instruction began with *Three Character Classic* (三字经 *Sanzijing*) and progressed to *Hundred Family Surnames* (百家姓 *Baijiaxing*) and *Thousand Character Text* (千字文 *Qianziwen*). The first words Hung memorized were *ren zhi chu xing ben shan* (人之初性本善, people at birth are naturally good). Hung's father wanted him to follow in his footsteps and become a magistrate. However, this future closed to him in 1905 when the Imperial Court abolished the 1,500-year-old examinations.

Though he hoped to attend the new Naval Academy in Shanghai, Hung eventually enrolled in the Anglo-Chinese College in Fuzhou. Run by the Board of Foreign Missions of the Methodist Church, the college taught all subjects, apart from Chinese literature, in English. Hung earned the nickname "Master Mencius" as he preferred Chinese and the Confucian classics to English and the Bible. But he quickly learned both. By his second year at the Anglo-Chinese College, Hung was awarded a set of the just-published *English-Chinese Dictionary* for having the highest grades in the whole college. As his knowledge of English and the Bible grew, he put it to use attacking Christianity. Hung argued that Confucianism and Christianity were incompatible. He wrote his dad asking him to come to Fuzhou to help defend Confucianism against Christianity. As his attacks grew more vocal, Hung attracted other students to his cause.

Faculty members responded by attempting to expel him. The principal's wife, Mrs. John Gowdy, came to his rescue. She argued for the impropriety of expelling an outstanding student simply because he opposed Christianity. A few months later Hung's father died suddenly. His opposition to Christianity softened as Mrs. Gowdy responded to his doubts and as he heard an impassioned evangelistic plea from Sherwood Eddy. Eddy argued that China had a rich history of prophets such as Confucius and Mencius and that the whole world had much to learn from China. Egan

30. Egan, *Latterday Confucian*, 8.

31. Hung and countless other Chinese students spent over 3,000 hours each year in school. In comparison, the average British primary student spends around 1,300 hours per year in school.

writes: "Eventually, Mrs. Goody's demonstration of Christian love and her liberal interpretation of Christian doctrine won Hung over."[32] Hung became a Christian and was baptized on New Year's Day 1913 by Bishop James W. Bashford. Two years later Hung graduated from Anglo-Chinese College and was offered a chance to study in the United States. He chose Ohio Wesleyan University.

In the fall of 1915 William Hung steamed across the Pacific Ocean on a Canadian ship, the *Empress of Manchuria.* He excelled academically and socially at Ohio Wesleyan. When he graduated magna cum laude in 1917, his eyes were set on Manhattan. The summer before Hung had met Timothy Tingfang Lew at a YMCA conference in New York, mentioned previously in this chapter. Lew traveled to Ohio to visit Lew and suggested that Hung join him in New York City where he could pursue his two academic passions: history at Columbia and theology at Union. Hung's years in New York City set the course of his life. Three German-trained professors had a particular influence on his theology and his approach to research. At Columbia, William Rockwell and James Harvey Robinson taught Hung how to do historical research.[33] Rockwell, despite his dry lectures, challenged Hung to distinguish facts from values then to apply a clinical objectivity to probe the values that groups held. Robinson subscribed to "New History," which emphasized people's actions and worldviews over economic trends and government policies. Through Robinson's supervision of his master's thesis, Hung came to realize the biased foundation of his seemingly profound understanding of Chinese philosophy. Robinson enjoyed mocking Christianity; his students nicknamed his course on Europe's intellectual history "The Downfall of Christianity." Despite Robinson's critique of Christianity, it was a Union professor, Arthur Cushman McGiffert, who challenged Hung's understanding of traditional Christian dogma. Chapter 9 details how McGiffert influenced Hung's theology. In 1920 Hung made six commitments that shaped the course of his life.

He committed to a life philosophy that he called: *sanyu, sanbu* (三与，三不). These "three positive, three negative" statements would set strict boundaries on what he would do and not do over the next three decades. On the positive side he decided to work towards specific achievements (与为 *yuwei*), to live a moral life (与守 *yu shou*), and to cultivate a childlike joy in life (与趣 *yuqu*). While these three positives are general

32. Egan, *Latterday Confucian*, 43.

33. See Hendricks, *James Harvey Robinson*, and Hendricks, "James Harvey Robinson."

and could apply to the ambitions of many people, it is the three negatives that distinctly marked Hung's life. He resolved to never become a political official, an ordained minister, or a principal or college president. Reflecting back on these resolutions, Hung told Egan:

> I resolved that I would never be an ordained minister. In other words, I wouldn't take religion as my profession. Then what could I do? I could be a teacher and a writer; but I would never be a principal or a college president, because in education there are politics too, and you have to hobnob with people who have money, catering to their desires, and mix with the politicians and financiers.[34]

Hung's resolutions as a twenty-six-year-old reflected a desire to live like a Confucian literati: concerned about the welfare of his people but leery of the apparatus of ruling, ready to teach but eager to remain free from external influences. For a brilliant man surrounded by wealthy Americans and ambitious Chinese, Hung's resolutions are striking. However, given Hung's concern about hobnobbing with wealthy people, it is ironic what he chose to do after graduating from Union in 1920.

Between 1920 and 1922 Hung went on the lecture circuit across the United States. He spoke at Rotary Clubs, church groups, Kiwanis Clubs, and anyone else who invited him. Praise followed Hung wherever he spoke. *The Congregationalist* in Boston reported:

> He speaks English not only with the utmost fluency, but with the richest vocabulary, and a rare sense of discrimination. A man of great practical sagacity, of keen analytical mind, he has also a deep sense of humor which is often the counterpart of unusual insight and sane judgment of men and events.[35]

These speaking engagements honed his skills as an articulate spokesman for China. He also worked part-time as the student secretary of the Methodist Church's Board of Foreign Missions. This job strengthened his ties with Chinese Christians scattered across the United States and established weak ties with influential Americans. In 1921 he met President Warren Harding. Hung's success on the lecture circuit, his academic prowess, and his

34. Egan, *Latterday Confucian*, 76. Hung used a clever but opaque analogy to explain his view of church/state relations: "I am very much interested in religion and in the church. The church is like the face, but religion is the smile. You have to have the face, and the face has to be washed clean for the smile to show. But if the face is dirty, the smile can't be appealing."

35. Egan, *Latterday Confucian*, 79.

leadership skills drew the attention of Yenching University. In 1922 Timothy Tingfang Lew wrote to advocate for his school. Lew told Hung about J. Leighton Stuart's upcoming trip to the US. The two men met. Hung took a quick liking to Stuart. Both men held similar views of Christianity and on Christianity's potential role in China's future. Stuart appointed Hung as assistant professor of church history at Yenching but asked him to remain in the States to help raise money for the university.

Hung joined Henry Luce, traveling throughout the United States to raise funds for the Beijing school. Hung and Luce made quite the team: Hung would speak on Chinese culture and history; Luce would follow with an appeal for financial support. Fifty-six years later, Hung reminisced on his fund-raising partnership with Luce: "I was the monkey and he was the organ-grinder."[36] Countless hours together on the road together blossomed into a close friendship. During their cross-country travels, Luce would read Hung the letters from his son, a Yale graduate who hoped to start a weekly news magazine.[37] Over eighteen months Luce and Hung raised two million dollars for Yenching University, over $27 million in today's dollars. Hung's experiences following his graduation from Union deepened his connections to wealthy Americans and ambitious Chinese. Despite his strict Confucian upbringing, Hung's eight years in the United States made him speak, act, and even think like an American. "Hung's years in America were so formative in shaping his view of life," explains Philip West, "that it became as easy for him to think in English as in Chinese."[38] In their interviews at the end of his life, Hung conceded to Egan that he became more comfortable with Americans than with Chinese.[39] As Hung changed, China was in the throes of immense social change.

In 1924 Hung became dean of Yenching's College of Arts and Sciences. Along with Lew, who led the School of Religion, Hung exerted profound

36. Egan, *Latterday Confucian*, 83. In the same series of interviews with, Hung described Luce in glowing terms. He compared him to the apostle Nathaniel, of whom Jesus said "Behold, an Israelite in whom there is no guile" (John 1:47). Hung on Luce: "He was so serious, so devout, so innocent, that he sometimes gave the impression of being an old little boy. . . . And people believed in him, because he was so obviously honest."

37. See ch. 5 for details on H. R. Luce's connections to Union and China. In the 1940s, Hung called on the now-famous younger Luce at the Time-Life Building. Luce gladly met with Hung, grateful for the moral support given him as he started his publishing enterprise.

38. West, *Yenching University*, 75.

39. Egan, *Latterday Confucian*, 85.

influence on the university. Stuart, Lew, and Hung became a triumvirate that ran Yenching in the 1920s. Despite the strength of their interpersonal tie, the friendship between Hung and Lew was tense. The strain began in New York when the two argued over that amalgamation of Cands and D&J secret societies. At Yenching they disagreed over whether or not the university should grant honorary degrees (Hung prevailed in opposing this plan) and whether Sun Yat-sen should have a Christian funeral (Lew won and the funeral happened). Hung's wife, Rhoda, disliked Lew: his short stature, poor health, and, in her opinion, his constant self-promotion.[40]

In a series of letters between 1926 and 1929, Lew and Hung wrote Stuart detailing the depth of their interpersonal conflict.[41] On May 10, 1928, Lew wrote Hung four dense pages, addressing the tension in their friendship and the spiritual crisis it caused.[42] Lew explained that his broken friendships at Yenching in 1925–26 almost caused him to abandon his faith. "It was a series of severe blows one after another inflicted upon my sensitive soul which almost crushed me spiritually," Lew wrote. He described his desire for Hung to succeed and be free from "even the shadow of my supposed interference." While admitting to his insistence on certain convictions, he faulted Hung with being unbending with his own ideas. Lew compared his broad planning with Hung's efficiency in carrying out details. He confessed his disappointment that they did not "supplement each other as Leighton always believe would be for the best of the University." He closed the letter by expressing his concern for Hung: "Dear William, you do not know how much I cared for you and the pain thus caused was in proportion to my genuine affection for you."

Timothy Tingfang Lew and William Hung both had impressive resumes and both made significant contributions to Yenching University, to the SFPE, and to Sino-American relations. Yet both men were human. Their interpersonal conflict humanizes them in ways that a direct accounting of

40. Egan, *Latterday Confucian*, 100. Around their home, Hung's wife called Lew "Chit" because she viewed him like a mouse: always looking for opportunities and boring into them.

41. December 6, 1926. MRL 6: Timothy Tingfang Lew Papers, ser. 1, box 1, folder 17. May 26, 1929. MRL 6: Timothy Tingfang Lew Papers, ser. 2, box 2, folder 5, Burke Library, Union Theological Seminary, NY.

42. Lew mentions Hung's "desire for a complete recovery of our old time fraternal relationships." This alleged desire for reconciliation, though, comes from letters from Stuart to Lew. It seems doubtful to me that this desire stems from Hung himself. Instead, it appears to be the hope of Stuart but not of Hung. MRL 6: Timothy Tingfang Lew Papers, ser. 2, box 2, folder 5, Burke Library, Union Theological Seminary, NY.

their achievements cannot. Their tension stemmed not from an adversarial relationship but from a close friendship where unresolved conflict festered. These capable, ambitious men did not like it when other people opposed their ideas.

Despite conflict with Lew, Hung left a considerable legacy at Yenching. He removed faculty members who were not academically qualified, especially those in Chinese history and literature. Not only was he unpopular among Chinese colleagues, students resented him, too, considering him to be a "fake Chinese." Hung certainly raised Yenching's academic standards. He introduced graduate courses in the College of Arts and Science, built up the university's Chinese collection, and founded the *Yenching Journal of Chinese Studies*. Egan contends: "It was under Hung's deanship that Yenching emerged from an obscure college run by Western millionaires to a nationally recognized Chinese university that participated fully in the intellectual life of China."[43]

Not only did Hung help raise Yenching's academics internally, he also boosted its reputation externally. The creation of the Harvard-Yenching Institute in 1928 provided the school with unique international stature. Hung served as director in 1934 and went to Harvard to lecture from 1928 to 1930 and 1947 to 1948. Hung's monumental work for the institute was developing and supervising the Harvard-Yenching Institute Sinological Index Series (HYISIS). In the HYISIS Hung and a small staff team systematically evaluated the most important books ever written in China. They would determine any textual variants of these classics and provide them with indices or concordances. The HYISIS transformed classical scholarship in China by establishing new criteria for formerly vague referencing in Chinese history and literature. Eventually the HYISIS included sixty-four titles. Hung put his historical training at Columbia to good use in the Index. In 1949 Hung was unable to support the Communist in Beijing or the Nationalist in Taipei so he moved permanently to Cambridge, Massachusetts, where he worked as a research associate at Harvard. He died on December 22, 1980. Timothy Tingfang Lew also spent the last years of his life in the US. Due to his worsening health and travel difficulties during World War II, he lived in Morningside Heights near Union from 1942 until 1947. He finally succumbed to tuberculosis, dying in a sanatorium in New Mexico on August 2, 1947.

43. Egan, *Latterday Confucian*, 110.

## Summary

On January 19, 1927, William Hung wrote Timothy Tingfang Lew and closed his letter: "Remember me to all the old friends at Union."[44] Union crops up over and over in the narrative of the SFPE. Throughout Republican China, the seminary drew outstanding Chinese leaders to its campus in Manhattan, across the street from Columbia University. The primary source of recruiting for Chinese Christians came from a network of Chinese and American alumni in China. This network's influence began in the church and academy and spread throughout Republican China. Union strengthened ties among Chinese and American Christians: absent ties became weak ones and weak ones became strong. This dense social network manifested itself in the Cross and Sword secret society. While in America ambitious Chinese Christians became an elite network. Back in China former Cands members exerted remarkable social power, which influenced Chinese Protestantism before and after 1949. Timothy Tingfang Lew and William Hung demonstrate this influence in Republican China and Y. T. Wu and K. H. Ting, in Communist China. Union helped equip Chinese leaders such as Lew and Hung to be bicultural communicators: equally comfortable in Chinese and English and competent in relating with influential people. In 1926 Lew kept a list of the "China Alumni of Union Theological Seminary." The list contained 101 names.[45] I now turn to one of the names on that list, Andrew Y. Y. Tsu, and to an organization that he helped lead, the Chinese Students' Christian Association.

44. MRL 6: Timothy Tingfang Lew Papers, ser. 3, box 1, folder 9, Burke Library, Union Theological Seminary, NY.

45. MRL 6: Timothy Tingfang Lew Papers, ser. 3, box 1, folder 13, Burke Library, Union Theological Seminary, NY. See Appendix F for a reproduction of the list.

# 8

# Union and the Chinese Students' Christian Association

Andrew Y. Y. Tsu and Siu-may Kuo

From its founding, Union Theological Seminary wanted to be an international institution in one of the world's most important cities. As New York's global importance grew, so did Union's. The school intended to change the world and it did. Both directly and indirectly the seminary exported its liberal theological views across the globe. In the case of China, however, Union's chief contribution came not from books or professors. Union intentionally attracted, and then funded, Chinese leaders in whom they saw leadership potential: people like Timothy Tingfang Lew and William Hung in the 1910s, Y. T. Wu in the 1930s, and K. H. Ting in the 1940s. Union Seminary became a social hub for leaders in the SFPE.

The school enabled interpersonal ties to be established and strengthened. These ties formed a network of elite Chinese Christians connected to influential American Christians. Union gave Chinese Christians access to a powerful social web. And, as I describe in the next chapter, the seminary also provided a distinct theology. The people in this web were patriotic and ambitious. They wanted to use Christianity to build China and were sure of the important role they themselves would play in China's transformation. Not only did they develop strong ties while in America, they also established and led organizations there. Timothy Tingfang Lew and William Hung formed the Cross and Sword secret society in New York City and then led Yenching University in Beijing. Now I turn to the formation of another organization, the Chinese Students' Christian Association (CSCA), and two of its leaders: Andrew Y. Y. Tsu and Siu-may Kuo. My narrative will take interludes to examine two intriguing and important families: the

Huies in New York and Gongs in Shanghai. I will conclude by describing the CSCA's infiltration by the Chinese Communist Party.

## Chinese Students' Christian Association

Unlike David and Jonathan and Cross and Shield, the Chinese Students' Christian Association was no secret. C. T. Wang (Yale), P. W. Kuo (Columbia), David Z. T. Yui (Harvard), and W. C. Chen (Michigan) organized the CSCA in New York City in 1909. The Association acted as the Student Christian Movement for Chinese students on American university campuses. It was affiliated with YMCAs in North America, China, and France. In 1917 the YMCA offered the CSCA office space in their New York headquarters and funding for a general secretary. According to a 1931 publication, the group had four aims:

> 1) To cultivate among the members and friends the Christ-like spirit and to apply His teachings in their daily lives and activities.
>
> 2) To build strong moral character and to foster the spirit of self-sacrifice and self-development by rendering service to members.
>
> 3) To unite those students in cooperative efforts for promoting programs and activities of the Association on various campuses.
>
> 4) To study and understand American life and society; and to interpret Chinese culture and civilization to America through writing, speaking, dramatics, and friendly contacts.[1]

In the 1940s membership reached two thousand people in twenty-five chapters.

During the 1940s the Tings' good friend Paul T. K. Lin (林达光 *Lin Ta Guang*, 1920–2004) served as the association's general secretary. Two aspects of the CSCA impressed Lin: its "moral leadership" and "mission of service to China."[2] Lin worked frantically as leader of the CSCA in the years following World War II. In both Boston and New York, he met with leading Chinese scholars and dignitaries, including Meng Chih (descendent of Mencius and longtime director of the China Institute), P. C. Chang (Chinese diplomat to Turkey, Chinese delegate to the United Nations, and professor at the University of Chicago), Hu Shih (leader of China's New

1. "Guide to the Archives of the C.S.C.A.," 4. Special Collections, YDSL, CSCA Archives, group 13.

2. P. Lin and Lin, *In the Eye*, 48.

Culture Movement, president of Peking University, and China's ambassador to the US from 1938 to 1942), Chang Chi-yun (China's leading geographer, founder of Chinese Culture University, and minster of education in the Republic of China from 1954 to 1958), and H. H. Kung (China's greatest financier and premier of China from 1938 to 1939). Why would China's most powerful men bother to meet with the head of the CSCA? The ranks of the CSCA, like Cross and Sword, included people of great social power. This was no marginalized, sectarian organization. CSCA members intended to play prominent roles in China's future development. They also had deep social connections with powerful Americans, as the interaction of Siu-may Kuo and Leighton Stuart later demonstrates. The CSCA represented an elite Chinese network. The association allowed students to strengthen ties with one another and to form weak ties with prominent Chinese and American leaders. In Granovetter's language, these weak ties had a strength all their own in that they allowed formerly disparate groups to connect. The CCP recognized the social power of the CSCA and infiltrated the group in the 1930s and 1940s. I will explain how in the closing pages of this chapter. I turn now to the life history, Union connection, and future influence of two CSCA leaders: Tsu and Kuo.

## Andrew Y. Y. Tsu (1885–1986)

Andrew Y. Y. Tsu was born into a Christian family outside of Shanghai on December 18, 1885.[3] The third of seven children, his parents gave him the Chinese-Christian name of *Yu-yue*, friend of fishermen, when he was baptized. His father, Tsu Yu-tang, moved the family to Shanghai in 1886. Ordained in the Episcopal church, the elder Tsu served as assistant chaplain at St. John's College, then as vicar of Church of Our Savior.[4] He died in 1901. Three years later his eldest son was in the first class at St. John's College to be awarded the BA degree. Tsu continued studying theology at St. John's, then followed his father into the pastorate in the Chinese Episcopal Church. After serving as a deacon in Jiangsu for two years, he won a scholarship to study at General Theological Seminary in New York.[5] While

3. Boorman and Howard, *Biographical Dictionary*, 3:321–25.

4. Church of our Savior Episcopal Church was built in 1853. See Richmond, *American Episcopal Church*.

5. Established in 1817, the seminary is the oldest seminary of the Episcopal Church in the United States. It is located in the Chelsea neighborhood of Manhattan, five miles

studying at General Seminary, Tsu also took classes in social sciences at Columbia University. In 1912 he received a BD from the former and a PhD from the latter. At the request of the bishop of Shanghai, Frederick Graves, the Episcopal Church ordained Tsu at the imposing Cathedral of St. John the Divine in 1911. Following graduation in New York, Tsu returned to Shanghai to teach at St. John's University.

Tsu joined St. John's mostly American faculty at a time when the school was flourishing. "St. John's was in its heyday of popularity," wrote Tsu, "and we basked in its well deserved prestige as one of the best colleges in the land."[6] Teaching in both the college and theological school, Tsu's students included future bishops (T. K. Shen and Kimber Den) and prominent members of the Chinese Communist Party (Pu Huaren).[7] In 1918 he joined a group of scholars in advising Sun Yat-sen on his book, *International Development of China*.[8] The group met weekly with Sun for several months to edit his manuscript. Tsu's circle of influence extended beyond church and classroom and into politics. Throughout Republican China, leaders in the SFPE had strong and weak ties to those in the halls of power. Sun's consultation of Andrew Y. Y. Tsu is one example of these ties; Truman's appointment of J. Leighton Stuart as the US Ambassador to China following World War II is another. In 1920 Tsu received a fellowship for graduate study at Union Seminary. Interestingly, in his autobiography Tsu describes nothing of his year of study at Union. Tsu remained in the United States for three years as executive secretary of the CSCA. Through the CSCA, Tsu immersed himself in a dense network of motivated, influential Chinese Christians. Another significant life event during this time was his marriage to Caroline Huie (1897–1970).

Caroline Huie was the fifth of ten children born into a prominent Chinese Christian family in New York City.[9] Her father, Huie Kin (许芹 *Xu Qin*, 1854–1934), founded and pastored the First Chinese Presbyterian Church in New York.[10] Huie immigrated from south China to San

south of Union.

6. A. Tsu, *Friend of Fishermen*, 27.

7. T. K. Shen served as bishop of Shanxi. His son, Shen Yifan, also became an Anglican minister and, in 1986, became the vice-president of the Chinese Christian Council. Kimber H. K. Den served as a pastor in Nanchang, then became a bishop. For more on Pu, see ch. 6.

8. The group included Tsu, David Yui, T. Z. Koo, John Y. Lee, and Chiang Mon-lin.

9. Most histories describe the Huie's nine children. But one of the ten children, Tom (1891–95), died in childhood.

10. C. Tsu, "Huie Kin." See also Bieler, *"Patriots" or "Traitors,"* 152–56.

Francisco in 1868. This fourteen-year-old emigrant began learning English and working on a farm in Oakland. Huie joined his German employers each Sunday at Broadway Presbyterian Church and eventually became a Christian. The minister there, Dr. James Eels, befriended Huie and suggested that he go east for collegiate training for Christian ministry.[11] After studies in Pennsylvania and Ohio, Huie was appointed by the Presbyterian Mission Board to begin Christian work among the Chinese community in Manhattan in 1885. In New York City he met and married Louise Van Arnam who was also serving as a Presbyterian missionary to Chinese emigrants in the city.

Huie located First Chinese Presbyterian Church in midtown Manhattan, accessible to the Chinese community in Chinatown and students at Columbia University and New York University. The church provided spiritual and social services for the Chinese community in New York: they offered a kindergarten for Chinese children, English classes, legal help, and assistance with hospital visits. The Chinese YMCA and Boy Scouts had their New York headquarters in the church. A dormitory on the third and fourth floors offered students a place to stay. The church became a key gathering place for Chinese students.

Future leaders in Republican China made Huie's church their Manhattan home. Huie reserved the room above the parsonage for Sun Yat-sen. In the winter of 1904 Sun secluded himself in that room with Wang Chung-hui. The Huie family later discovered that Sun and Wang were writing the Constitution of the Republic of China.[12] Another Yale student who spent time in the Huie parsonage was C. T. Wang. As discussed earlier, C. T. Wang helped found and then lead the Chinese Students' Christian Association. The Huies nursed Wang back to health when he came down with pneumonia at Yale. Rev. Huie attended the inaugural meeting of the CSCA in 1909. A robust network of Chinese Christians, future leaders in Republican China, gathered frequently in the Huie's church and home. Hayford suggests that the David and Jonathan secret society could have been founded in the Huie parsonage.[13] Interestingly, all six Huie sisters married Chinese

11. Eels's daughter later married Henry Sloan Coffin, president of Union Theological Seminary.

12. C. Tsu, "Huie Kin," 24.

13. Hayford, *To the People*, 21.

students in New York and moved to China to positions of great influence in Republican China.[14]

Chinese students arriving into Manhattan's piers or Grand Central Station would find a beaten path to the Huie's church and residence. More than any other family in New York City, they played a pivotal role in networking Chinese Christians.[15] Andrew Y. Y. Tsu met the Huie family during his first stay in New York. Reminiscing on these years, he wrote: "The best thing that happened in my American sojourn, 1909–1912, was the opportunity to get acquainted with the Rev. Huie Kin."[16] In his first visit Caroline Huie was only twelve years old. They renewed their acquaintance in 1919 when she came to Shanghai to work with the YMCA. When Tsu returned in the 1920s for the Union fellowship, she was in her twenties, no longer a child. The couple married in February 1924.

A few months later the newlyweds moved to Beijing. Tsu became chaplain of the recently established Peking Union Medical College. In 1925

14. Harriet Huie (1893–1991) married F. L. Chang (*Zhang Fuliang*, 1889–1984). Chang attended St. John's Middle School and took a Boxer Indemnity scholarship to study at Yale in 1909. He taught at Yale-in-China, directed the Rural Welfare Service, and served as general secretary of the Chinese Industrial Cooperatives. Alice Huie (1895–1980) married Y. C. James Yen (*Yan Yangchu*, 1893–1990). Yen attended Yale from 1916 to 1918, where he was a member of the David and Jonathan Society. He worked as head of the Department of Popular Education in the YMCA. Urban literacy work was Yen's passion. He launched education movements in China and the Philippines. For this work, he received honorary degrees from St. John's University, Syracuse University, the University of Maine, Temple University, and the University of Louisville. In New York in May 1943, he received a Copernican Award along with nine other world-changers, including Albert Einstein, Orville Wright, Walt Disney, Henry Ford, and John Dewey. Helen Huie (1899–1995) married Paul Chi-ting Kwei (1895–1961) who was a prominent physicist and dean of the School of Science at Huachung University in Wuhan. Ruth Huie (1901–90) married Henry Hsieh-Chang Chou (1892–1945) who was dean at Yenching University. Dorothy Huie (1902–99) married Amos Yi-hui Wong (1899-?). Wong taught obstetrics and gynecology at Peking Union Medical College and St. John's University. He was the attending physician for Sun Yat-sen.

15. In 1935 Mrs. Huie visited her daughters in Shanghai. Old friends often invited her out, leading the family to joke about her popularity "with the young Chinese men who were connected to the mission in New York City." Tsu to "Friends at the Cairn," February 25, 1935. RG 275, box 1, folder 6, archives of the Episcopal Church, Austin, TX. Reprinted by permission.

16. A. Tsu, *Friend of Fishermen*, 21. Charles Hayford suggests that Sun and Wang used this time to write the "The True Solution of the Chinese Question." In this pamphlet they argue that China would be a better neighbor if she were rich and intelligent and that it would benefit America to have a Chinese Revolution based on American democracy. Hayford, *To the People*, 21.

he joined Timothy Ting-fang Lew in officiating the Christian memorial service for Sun Yat-sen in the school's auditorium. Tsu, like Lew and Hung, played a prominent role in the SFPE in Republican China. The web of relationships proved to be deep and influential. These Chinese and American Christians favored theological modernism, as I will detail in the ensuing chapter and illustrate with one incident from Tsu's time in Beijing. In the summer of 1926 Rufus Jones, a philosopher from Haverford College in Pennsylvania, visited China at the invitation of the YMCA. Jones invited prominent American and Chinese Christians, including Tsu, to join him at Taishan.[17] The group discussed various interpretations of the person of Jesus on one of China's most sacred mountains, located next to Confucius's hometown. Just as Confucius had climbed Taishan to ruminate on life, the group gathered there to reinterpret Jesus from a Chinese perspective. The geographical significance of Jones's talks would not have been lost on the assembled group. Jones continued his Eastern journey by visiting Buddha's birthplace and meeting with Mahatma Gandhi. The Taishan gathering helps demonstrate the social influence and theological elasticity of this social network. This Christianity would prove malleable enough for many of these Christians, but certainly not Tsu, to join the CCP. Over the next decade Tsu assisted in famine relief work in Inner Mongolia and taught as a visiting lecturer in the United States. In 1933 he "finally succumbed to the dictates of conscience and persuasive words of friends" and joined the National Christian Council (NCC).[18] After two years with the NCC, the council asked Tsu to succeed C. Y. Cheng as general secretary. He declined and instead opted for the university classroom.

Tsu returned to St. John's University in 1935 to teach sociology.[19] In deciding between the NCC and St. John's, Tsu sought the confidential advice of his good American friends: the Bruglers. Writing on August 6, 1934, he

17. David Yui, L. T. Chen and Eugene Barnett (YMCA), Frank Rawlinson (*The Recorder*), R. O. Hall (Student Christian Movement and future bishop of Hong Kong), E. C. Lobenstine (National Christian Council), and William Hung.

18. Letter of October 16, 1933. RG 275, box 1, folder 6, archives of the Episcopal Church, Austin, TX. Reprinted by permission. Each year Tsu sent a circular letter to friends in the United States. These letters, held in the archives of the Episcopal Church, were written to Rev. Charles E. Brugler and Mary L. H. Brugler. Rev. Brugler served as Rector of St. Peter's Church, Portchester, NY, beginning in the 1890s. When Rev. Brugler died in 1936 he left a bequest of $75,000 to St. John's to establish and maintain the Brugler Chair of Religious Research.

19. St. John's Faculty and Administration, Shanghai Municipal Archives (*Shanghai shidangan guan)*, U104-0-77-79.

explained the difficulty of the decision: "Both calls afford fine opportunities; the difference is that the NCC type of work is more impersonal, while the SJU service is more personal, having to do with young men directly."[20] Tsu opted for the appointment at St. John's, excited to return to his alma mater.[21] He was swayed, perhaps, by Potts's insinuation that Tsu would succeed him as university president.[22] The teaching job fulfilled Tsu's desire for direct contact with young men. One of his students in his first year at St. John's happened to be a third-year student from Shanghai, K. H. Ting.[23] When St. John's opened to women, Caroline Tsu became the first dean of women. This allowed her to interact with a student from Shanghai who transferred to St. John's from Yenching University: Siu-may Kuo, Ting's future wife.

Shortly after Ting graduated from St. John's in June 1937, the Japanese bombed and captured the city. The St. John's community relocated to the International Settlement in Shanghai. As refugees poured into the foreign-protected settlement, an International Red Cross Society was established with Tsu as the executive secretary. In his annual Christmas letter Tsu explained the situation in Shanghai to friends in America:

> Tho [*sic*] destruction and desolation surround us, we believe the Star of Bethlehem still broods over the earth, pointing to the Way of Peace, if the nations would but follow its gleams. For three long months we in Shanghai lived day and night in the midst of racket of machine-guns, naval shellings and aerial bombings. Then on Nov. 10, the last battalion of Chinese defenders withdrew leaving a silence over the countryside like unto the silence

20. RG 275, box 1, folder 6, archives of the Episcopal Church, Austin, TX. Reprinted by permission. In another letter in the same folder, dated February 25, 1935, he wrote: "It is lots of fun to be working about young people. They are the same everywhere and in all ages, vivacious, social, ambitious."

21. In a January 3, 1935 letter Tsu wrote: " Fifteen years ago, in 1920 I withdrew from St. John's, and carrying my worldly possessions in a knapsack, so to speak, for I was a lone bachelor, wandered all over the world. Now I am retracing my steps and a warm welcome awaits the 'prodigal son,' but not me alone, for I am going back with a good wife and four fast growing children." A. Tsu, *Friend of Fishermen*, 45.

22. "This time, Dr. Pott has repeated the invitation and indirectly suggested that hope of my succeeding him on his retirement (very confidential), and it comes with the approval of this Bishop." Tsu letter to Bruglers, August 6, 1934 (emphasis his). RG 275, box 1, folder 6, archives of the Episcopal Church, Austin, TX. Reprinted by permission.

23. 1935/1936 grading report for Ting Kwang-Hyuin, St. John's University: School of Arts and Science, Shanghai Municipal Archives (*Shanghai shidangan guan*), Q243-41-1115-337. Ting received a B his first semester, an A in the second, and finished the year with an A average.

> of death. . . . Terrible as the material destruction has been, the suffering brought to millions of civilians in the war area beggars description. The International Area of Shanghai with its normal population of one and half million is now caring for 750,000 of whom 250,000 are destitute.[24]

Six months later Tsu journeyed to Wuhan to meet with Chiang Kai-shek.

Chiang asked Tsu and W. Y. Chen to serve as his advisors in establishing a youth training corps that would prepare young men for military service and reconstruction work.[25] As this role expanded beyond its original six-month contract, Tsu grew troubled by the lack of adequate medical services on the war-front. To address this problem, he began working with the Shanghai Medical Relief Committee. The war forced the Nationalist government to flee Wuhan to Changsha and eventually to Chongqing. In Changsha he was reunited with Caroline, who was serving as president of the YWCA in China. Despite China being in the midst of a war, the Chinese Episcopal Church (*Sheng Gong Hui)* decided to create a new missionary diocese in 1940. The church consecrated Tsu as assistant bishop of Hong Kong and appointed him as the bishop of Kunming, responsible for the newly created district. In the midst of pastoral duties at St. John's Church in Kunming, war relief efforts, and administrative duties as bishop, Tsu also represented China to the West.

In 1943 Chiang Kai-shek asked him to join a group of scholars representing China in the United States. For a year he toured Canada, the United States, and England, making speeches on behalf of the Nationalist government.[26] He also advocated for freedom for the Chinese church to elect

24. Letter of December 1, 1937. RG 275, box 1, folder 6, archives of the Episcopal Church, Austin, TX. Reprinted by permission.

25. Chen earned a PhD from Duke University in 1929, then taught at Fujian Christian University. In 1936, he was elected as general secretary of the National Christian Council. He became one of China's four Methodist bishops. *Time* once designated him as "China's No. 1 Protestant."

26. Chiang Kai Shek understood the importance of having good relations with influential American Christians. After John R. Mott, of the Student Volunteer Movement, won the Nobel Peace Prize, Chiang sent him a personal telegram on December 17, 1946. Chiang wrote: "Please accept my sincerest congratulations on your being awarded the Nobel Peace Prize which your splendid accomplishments for peace have deservedly earned for you. May greater success attend you [*sic*] untiring effort in fostering closer and better relations among men and nations so that this world will be made free and happier for all." John R. Mott Papers, Special Collections, YDSL, CSCA Archives, group 45, ser. 1, box 15, folder 276.

bishops for the *Sheng Gong Hui* regardless of their nationality. In London Tsu met the archbishop of Canterbury and preached in Westminster Abbey. He accepted an invitation from the United States Army in January 1945 to serve as chaplain to Allied troops traveling on the international highway in his diocese known as the Burma Road.[27] Andrew Y. Y. Tsu proved to be a valuable asset to the Nationalist as he represented their government to the West. He served both China and the United States in sacrificial ways throughout World War II.

Following the war Tsu became the general secretary of the *Sheng Gong Hui*, leading their negotiations for the return of church properties seized by the Japanese Army during the war. In 1948 he attended the Lambeth Conference of the Bishops in the Anglican Communion and the Amsterdam Assembly of the World Council of Churches. He spoke on the "The Significance of the Younger Churches in the Life of the Church Universal" in the former and on "The Chinese Church in Action" at the latter. When Tsu returned to Nanjing he found a city torn apart by fighting between the Nationalists and Communists. He announced his retirement in 1950 and left Shanghai to join his family in the United States. When Y. T. Wu wrote the "Christian Manifesto" and formed the TSPM, Tsu and thirteen other Chinese church leaders were denounced as "imperialist agents under the cloak of religion."[28] Other Chinese Christians affiliated with Union played central roles in the development of the Three-Self Patriotic Movement. But not Tsu. In fact, he became a vocal opponent of the TSPM. So, why include Tsu in this study?

At first glace, the inclusion of Andrew Y. Y. Tsu in these pages might seem inappropriate. Tsu went to Union on a fellowship in 1920 but never enrolled as a student. He held vital posts in the SFPE in Republican China but never in the TSPM. Yet Tsu plays an important role in this narrative. Union linked influential Chinese and American Protestants. This network extended beyond the church into the academy, business world, and even the state. On September 2, 1938, Madame Chiang Kai-shek (*Mayling Soong Chiang)* wrote Tsu to thank him for the two prayer books that he had sent her husband, the generalissimo. She makes it clear that the Nationalist government wanted, and needed, the support of Chinese Christian leaders:

27. Tsu became known as the "Bishop of the Burma Road." Tsu was the only Chinese chaplain in the United States Army in China. He was awarded a Citation for Meritorious Civilian Service. AP, "Andrew Tsu of China."

28. Boorman and Howard, *Biographical Dictionary*, 3:324.

> We need men like you to support the Government and to inspire confidence of the public both at home and abroad. . . . This confidence, to my mind, can only be gained when men like yourself, who are socially minded and who are known to be interested in the welfare of the people, participate actively in the Government's programme to reach the people and to ameliorate existing social conditions.[29]

Chinese Christians affiliated with Union had access to the highest echelons of power in the Republic of China. The same would be true in the People's Republic of China, demonstrated by Y. T. Wu's interaction with Zhou Enlai. Leaders in both governments coopted Christian leaders to serve their political ends. In a letter dated December 10, 1936, Tsu described Chiang to his American friends. As China celebrated the generalissimo's fiftieth birthday, Tsu wrote: "Barely ten years ago he was practically unknown at home and abroad. Rarely has there been such a happy combination of statesmanship, military genius, capacity for work and personal magnetism as made Chiang Kai-shek the great leader of the Chinese nation at this critical hour."[30] Between 1911 and 1949 Union Seminary had a magnetic appeal, pulling Chinese Christians into its influential network. Such was the case of both Andrew Y. Y. Tsu and Siu-may Kuo.[31]

## Siu-may Kuo (1916–95)

Siu-may Kuo (*Guo Xiumei*) was born in Wuhan on May 5, 1916.[32] After her mother died Kuo's father remarried and moved the family to Shanghai. She attended secondary school at St. Mary's Hall, St. John's sister school. In 1936 Kuo went to Beijing to study at Yenching University. Health problems

29. RG 275, box 1, folder 6, archives of the Episcopal Church, Austin, TX. Reprinted by permission.

30. RG 275, box 1, folder 6, archives of the Episcopal Church, Austin, TX. Reprinted by permission.

31. The question of how to refer to Chinese women after marriage in historical writing is tricky. In modern China, women do not change their surnames after marriage. However, in Republican China many Chinese women—especially those educated in the United States—intentionally took their husband's surname. Such was the case for Siu-may Kuo. I will refer to her as Kuo or Siu-may and to the couple as the Tings.

32. Wickeri, *Reconstructing Christianity in China*, 53. Though I will refer to Kuo as Siu-may Kuo, which she typically preferred, she sometimes referred to herself as Siu May Ting.

forced her to withdraw and return home to Shanghai. After recuperating, she enrolled in the newly coeducational St. John's University where Caroline Tsu had just been installed as the dean of women.[33] Kuo learned about Christianity through the student Christian work in Shanghai. She was baptized in 1940 and graduated from St. John's in 1942. Two of Kuo's classmates at St. Mary's and at Yenching—sisters Gong Pusheng (龚普生 *Kung Pu-sheng*, 1913–2007) and Gong Peng (龚普生 *Kung Peng*, also known as *Gong Weihang*, 1914–70)—played an important role in her engagement to K. H. Ting and in China's future. Gong Pusheng worked as Ting's counterpart in the student department of the YWCA and introduced him to Kuo. After a brief courtship, Ting and Kuo married on June 12, 1942, at the Church of Our Savior. Before describing the first decade of the Ting's marriage, I pause to consider the Gong family.

The family patriarch, Gong Zhengzhou (1882–1942), was a Christian and a revolutionary in late Qing China.[34] Sun Yat-sen appointed him commander of the Humen military fortification in 1917. At Yenching University the Gong sisters helped lead the student union. They participated in the anti-Japanese demonstrations in 1935, known as the December 9 Movement, and led a press conference on the Beijing campus to answer questions about the movement. The audience included Edgar Snow, who later interviewed Mao Zedong and wrote *Red Star over China*. Gong Peng joined the CCP in 1936, and Gong Pusheng, two years later. After graduating from Yenching, Gong Peng moved to south China to join the Red Army. In 1940 she became Zhou Enlai's private secretary and English interpreter. Like Zhou, Gong Peng "was good at making friends and winning people over to the communist cause through gentle persuasion."[35] The CCP appointed her as head of the Information Department in the Foreign Ministry in 1949. Her husband, Qiao Guanhua (1913–83), also held prominent roles in the Foreign Ministry.[36] Despite Gong Peng's extraordinary career, her older sister is more important for this study.

33. When St. John's became co-ed in 1936, it was limited to graduates of St. Mary's. Tsu letter, December 10, 1936. RG 275, box 1, folder 6, archives of the Episcopal Church, Austin, TX. Reprinted by permission.

34. Lee, "Gong Pusheng."

35. Lee, "Gong Pusheng," 178–79.

36. Qiao Guanhua's extraordinary life included studies at Tsinghua University in Beijing and Tokyo Imperial University and a PhD at the University of Tübingen. He worked directly for Zhou Enlai in the 1940s. He served as foreign minister and played an important role in the talks with Henry Kissinger. His daughter Qiao Songdu wrote a biography

Gong Pusheng represented China in 1939 at the World Congress of Christian Youth in Amsterdam and attended the World Union of Students assembly in Paris. At the end of 1939 she met with Zhou Enlai in Chongqing to describe her time in Europe. He told her:

> You should go to America where you can tell the whole world about the Chinese people's war against Japan's invasion and win international support and sympathy. You need to make friends there and learn more about America. You have the ability to work on the international united front.[37]

Without telling her sister of her CCP membership or Zhou's advice, she journeyed to New York to attend Columbia University. While there, she also enrolled at Union Seminary in 1941.[38] Before finishing her MA in religion, Gong befriended Eleanor Roosevelt, Pearl Buck, and other well-known Americans. Gong Pusheng illustrates well the elite network of Chinese students connected with Union who developed strong and weak ties with prominent people in both China and America. Gong graduated from Columbia in 1942. The university published Gong's thesis, entitled *Student Christian Movement in War Time China*. She returned to China in 1942 to attend her father's memorial service. Zhou Enlai ordered her to return to the United States to pursue a PhD. The war made immediate travel back to New York impossible. She returned to Manhattan in 1945 and, one year later, began work in the Human Rights Commission of the newly established United Nations.

A Communist victory over the Nationalist seemed imminent in 1948 so Gong returned to China. She soon married Zhang Hanfu. Zhou Enlai's wife, Deng Yingchao, emceed their wedding ceremony. After the establishment of the People's Republic of China, Zhang became the executive deputy minister of foreign affairs, and Gong, the deputy director of the International Organization and Conference Department of the Foreign Ministry. In 1958 she became director of that department. Throughout her career Gong Pusheng proved to be a skilled representative of China on the international stage.[39] Lee explains that both Gong sisters "distinguished themselves in the

of her parents: Qiao, *Qiao Guanhua and Gong Peng*.

37. *Jianghuai Morning News*, "Gong Pusheng."

38. Alumni Office of Union Theological Seminary, *Union Theological Seminary*, 210.

39. In 1950, Gong was the only Chinese female delegate at the UN Security Council. The delegation protested the US invasion of Korea. Seven years later, she led the Chinese delegation to the Nineteenth International Conference of the Red Cross in India. In

field of foreign affairs." Both they and their husbands were "unique in that all four were prominent in the same field," a field where their contribution and influence was "considerable."[40] Y. Y. Tsu and Caroline Tsu embodied Chinese Christians with direct access to the top echelon of leaders in Republican China, and the Gong sisters, in Communist China. And it was the very same sisters through whom Siu-may Kuo met K. H. Ting in Shanghai.

After their wedding the Tings labored to help build a war-torn Shanghai. Siu-may Kuo taught at St. Mary's and St. John's and then wrote for the *United Daily*, a publication of the Central News Agency. She served with the United Nations' Relief and Rehabilitation Agency after the war ended. Kuo spent her free-time helping her husband with his new work responsibilities. Beginning in 1942 Ting served as acting pastor of Community Church. The American pastor of the nondenominational, English-speaking Community Church, nicknamed the "American Church" and now known as the International Church, was in a Japanese internment camp. K. H. Ting preached, conducted weddings, and visited members in their homes or in the internment camps.

The Tings also started the nondenominational Student Church, which met at Community Church on Sunday afternoons, in August 1942. The Tings' vicarage, Scout House, became the meeting hub for the new Student Church. Chinese students engaged in fierce discussion and resistance activities in these gatherings. Even though Japanese soldiers kept the church under surveillance, students could meet and talk freely in the Community Church and Ting home. Many students learned about the Chinese Communist Party through the Student Church. "This was clearly part of its purpose," writes Wickeri. "The Student Church was an ecumenical fellowship that also became a cover for student activities organized by the CPC underground."[41] In their first years of marriage, the Tings led the most influential international church in war-torn Shanghai and, on the side, a Student Church that covertly recruited young people to the Communist cause. They proved to be a capable team: Kuo's extroversion and exuberance mirrored Ting's introversion and deliberation. The couple repeatedly demonstrated an extraordinary ability to juggle disparate realms: international and Chinese, Christian and Communist. After the Japanese surrendered the Tings accepted an appointment with the SCM in Canada in 1946.

1979, she was appointed as ambassador to Ireland.

40. Lee, "Gong Pusheng," 182.

41. Wickeri, *Reconstructing Christianity in China*, 56–57.

Since I described K. H. Ting's experiences in North America in chapter 6, I now turn to Kuo's life during those same years, 1946–51. For twelve months the Tings traveled across Canada, describing China, its needs, and their experience as Chinese Christians. They advocated a distinct political and theological perspective. Two incidents from their time in Toronto, one humorous and one tragic, illustrate well the extent to which Kuo shared her husband's Communist and Christian commitments. On one occasion, she spoke to a church group and referred to the Communist-controlled areas of China as the "Liberated Areas." After a local Canadian newspaper described Kuo's pro-Communist statements, the Chinese Embassy phoned Ting to register its disapproval. They told Ting to keep better control of his wife, "especially her tongue."[42]

After arriving in Canada Kuo gave birth to a baby boy. He died three days later. In a circular letter to friends on January 12, 1947, she explained what happened. Kuo described the "joy and expectations the little heartbeats and kickings" of the pregnancy and the three "eternally long and yet short" days filled with "all the depth of hope, worry, and anxiety as only a mother can." Then, she writes, "everything ceased—so abruptly." First, she blamed herself: "My first thought was that of self-blame. I felt as if I had murdered him because if I had been more careful, he would have lived." Her thoughts then turned to her homeland and its struggles. This section testifies to her mindset even in midst of her pain.

> Yet, as I look into it more closely; strangely, the little face is not condemning. It just reminds me of the deserted babies which I have too often seen on the street corners in Shanghai and countryside in China. Then I remember millions of mothers in China who have to suffer, and millions of babies who have to die because of ignorance, superstition, financial inabilities, and of lack of midwifery care—of reasons far different from mine; for I had the best of medical care and all that scientific advance at this stage of human progress could offer. So I think that sight of the little face gasping for life is just a signal from God calling me to work more earnestly and more vigorously for a better China, a better society where there will be no unreasonable reasons for mothers to suffer and babies to die—as far as man can conquer nature. Personally there will be an emptiness in my heart and this in my life left by that thing buried, unmarked in Mount Pleasant cemetery, and that

42. Kuo interview with Wickeri, Nanjing, China, June 9, 1991. In Wickeri, *Reconstructing Christianity in China*, 67.

> once has been life—an emptiness which nothing can fill up again. But as God wills it. It is only through pain you can really know pain; it is only through suffering you can really understand suffering; and it is only through tears you can really see tears. Through this, God has made me to feel for certain things and certain people with an intensity I did not have before.[43]

Both Ting and Kuo cared deeply about China. Even in the worst of times personally, China's national salvation never drifted far from their minds. The vision of using Christianity to build a better China drove their lives. At the end of their time in Toronto, the Canadian SCM chairman commended the Tings' presence as the most significant accomplishment by the missionary committee for that year. The "talented and consecrate" couple gave the SCM a "new vision of the meaning of the World Church."[44] Following their time in Toronto, they decided move south.

Like her husband, Kuo wanted to move to New York City for various reasons. First, she had a brother there. Two SCM leaders and friends of Kuo exchanged letters that addressed her feelings about the move. Harriet Christie wrote Hilda Bensen on March 11, 1947: "She is feeling somewhat strange about [New York], not having been there before, although she does have a brother there."[45] Second, Kuo wanted to study in New York. In a letter to Hilda Bensen on February 27, 1947, Ting expressed his wife's "hopes to come to New York to study" at either Teachers College or the New York School for Social Work.[46] He also sought advice on how they could obtain scholarships for study in New York. Kuo received a scholarship at Teachers College and enrolled as a full-time student in September 1948. When not in class Ting and Kuo immersed themselves in New York's Chinese student community. Their good friend Paul T. K. Lin served as general secretary of the CSCA. So, naturally, they joined the association. Their student apartment at Union became a boardinghouse for their Chinese friends. When

43. Kuo, circular letter, January 12, 1947. Special Collections, YDSL, SVM group 42, ser. 6, box 491, folder 5877A. All preceding quotations in this paragraph come from this letter.

44. Thompson, "Report of the National Missionary Committee, 1946–47," 14. In Wickeri, *Reconstructing Christianity in China*, 71.

45. Special Collections, YDSL, SVM group 42, ser. 3, box 372, folder 4427. I have been unable to ascertain the name or circumstances of Kuo's brother in New York City. It is possible that she referred to a cousin or close family friend as a brother when she spoke with Harriet Christie.

46. Special Collections, YDSL, SVM group 42, ser. 6, box 491, folder 4877A.

Lin returned to studies at Harvard in 1949, the association began searching for a new leader. Lin writes: "I was delighted when the search committee chose Siu May Kuo (Mrs. K. H. Ting), who brought to the job both a deep intellect and recent experience working with students and the YMCA in China."[47] Both Andrew Y. Y. Tsu (1921–24) and Siu May Ting (1949–51) led the CSCA. The CSCA illustrates the density and influence of the elite network of Chinese Christians in the US. One organization understood the importance of this network of Chinese Christians: the Chinese Communist Party.

In the late 1930s and 1940s the CCP engaged in systematic and extensive infiltration of the CSCA.[48] The CCP in Jiangsu secretly established groups in 1938 to subvert the Christian student groups. These committees were called the Youth League in the Federation of Christian Students' Groups in Shanghai and the CCP Committee of the Christian-School Students' Movements. Yu Pei-wen, director of the former and the first secretary of the latter, served on the National Committee of the CSCA in 1947. Yu became friends with Ting when they were both serving in the student department of the YMCA in the late 1930s.[49] In the early 1940s the Shanghai and South Bureaus of the CCP began sending party members to study in the United States in order to encourage Chinese students to return home to rebuild a new China.[50] Some of these students became members of the CCP Leading Group in America and others became key leaders of the CSCA. It is no surprise then that by 1948–49 four of the nine members of the National Committee were members of the CCP.[51] The Communist intentions of CSCA leaders manifested as early as 1945. In December of that year, two brothers studying at Harvard, Pu Shouchang and Pu Shoushan, began publishing *Chinese Students Opinion*. This quarterly journal, produced by and for members of the CSCA's Boston branch, began as nonpartisan. But under the leadership of the Pu brothers, the publication began propagating

47. P. Lin and Lin, *In the Eye*, 56.

48. Zhao, "Chinese Communist Party." The information in this section is based on Zhao's paper.

49. For photo of Ting, Kuo, and Yu in Shanghai in 1945, see Wickeri, *Reconstructing Christianity in China*, 43.

50. The instruction for the South Bureau came at the behest of Dong Biwu and included Ji Suhua, Xu Ming, Lai Yali, Xue Baoding, Lan Yuzhong, Yang Gang, Gong Pusheng, Hong Xianglin, and Tu Guanzhi. The Shanghai Bureau sent Chen Yiming, Chen Xiuaxia, and others.

51. Yu Peiwen, Chen Lisheng (later, Chen Hui), Chen Xiuxia, and Xu Ming.

Communist ideology. The brothers joined the American Communist Party in 1944 and 1945. They transferred into the CCP and led other Chinese students to do the same. Eventually both brothers would serve in prominent roles in the CCP.[52] This pattern repeated itself: many CSCA leaders would rise to positions of prominence in the CCP.

Xu Ming joined the CCP in 1938. After leading a party committee in Chengdu, the CCP's South Bureau assigned him to study in the United States in 1944. He enrolled at Clark University in Boston and became active in the CSCA. Soon he took charge of mobilizing Chinese students in the CCP Leading Group in America. In 1949 he returned to China, reporting his activities to Zhou Enlai. At Zhou's behest he returned to the US later that year to continue advocating for Chinese students to return to their homeland. Later, Xu worked in the Information Department of the Ministry of Foreign Affairs and as director general of the Foreign Affairs Bureau of the State Committee of Planning. Xu, the Pu brothers, and other leaders in the CSCA who were CCP members were well rewarded in their future careers in the People's Republic of China. As CSCA leaders began endorsing the Chinese Communist Party, tension arose with the YMCA. The Y worried that the Chinese Students' Christian Association had become "too political."[53] The 1949 elections for the CSCA National Committee would confirm the Y's concerns. Now eight of the nine members of the National Committee were members of the CCP. The chairman and vice-chairman of the CSCA both joined the CCP in New York in 1949. Another member of the National Committee was Siu-may Kuo. She succeeded Paul Lin to becoming the CSCA's first woman general secretary.

In the summer of 1948 Siu-may Kuo graduated from Teachers College and K. H. Ting, from Union Seminary. Ting accepted a job with the World Student Christian Federation in Geneva and sailed for Europe two weeks after graduation. Kuo remained in New York to continue her role in the CSCA and prepare for the birth of their son, Stephen Yenren Ting. Part of Kuo's role with the CSCA involved public relations and fund raising. On August 12, 1949, she wrote to the American Ambassador to China,

52. Pu Shouchang was the English interpreter of Zhou Enlai, the vice minister of the Ministry of Foreign Affairs, and a translator of the English edition of *The Selected Works of Mao Zedong*. Pu Shoushan, who changed his name to Pu Shan, was deputy director of the Institute of International Problems of the Ministry of Foreign Affairs and director of the World Social and Economic Institute of the Chinese Academy of Social Sciences.

53. Wickeri, *Reconstructing Christianity in China*, 73.

J. Leighton Stuart, asking if she could interview him.[54] Kuo reminded Stuart that she had been a student at Yenching University, where he served as president. In addition she had given the opening speech when Stuart visited student Christian workers in Shanghai in 1939. Stuart responded three days later: "Of course I remember you quite distinctly and have a great admiration for your husband."[55] A few weeks later Ting and Kuo met with Stuart. They told him about the CSCA and elicited his support. Following their meeting, Stuart donated fifty dollars to the CSCA and wrote a statement of endorsement:

> The Chinese Students' Christian Association in North America has always been a useful agency for conserving Christian faith among those students who have come here from China as Christians as well as for extending religious influence among others. But in view of the especial perplexities all Chinese students in this country are now facing, I am impressed by the unique value of this organization in promoting the cause for which it exists.[56]

President Truman appointed Stuart as the American Ambassador to China in 1946 because of decades of experience in leading Yenching. Stuart knew China well. But it is highly unlikely that Stuart knew about the Communist infiltration of the association. It has taken the academic community over sixty years to recognize and write about the links between the CCP and the CSCA. Zhao concludes: "Under the leadership of numerous underground party members whose public identity were foreign students, the CSCA gradually turned into a Christian students' organization which sympathized with the CCP" which "indirectly provided a religious camouflage" for the promotion of the CCP.[57] The CSCA challenged many Chinese students in the US to return home to help build a new China.

On June 24, 1949, Kuo wrote William Fenn, the associate executive director of the United Board for Christian Colleges in China, to address the question of students returning to help rebuild China. Five days later Fenn responded. He agreed that Chinese students in the US should "return to China as soon as possible" because they are "badly needed" throughout the

54. Special Collections, YDSL, CSCA Archives, group 13, box 2, folder 28.

55. Letter dated August 15, 1949. Special Collections, YDSL, CSCA Archives, group 13, box 2, folder 28.

56. Letter dated September 3, 1949. Special Collections, YDSL, CSCA Archives, group 13, box 2, folder 28.

57. Zhao, "Chinese Communist Party," 3.

country. He believed it was possible that the influence of these students in a "relatively fluid situation may prove many times greater than any influence they can exert once the pattern has taken final form."[58] In August 1949 the leaders of the CSCA led nearly two hundred Chinese students home on the *President Wilson* steamship. Fenn's words would prove to be prophetic in regards to how influential some of these students would become in the People's Republic of China. Significant to this study is the dense social network represented in and by this group of Chinese Christians in America. Ting and Kuo planned on returning to China in the summer of 1950. However, the Korean War disrupted travel. The Tings worried about their prospects of returning to China as the war grew and Sino-American relations worsened. Their determination to return remained but they knew they must wait. Ting accepted a one-year extension of his job with the WSCF. Kuo and their son joined him in Geneva for one year. Despite dire warnings from friends, the Tings returned to China in the summer of 1951.

On August 29, 1951, the Tings trained from Hong Kong to Shanghai. A few months later Ting journeyed to Beijing to visit his old friends, Gong Peng and Gong Pusheng. Gong Peng told Zhou Enlai about Ting's visit. The premier suggested he remain in Beijing a few days and set up a personal meeting. Ting met Zhou for a meal at his home in Zhongnanhai, the ancient imperial compound next to the Forbidden City. "From this time forward, Zhou Enlai became a powerful friend and promoter of K. H. Ting," writes Wickeri. "They had a personal relationship that was of critical importance for Ting's public life, a relationship based on common commitment and mutual affection, not on political expediency."[59] Though an important comment, Wickeri's assessment fails in his final words. Zhou and Ting's relationship was based very much on political expediency: what Zhou could do for Ting in Communist circles and what Ting could do for Zhou in Christian ones. Reflecting back on the conversation, Ting recalled Zhou's emphasis that the CCP was not opposed to religion and that religion could be used to make people progressive.[60] As detailed in chapter 6, Ting went

58. Special Collections, YDSL, CSCA Archives, group 13, box 2, folder 28.

59. Wickeri, *Reconstructing Christianity in China*, 101.

60. Wickeri, *Reconstructing Christianity in China*, 101. Six years later Zhou Enlai wrote: "Religion will continue to exist for a long time, and its future development will depend upon future conditions. But as long as there are questions which people are not able to explain and resolve on an ideological level, the phenomenon of religion will be unavoidable." Zhou Enlai, "Several Questions on China's Nationalities Policy," translated and quoted in Wickeri, *Reconstructing Christianity in China*, 93.

on to become one of the most important leaders of the TSPM in the ensuing decades. In 1952 K. H. Ting moved to Nanjing to become principal of the newly established Nanjing Union Theological Seminary. Kuo and their two boys joined in 1954. The Tings remained in Nanjing for the remainder of their lives. For decades Kuo taught English at Nanjing University.[61] She died in her family home in Nanjing on September 24, 1995.

## Summary

In this chapter I described the lives of Andrew Y. Y. Tsu and Siu-may Kuo and their involvement in the Chinese Students' Christian Association. These two case studies might seem peripheral to our contention that Union Seminary exerted a profound influence on Christianity in twentieth-century China. After all, neither Tsu nor Kuo graduated from Union. Tsu received a Union fellowship in 1920. Kuo lived on Union's campus in 1947 while her husband studied there and she took classes across Broadway, at Teachers College. Both are present in this narrative and critical to its argument because the CSCA is a prime example of a dense network of Chinese Christians in Morningside Heights, the neighborhood surrounding Union, Columbia, and Teachers. The narrative even veered to describe two remarkable families: the Huies in New York City and the Gongs in Shanghai. These two families illustrated the depth and interconnectedness of these social networks in the US and in both Nationalist and Communist China.

Union's dense social network and distinct theological vision most directly impacted China through the thirteen Christian colleges and the YMCA. The school served as a social catalyst for prominent American and Chinese Christians. General Seminary, Y. Y. Tsu's alma mater, was also located in Manhattan. It had the advantage of being older and affiliated with the Episcopal Church. So why did this school not influence the SFPE in the same way that Union did? From its founding Union's eyes were on the entire world. The seminary helped China's Christian leaders meet each other and network in powerful circles of American Christians. Union provided more *guanxi*, social capital and connections, to Chinese Christians than any other seminary in the West. In the years of Republican China the school it gave these students relational ties to prominent American Christians. The

61. Before her death, she wrote two books on the Bible as literature: *Venturing into the Bible* and *Journeying through the Bible*. The books are based on her English classes at Nanjing University.

school also exported a distinct, modernist theological vision to China. I now turn to explore Union's particular theological vision and its impact on Chinese Protestantism.

# Part III

# Union Seminary Exports a Progressive Theology

# 9

# To China's Three-Self Patriotic Movement

THIS BOOK HAS EXPLORED the impact of Union Theological Seminary on the SFPE in Republican China (1911–49) and the TSPM in Communist China (1949–present). Union influenced Christianity in twentieth-century China through a dense social network. The New York seminary helped influential Christians established and strengthened their relational ties. Over time these strong and weak ties formed a web of relationships that influenced Sino-American relations and Chinese Protestantism. Apart from Xu Yihua, scholars have overlooked Union's impact on Chinese Protestantism. By combining Hunter's concept of a dense social network and Granovetter's theory of the strength of weak ties, the influence comes into clearer focus.

Though I have demonstrated *that* Union influenced the SFPE and TSPM, I have not yet fully explained *how.* The door now opens for several avenues of scholarship. I could explore Union's geopolitical role in Sino-American relations in Republican China or the precise ways that Union influenced specific leaders in the SFPE and the TSPM. Rather than concentrating on one of these lines of inquiry, in this chapter I will explore the theological impact of Union Seminary on Chinese Protestantism. I intend to answer this question: Did Union help provide a theological framework that enabled Chinese Christians to more readily work with the Chinese Communist Party in forming the TSPM? More precisely, did Union's theological liberalism enable its Chinese graduates to more readily accommodate to Communism? The answer, I propose, is: *It varies.*

The extent of Union's theological influence varies depending on several factors: the age and life experiences of these Chinese students, their purposes in coming to the seminary, their personalities, and their role back in China. There are three types of Chinese graduates from Union: 1) those who acknowledged and embraced the seminary's impact on their theology, 2) those who recognized and rejected it, and 3) those who did not acknowledge any influence Union might have had. This chapter will thus be divided into three categories, each with a representative example. Some Chinese leaders have described how Union influenced them theologically or philosophically. Such is the case with William Hung and John Sung. The case of William Hung will require the least amount of space because in his case the answer is quite clear but more space will be given John Sung as I recast the historiography surrounding his time at Union. The last group denied, minimized, or never discussed how Union impacted their theology. Such is the case with Y. T. Wu and K. H. Ting. Both men sought to distance themselves from the influence of any "imperialistic" Western missionary or institution, including Union. I turn to an assessment of Ting's writing to determine if and how Union influenced his theological perspective. Tracing theological impact is a difficult task. So I will give more attention to Ting's theology than that of Hung or Sung. The breadth of this chapter might frustrate some readers hoping for a deeper analysis; however, I hope to at least open the door for future research.

## Chinese Graduates Who Embraced Union's Theology: William Hung

William Hung left no doubt how Union impacted his theological views. Six decades after studying at Union, Hung reminisced on exactly how the seminary transformed his theological perspective.[1] To begin, Arthur Cushman McGiffert, the Washburn Professor of Church History and Union's president from 1917 to 1926, taught Hung to scrutinize Christian belief. McGiffert's 1897 book, *A History of Christianity in the Apostolic Age*, created considerable controversy in the Presbyterian Church. The General Assembly brought heresy charges against McGiffert after he refused to change his views. Eventually he withdrew from the Presbyterian Church and joined the Congregational Church. McGiffert argued that historical change relativizes all religious teaching. There was, in his mind, no essence of history. Hung learned from McGiffert the futility of searching for consistency in an individual's philosophy. Instead, one should identify their subject's main idea, their strongest point, and from this extrapolate their weakest point, the place where they overreached.

1. Egan, *Latterday Confucian*, ch. 8. From 1978 to 1980 Hung spent two hours most Sunday afternoons telling his life story to Egan at his home in Boston.

As with individuals, McGiffert contended, so with the history of Christian thought. Hung once viewed the Christian creeds as statements of faith agreed on by Christian thinkers. But McGiffert taught that Christian dogma was negative, written to exclude people who did not subscribe to those ideas. His days of study under Adolf von Harnack had honed his skills in dissecting theology. In the preface to his controversial book, McGiffert praised his "honored teacher" in Berlin, noting "I find myself, I am happy to say, in general agreement with Harnack in most of the matters upon which he touches."[2] McGiffert traced each point of the Christian creeds to specific attempts by the church to suppress particular heresies. What should Hung do with his traditional understanding of Christianity? In the words of Egan, Hung salvaged his Christianity "by detaching it from churches" and the "thought of becoming a minister became daily more distasteful to him."[3] With transformed views of Christian dogma, Hung was drawn to the theology of a new Union professor, Harry F. Ward.

Ward joined Union's faculty in 1918. He articulated a vision for the kingdom of God that appealed to Hung: the social gospel. Though born outside London, Ward had been a Methodist pastor in Chicago. He read Marx during a sabbatical in 1905. Marx's ideas resonated deeply with Ward's experience of living among the poor in Chicago's stockyard area. Ward's biographer, David Nelson Duke, argues that Marxism provided "labels for an interpretation of what he knew firsthand . . . a theoretical framework for his indefatigable social passion."[4] Later, when asked if he was a Communist, Ward would respond:

> As for myself, I belong to no party or economic faction. I am neither Socialist nor Communist. In answer to that question, I usually say, "I am something worse than that, I am a Christian." That is, to say, I expect to follow the teachings of Jesus wherever they may lead.[5]

In 1920 the New York State Joint Legislative Committee to Investigate Seditious Activities, known as the Lusk Committee, delivered its verdict on Ward and Union. They named Union Theological Seminary where Ward taught Christian ethics as one of the nations two most dangerous centers of socialist thought. Ward taught, in the view of the committee, a

2. McGiffert, *History of Christianity*, viii.
3. Egan, *Latterday Confucian*, 70.
4. Duke, *In the Trenches*, 55.
5. Duke, *In the Trenches*, 117.

kind of Bolshevism far worse than the communism in Russia. Like Union professors before and after him, Ward visited China in 1925. A year later his talks were translated and published in Shanghai under the title *Geming de Jidujiao* (A revolutionary Christianity). In his foreword to the book, Jian Youwen argued that it was "appropriate and timely" to publish a book on Christianity's revolutionary nature in an era of revolution. He elaborated:

> If all members of Chinese Christianity continue to proceed in this direction, then critics of Christianity could no longer charge Christianity as "anti-revolutionary." Positively speaking, Christianity might even play a role in the great movement of social reform in the nation's renaissance. By that time, people may talk about religion as the stimulant of the people rather than religion as the opium of the people. And the life of Christianity will last forever in tandem with the Republic of China.[6]

Like William Hung, Timothy Tingfang Lew expressed his appreciation for Ward's ideas. Lew acknowledged his debt to Ward and the potential for his ideas to address China's pressing needs.[7] For some Chinese Christians, Union's professors forced a welcome re-examination of orthodox Christian theology. They learned to doubt traditional dogma and to reinterpret Christianity. While Hung and Lew acknowledged their appreciation for Union's theological influence, other Chinese students at Union had the opposite response. Most notable in Chinese Christian circles is John Sung.

## Chinese Graduates Who Rejected Union's Theology: John Sung

Upon mention of Union Theological Seminary, many Chinese Christians today think of Sung, the greatest evangelist of twentieth-century China. The sixth child of a Methodist pastor, John Sung was born in Fujian Province in 1901. He attended mission schools in China before moving to Ohio in 1920 to study chemistry. After finishing a bachelor's degree at Ohio Wesleyan University in three years, he earned a master's degree from Ohio State University in 1924 and a PhD in 1926. Sung excelled at each stage of his studies in Ohio. After graduation several teaching opportunities opened to him. But rather than returning to China to teach chemistry he decided to study theology at Union. Sung recalled his "personal agenda"

6. Jian, "Foreword," 7.

7. Wu, "Idea and Practice." See also Lew's introduction of Ward's theology in Tingfang, "Jidujiao de shehui fuyin."

that made him interested in Union: he could gain theological knowledge there while he lived in the "great city" of New York.[8] In addition Union's proximity to Columbia University would also allow him to pursue further scientific research. Daryl Ireland correctly observes how Sung "pressured former professors and friends" to help him gain admittance and funding to Union with "characteristic determination."[9] The seminary admitted him, like they had other brilliant Chinese Christians of era, and offered an Oriental Scholarship, granting full tuition and an annual living allowance of $200. Recalling Union's scholarship, Sung wrote: "Now, that bargain would be too good to pass up!"[10] Sung was drawn to Union for the same reason as other Chinese Christians in Republican China: the seminary itself and the scholarships therein, Union's connections to Columbia and Teachers College, and a chance to live in the world's greatest city. In his application dated May 25, 1926, Sung wrote that it was his intention to study two or three years to prepare for "any form of religious work."[11] He wrote his parents, explaining to them that he turned down job offers at Peking University and Ohio University in response to God's call on his life. Sung's time at Union ended up being far shorter than he planned. What happened then forever impacted Chinese Christianity and the future perception of Union.

In his first term at Union, Sung jumped into classes in the Bible, theology, and philosophy. He asked for permission to complete the three-year course in one year, knowing it would involve an extra seven to eight hours of study each day. Sung soon realized that he had landed, in his words, in a seminary "devoid of any spiritual life" that discarded truth "by the wayside."[12] Union approached hermeneutics from the perspective of philosophy and evangelism, from psychology. The school dismissed the Bible when it seemed incompatible with science. Leslie Lyall describes how Union shook Sung's Christian faith to its core:

> Every problem was discussed in light of human reason. Anything in the Bible which could not be justified scientifically was rejected as being unworthy of belief. Genesis was held to be unhistorical and belief in miracles unscientific. The historical Jesus was presented as

8. Song, *Journal Once Lost*, 37.

9. Ireland, "John Sung," 22.

10. Song, *Journal Once Lost*, 37.

11. Sung, application letter. UTS 2, ser. 10A, box 4, folder 9, Burke Library, Union Theological Seminary, NY.

12. Song, *Journal Once Lost*, 39.

> an ideal to imitate, while the substitutionary value of His death and His physical Resurrection were denied. . . . To dissent from such views and opinions was to become an object of pity or derision.[13]

Sung's traditional Christian faith was being replaced with the "giant melting pot" of the social gospel.[14] He began exploring Eastern philosophy, translating the Dao De Jing into English. Sung attacked sincere believers as overly emotional or superstitious. Soon a deep and debilitating crisis set into Sung's soul and body. He wrote: "My soul wandered in a wilderness. I could neither sleep nor eat. My faith was like a leaking, storm-driven ship without captain or compass. My heart was filled with the deepest unhappiness."[15] Soon he decided that neither science nor religion could bring him any peace. In the midst of this spiritual crisis and mental breakdown, he considered starting a new religion. Then, in October 1926, he attended an evangelistic service at Calvary Baptist Church on West Fifty-Sixth Street.

To his surprise a teenage girl went on stage. Dressed in all white, the fourteen-year-old from California opened a gilded Bible and preached on the cross of Jesus Christ. In dramatic fashion Uldine Utley explained her "baptism of the Holy Spirit" at a revival meeting in 1921.[16] Sung concluded that he was not baptized by the Holy Spirit and resolved to pursue a new life in Christ. He spent the next months reading Christian biographies and praying for spiritual power. Weeks spent in tears and desperate prayer culminated on February 10, 1927. That night he read Luke 23 and imagined himself joining Jesus at Golgotha, weighed down by his sins. He cried out for the forgiveness of his sins. The overwhelming experience left him spiritually and physically depleted; he felt as if he had suffered a major injury and believed that God allowed him to feel the pain of the crucifixion. He changed his name to John, after John the Baptist.

He began telling everyone what God did for him that night. Sung pointed out the sins of pastors and professors, calling them to repentance. He burned his theology books because they were demonic. He told his homiletics professor, Harry Emerson Fosdick: "You are of the devil. You made me lose my faith, and you are causing other young men to lose their faith."[17] Sung later wrote that many people at Union thought he was out

13. Lyall, *John Sung*, 30.

14. Song, *Journal Once Lost*, 39.

15. Cited in Lyall, *John Sung*, 31.

16. Utley, *Why I am a Preacher.*

17. Schubert, *I Remember John Sung*, 20, 94. See also Xi, *Redeemed by Fire*, 141.

of his mind. One week later, on February 17, Sung went out to buy a new Bible. On his way back to campus he saw an angelic looking boy writing the word "REST" on the street. He saw this two more times before returning to Union. At Union a professor met Sung at the gate to tell him that he was under great emotional strain and needed some rest in a quiet place. According to Sung, he was not allowed to gather his belongings but was taken straight to Bloomingdale Hospital in White Plains, New York. During his time at the asylum, Sung read the Bible forty times, using a different scheme of study each time. He wrote: "I devoured the Bible as a thirsty man would yearn for water. The Word was most nutritious, without which I would not have been able to move forward."[18] Sung expected his stay to last 40 days but it stretched to 193 days. He even tried to escape, making it several miles from the hospital before a police dog sniffed him down. Eventually his good friend, Rev. Wilbur Fowler, acted as a guarantor to help secure his release from Bloomingdale.

Later in life Sung concluded the "asylum was God's special theological college for me" and his 193 days there "were truly the most valuable period of my life."[19] Sung repeated his story about his time in the New York asylum when he returned to China. He insisted that he never went insane but that Union put this label on his born-again experience. On February 10, 1928, W. B. Cole of the Methodist Episcopal Church in China wrote to his friends at a church in Illinois to explain Sung's experience at Union. "Union decided he was going insane so they got him to a hospital on the pretext that he was going there sightseeing," Cole wrote. "His experience turned him back from modernistic paths to a renewed faith in the Bible and its message."[20] After his failed attempt to escape, Sung decided that his "prison" was intended by God to be like the apostle Paul's time in Arabia. For decades this story has shaped how Chinese Christians view Union. Sung's story has become apocryphal; it is unclear what actually happened.

Letters in Union's archives present a different story of what happened to Sung in 1927. This alternate historiography relies on letters to and from Harry Ward in May 1928 and from Sung himself, during and after his time at the asylum.[21] Ward knew Sung well in both the classroom and his home;

18. Song, *Diary of John Sung*, 34.

19. Song, *Diary of John Sung*, 32.

20. Letter from Cole to friends, February 10, 1928. UTS 2, ser. 10A, box 4, folder 9, Burke Library, Union Theological Seminary, NY.

21. Letters from Ward to Semans, May 8, 1926; Ward to Swift, May 10, 1926; Ward to Coffin, May 8, 1928. UTS 2, ser. 10A, box 4, folder 9, Burke Library, Union Theological

he first met Sung he enrolled at Union. In the weeks leading up to his admission to the asylum, Sung visited Ward in his Union office and announced that he was a "prophet of a new Dispensation . . . clothed all in white with a great girdle about my waist [and] a cross always in my right hand and a Bible in my left." Sung described the visions he was having and showed Ward writings that demonstrated "the same unbalanced state of mind." Ward wrote: "He went to the hospital gladly, admitting that his mind 'needed a rest.'" According to Ward's letters, and contrary to Sung's recollection, he went of his own volition to the Bloomingdale Asylum. The decision was based on the assurance of Charles Lambert, a noted psychiatrist at Columbia, that Sung was "mentally unwell." Ward asked a former student, Walker Alderton, to clarify his memory of Sung's admission to Bloomingdale.

In a letter to Ward dated May 17, 1929, Alderton recalled how Sung packed his own suitcase and took a taxi with Henry Busch and Dr. Lambert to Central Station on that day.[22] As the trio trained to Bloomingdale, he told them about his experiences in America and sudden decision to come to Union. Sung "seemed happy at the opportunity of having a rest." Earlier, students had noticed Sung standing outside in the cold of Union's quadrangle staring into space for hours on end. He remained motionless and silent even as other students spoke to him. Given Sung's behavior, Alderton observed: "All seemed to indicate that his difficulties were mounting to a crisis." Union Seminary covered Sung's hospital bill of $713.75. Yet Sung would paint a different picture of what happened surrounding his admission to Bloomingdale, forcing Union to clarify their perspective on what happened to him.

In 1931 Sung visited Paul Hays, a Union alumnus who served as a missionary in Wuhu, China. Sung expressed his frustration at being poorly treated at Union, especially in his admission to Bloomingdale. Hays wrote Ward to ask for more information. Gaylord White, Union's dean of students, responded to Hays on the school's behalf.[23] White detailed Sung's condition at Union and the reasons they admitted him to the Bloomingdale Hospital. When Sung entered Union in 1926 there was a "mystical quality about his state of mind bordering almost on the fantastic which might

Seminary, NY.

22. Letter from Alderton to Ward, May 17, 1928. UTS 2, ser. 10A, box 4, folder 9, Burke Library, Union Theological Seminary, NY.

23. Letter from White to Hays, May 12, 1931. UTS 2, ser. 10A, box 4, folder 9, Burke Library, Union Theological Seminary, NY.

have forewarned us that Dr. Sung was not by any means an ordinary type." Toward the middle of the academic year, other students became anxious about Sung who seemed "a little queer." White, who was responsible for Sung and the other students at Union, concluded: "There is no question that Dr. Sung's mental condition was serious and I think you will agree that the steps which the Seminary took for his recovery were dictated not only by professional advice and common sense but also by Christian sympathy and a genuine interest in the young man's welfare." White included a letter from the medical director of Bloomingdale Hospital. In this May 22, 1931, letter, the director expresses his concern for Sung if "he were so unfortunate to become ill again."[24] He confirmed that Sung was comfortable when he left the hospital in September 1927 and understood why he had been admitted. The physicians at Bloomingdale believed they had saved him from insanity. On February 3, 1932, Daniel Fleming responded to a letter from Ruth Bayliss.[25] Fleming highlights several reasons—the diagnosis of psychiatrists, the seminary's expenditure of his own funds, and Dean White's compassionate care—that the facts in Sung's case differ "vastly from the interpretation which you report."

Rev. Wilbur Fowler, who secured Sung's release from Bloomingdale, wrote a pointed letter to Union's president, Henry Sloane Coffin, on September 24, 1927. Sung planned to return to China in two weeks so Fowler sought the return of seventy dollars that his friend had deposited into the seminary bookshop and two honorary Greek letter keys. Fowler expressed concern that Sung was not allowed to pack his clothes and valuables when he was hurried off to the hospital. He left no doubt what he expected of Coffin: "I consider you two [Coffin and Dr. Hamilton] entirely responsible for all the things that are missing." He closed: "I am sure you agree with me that we owe Dr. Sung a great deal of thought and consideration to try to make up for what he has suffered. He is quite well and normal and he is trying to believe in the sincerity and the Christianity of this friends who sent him to the hospital." Three weeks before Fowler sent his letter, Sung himself wrote the dean from Fowler's home in Cincinnati.[26] Sung's attitude toward Union, though, contrasted from Fowler's perspective.

24. Letter from medical director to White, May 22, 1931. UTS 2, ser. 10A, box 4, folder 9, Burke Library, Union Theological Seminary, NY.

25. Letter from Fleming to Bayliss, February 3, 1932. UTS 2, ser. 10A, box 4, folder 9, Burke Library, Union Theological Seminary, NY.

26. Letter from Sung to Dean White, September 1, 1927. UTS 2, ser. 10A, box 4, folder 9, Burke Library, Union Theological Seminary, NY.

Sung actually asked if he could return to Union. He explained to Dean White that President Coffin had promised him a return to the seminary as soon as he was well. He wrote: "Now I am in perfect good health and decide to take up my study again next fall. Will you kindly reserve a room for me?" Even after being released from the asylum, Sung still wanted to return to Union. This picture differs sharply from the narrative that he would use back in China. In fact, a letter that Sung wrote to President Coffin from the asylum on April 27, 1927, confirms his, at that time, positive view of the seminary. He wrote:

> Spiritually in deepest gratitude to your spiritual love and mystical sympathy will pen this epistle of love as our token of gratitude. Our past misunderstanding has created a spiritual gulf between us. We must learn to forgive each other and follow the wisdom of turtle. U.T.S. is the best theological seminary in which many prophets are playing the music of love dancing in the spiritual air.[27]

He closed the letter by saluting all "with a holy kiss," then asked Coffin to keep the letter a secret. The point of recounting these letters is simply this: Sung's mindset toward Union in 1927 when he was in the United States differs from what he describes after he returns to China. Even after being in the asylum for 193 days, he still wanted to return to Union. The story regarding Sung's time at Union has been told and retold by Sung himself, Leslie Lyall, and William Schubert. The existing historiography follows these lines: Sung had a dramatic conversion in February 1927 filling him with evangelistic fervor. This fervor put him at odds with his professors at Union who labeled him insane and sent him to an asylum against his will. In the Bloomingdale Asylum Sung read the Bible forty times, which restored his faith and confidence in the Bible. He left the asylum, determined to return to China as an evangelist. Though this is the common view of Sung's time New York City, the reality is more complex.

Sung arrived at Union with many questions. Personally, he was torn between his desires for greater scientific research and wholehearted service to God. Theologically, he wanted a deeper understanding of what the Bible really meant. Sung encountered a modernist view of the Bible and Christian theology that compounded his questions. He attempted to complete three years of theological study in one year, deepening his physical exhaustion. The workload, the intense struggle with his life calling, and the challenge

27. Letter from Sung to Coffin, April 27, 1927. UTS 2, ser. 10A, box 4, folder 9, Burke Library, Union Theological Seminary, NY.

of Union's liberal theology led Sung to the brink of a nervous breakdown. His conversion in February 1927 came in the midst of this physical, emotional, and spiritual breakdown. In light of Sung's paranoia and exhaustion, Union's faculty acted in his best interest in having him evaluated by a psychiatrist and sent to Bloomingdale. Union's particular theological outlook did not send Sung to the asylum but it exacerbated the tension on an already-strained mind. He needed the rest and professional care. During and after his time there, he wanted to return to the seminary. The story of John Sung's experience in New York provides an archetypical example of the theological war afoot in the 1920s/30s. Daryl Ireland captures well how the narrative played out:

> The story was powerful because in the contentious context of China, UTS-the flagship seminary of modernism—could be drawn into binary opposition to Sung (UTS/modern/bad—Sung/fundamentalism/good). Such a mythic narrative framework easily emerged from a divided Christian community and allowed Sung to reverse the polarities of suspicion about his mental state. Among fundamentalists at least, if any party in this new story was deluded, it was Union.[28]

Perhaps Sung's animosity toward the seminary was related, at least partially, to their decision to not allow him to return in the fall of 1927.

Sung rejected Union's modernism. But, given his fragile mental and emotional state, how valuable is his assessment? In 1931 Sung summarized his understanding of liberalism in his diary: distorting the Bible at will, not believing in miracles, using psychology to explain prayers, using hypnotism to explain miracles from God, viewing all those who are demonized as mental patients, viewing the spiritual and inspirational as emotional, replacing faith with reason, and interpreting the Bible with science rather than the power of God.[29] Sung reflected back on what he had learned and rejected at Union. This new archival material nuances how we assess Sung's time at Union. As Ireland points out, these documents "demonstrated Sung's proclivity to exaggerate, fabricate, or silence events for rhetorical effect."[30] While interesting historically, Sung's reflections on Union fail to offer a robust understanding of the seminary's theology at the time. But there is another source that does: the letters of Dietrich Bonhoeffer. Given

28. Ireland, "John Sung," 48.

29. Song, diary entry from February 23, 1931. Cited in Song, *Diary of John Sung*, 29.

30. Ireland, "John Sung," 10. See also Ireland, *John Song*.

his previous theological training and stable mental state, Bonhoeffer offers a clearer assessment of what Union was like in the 1920s and 1930s.[31] The third and final group, those who deny Union's influence, became the founders and leaders of the TSPM.

## Chinese Graduates Who Denied Union's Influence: K. H. Ting

The final group of Chinese students at Union, men like K. H. Ting and Y. T. Wu, came to Union with their theological views well formed. Their time at Union was probably not the most important factor in shaping their theology; however, it seems to be a factor. At the least, the school confirmed their theological orientation. Union influenced Chinese Christians in and through its dense social network before they arrived in Morningside Heights. Even if Ting and Wu were not impacted while *at* Union, they were certainly influenced *through* the seminary. I propose that Union did in fact influence Ting's views. Certain themes stand out in Ting's collected works: Ting's curious silence regarding Union, his critique of fundamentalism and the way he sought to reconstruct theological thinking.[32] My goal here is not a thorough analysis of Ting's theological system. Instead I will attempt to trace echoes of Union's influence in his writings.

First, it is curious and revealing that Ting remained silent about Union Seminary. *God Is Love* contains Ting's speeches from around the world. In many of these international speeches, Manila in 1993, Sydney in 1984, Hollywood in 1993, Toronto in 1979, and Budapest in 1986, he followed a similar pattern.[33] He began by thanking his hosts, describing a personal connection to the site or mentioning the historical significance of that location. In Manila he thanked Union Theological Seminary in the Philippines and the seminary's president for honoring him and the church in China. In Budapest he celebrated his chance to preach from an "august pulpit" below which Jews had been hidden from Nazis in a secret room in World War II. He then praised Hungarian Christians for not simply being preachers and hearers of the Bible but doers of it in the midst of danger. At Timothy Easton Memorial Church in Toronto he praised the church for sending Jim

31. Ch. 3 detailed Bonhoeffer's views on the theology at Union.

32. K. Ting, *God Is Love* and *No Longer Strangers*. I decided to base the following section on these collected and, at times, translated works for several reasons: 1) ease of reference, 2) simplicity, and 3) accessibility in English.

33. K. Ting, *God Is Love*, 36–47, 56–61, 151–55, 164–70, and 315–18.

Endicott to be a missionary in China. He even joked at All Saints Church in California that he never thought he would be in Hollywood meeting so many movie stars. The point here: Ting usually began his international speeches by connecting to his audience.

But when he spoke at Union Seminary and at Riverside Church, he broke this practice. At Riverside Church in 1979, Ting mentioned no personal connection to the place. One would expect mention of the honor of preaching in the pulpit of Riverside's founder, Harry Emerson Fosdick.[34] But he was silent. He returned to Morningside Heights fifteen years later to be honored at Union. In 1994 the seminary's board of trustees awarded him the Union Medal, the school's highest honor for his "faithful and visionary ministry in China."[35] Yet, once again, he remained silent regarding Union. He neither thanked the school or any of his former professors nor acknowledged any indebtedness to the school.[36] Union Seminary and its professors never come up in any of Ting's writings in *God Is Love* and *No Longer Strangers.* He makes slight reference to Tillich, Niebuhr, and other theologians who have been translated into Chinese.[37] In these two collections, Ting's only mention of Union comes at the close of his speech at the seminary: "We like to think that, in our small way, we are doing an experiment on behalf of the Church Worldwide. As a Union alumnus and as the recipient of the Union medal tonight, I like to think that we are doing this with the blessing of Union Seminary."[38] Why would Ting not follow the same pattern of other international speeches when he spoke at and near Union Seminary? Why this strange refusal to acknowledge any debt to Union, any influence from the seminary? The silence here speaks loudly. And the answer is simple.

Following the establishment of the TSPM, K. H. Ting sought to disavow any connection to Union Theological Seminary or any impact on his theological views. Smart and politically cautious, Ting knew that he could not simultaneously rail against the imperialism of Western missionaries and admit to the personal influence of a particular Western institution.

34. K. Ting, *God Is Love*, 376–81.

35. Rosen, "Union Medal," 14.

36. K. Ting, *God Is Love*, 469–75.

37. "Christian theology is valued as a branch of Western philosophy and for that reason Chinese intellectuals have translated a great many of Western theologians into Chinese, including Tillich, Niebuhr, Hans Kung, Rahner and Moltmann." K. Ting, *God Is Love*, 471.

38. K. Ting, *God Is Love*, 475.

Acknowledging Western influences makes the TSPM less indigenous. Y. T. Wu and K. H. Ting called the Chinese church to be self-supporting, self-propagating, and self-governing. They wanted to eradicate any foreign influence and make the TSPM fully patriotic. But how do you eradicate ideas fundamental in your own thinking? Hung and Tsu gladly acknowledged Union's influence on their thinking because they could.

But Wu and Ting did not admit to any Union influence because, politically, they knew they could not. Ting's praise of Wu in 1989 helps us understand why:

> He differed from most other Chinese theologians in that he did not worship foreign books, nor did he lightly accept the official KMT propaganda. His own theological ideas developed through his dialogue with this times, especially through his dialogue with the young people who represented progressive trends.[39]

Both Wu and Ting knew the political connections represented in the dense social network at Union Seminary. It had close ties with America's power elite, not just in religion but in politics as well. Even though Union's professors held a plurality of views, the school fundamentally represented Western liberalism and a particular view of the nation-state. More specifically, Union was aligned—albeit directly or indirectly—with American political leaders who had supported Chiang Kai-shek and the KMT. In political philosophy and personal connections, Union represented what Ting had rejected. Acknowledging Union's influence would have been foolish for Ting in the People's Republic of China, where every foreign connection was held suspect. I wonder if Zhou Enlai or Mao Zedong recognized the depth of Wu and Ting's relationships in the United States. Given Zhou's relationships with Gong Pusheng, I suspect he knew but kept this knowledge from Mao. Because Wu and Ting were silent on Union's influence, scholars, to this point, have failed to see it.

Ting's biographer and good friend, Philip Wickeri, says no, Union did not impact his theology. Wickeri met with Ting weekly from 1981 to 1983. He argues that other factors, such as his Anglican formation and his involvement in the Student Christian Movement, diminished any deep contribution made by Union. The social setting in Shanghai in the 1930s and 1940s and Ting's experience and relationships therein "mitigated against the theological outlook that Union had to offer." Wickeri adds: "He was

39. K. Ting, *God Is Love*, 505.

interested in what his teachers had to say, but there is no evidence that he was particularly attracted to the thinking of Union's leading Protestant theologians, or to van Dusen's ecumenical vision."[40] Despite what Ting himself or Wickeri says about Union's influence, what does the evidence suggest?

The evidence that could demonstrate Union's influence on Ting might include journal entries, personal interviews, or essays from his days at Union. But such evidence is not available. Instead, scholars are left to probe Ting's writing to find what influence Union might have had. Recent research by Alexander Chow reinforces the influence of the Anglican-Episcopalian tradition on Ting.[41] Anglican thought at the turn of the twentieth century was shaped by the *Lux Mundi* tradition after Charles Gore and by the social theology of William Temple.[42] These Anglican concerns, argues Chow, influenced Ting more than the Christocentric debates revolving around Reformed themes in continental theology. My goal here is not to refute the impact of Anglican thought, Y. T. Wu's friendship, or Shanghai's social setting on Ting's theology. I am simply suggesting that Union exerted more influence on Ting's theology than Ting admits or that current scholarship recognizes. I turn now to examine a sampling of Ting's writing for particular themes and potential influences.

Throughout his writings, Ting disliked fundamentalism on political and theological grounds.[43] Politically, it bothered Ting that most fundamentalists opposed the CCP and sided with the Nationalists. How could they not be impressed with the ideology and lifestyle of the Communist revolutionaries? Not only did the Communists address China's crippling social problems, they also lived sacrificially to serve the nation. Ting believed fundamentalism contained several theological flaws: portraying the world as Satan's realm and condemned to imminent destruction, not loving the world, establishing an antithesis between belief and unbelief and

40. Wickeri, *Reconstructing Christianity in China*, 72.

41. Chow, *Theosis, Sino-Christian Theology*, 89–111.

42. Ramsey, *From Gore to Temple*, 40–59; Sachs, *Transformation of Anglicanism*, 155–59.

43. Marsden suggested three key features of fundamentalism as a movement: 1) it takes on the role of the beleaguered minority and develops strong sectarian or separatist's tendencies, 2) it relates to the American religious tradition of revivalism and pietism that stressed the "Bible alone," and 3) it contrasts faith and reason, distrusting the intellect. Marsden, *Fundamentalism and American Culture*, 7. See ch. 5 on Harry Emerson Fosdick.

making belief in Christ the prerequisite for doing good, and using the doctrine of security of salvation to ensure freedom of action for God's elect of God but condemning all others to hell regardless of how good their work may seem.[44] Fundamentalists were "antinomian reactionaries" who worked against all the goodness in the people's liberation movement.

By stressing justification by faith, conservative Christians became antinomian and advocated a lawlessness that permitted everything. In the end justification by faith denied morality. Ting wrote:

> The idea is that anyone who believes will go to heaven after death, and those who do not believe will go to hell. This is an idea that denies morality. By extension, Hitler and Mussolini, as Christians, would be in heaven, while Confucius, Laozi, Mozi and Zhou Enlai, non-believers, would be in hell.[45]

Ting longed to rid the Chinese church of this "deceptive talk" that vilified God by making him "unbearably cruel and brutal" toward humanity. The fundamentalists stress that the Bible is "God's word," which means "each chapter, each verse, each phrase, even each word, each punctuation mark and each stroke of each character must all be completely without error." But, Ting argues, "reality is not like this."[46] Like many of his professors and classmates at Union, Ting thoroughly rejected fundamentalism. He did so for theological reasons—their views of God, the Bible, eschatology, soteriology, and ethics—but also on their stubborn refusal to join the TSPM. He saw the fundamentalists as opposed to Christian unity. One Beijing pastor epitomized this opposition most vividly: Wang Mingdao.

Nowhere was Ting's pen more ferocious than in his attacks on Wang. Ting and Wang represented two opposite expressions of Christianity in China: modernist vs. fundamentalist, TSPM vs. unregistered churches. An old Chinese Christian in Beijing told a Western reporter "Understand two men, and you will understand Chinese Christianity." The journalist replied, "Which two?" the reporter replied. "Wang Mingdao and K. H. Ting!"[47] Ting disliked Wang because he opposed the unity that Ting delighted in. Through his sermons and quarterly magazine, *Spiritual Food* (*Lingshi jikan*), Wang spoke against registering with the TSPM. Wang had refused to

44. K. Ting, *No Longer Strangers*, 31–35. See also K. Ting, *God Is Love*, 61–74. The latter is fuller version of Ting's talk at Doshisha University.

45. K. Ting, *God Is Love*, 125; see also 171–77.

46. K. Ting, *God Is Love*, 51.

47. T. Harvey, *Acquainted with Grief*, 7.

join a church association mandated by the occupying Japanese in the 1930s and refused again to join the TSPM in the 1950s. His Beijing church, he argued, was already self-propagating, self-governing, and self-supporting. Not only did he refuse to register his church, he also berated modernist Christians as "unbelievers."

Ting spared no barbs in attacking Wang: "clearly he is filled with hatred for China and is absolutely against rational assessment" because he "refuses to talk about the crimes of aggression the imperialists have committed against China."[48] Wang not only refused to join the Three-Self movement, he also spoke against it. In doing so, he "unscrupulously distorts the meaning of the church's self-governing, self-supporting, self-propagating movement in an attempt to cause Christians to misunderstand the Three-Self Patriotic Movement."[49] In Ting's mind Wang hated the TSPM; this was his cardinal sin. By not joining the TSPM, Wang opposed unity and was unpatriotic. Ting minced no words in describing Christians who did not support the CCP:

> Patriotism impels us to support the new social system won by the people, to defend it, to eliminate the remaining bad parts, and to correct and improve it. The theory which opposes itself to any and every authority is not in accord with patriotism but with anarchy, subversion and counter-revolution.[50]

In advocating a Christian faith that distinguishes between Christians and non-Christians, Wang further struck against the theology that Ting endorsed. K. H. Ting disliked fundamentalists as unpatriotic and an affront to unity. He offered an alternative view of the world, non-Christians, Jesus Christ, and God.

In the 1990s K. H. Ting realized than many Chinese Christians in registered and unregistered churches and even in Nanjing Union Theological Seminary were evangelical in their theological orientation.[51] This trend concerned Ting so he advocated a "reconstruction of theological thinking"

48. K. Ting, *No Longer Strangers*, 141.

49. K. Ting, *No Longer Strangers*, 142.

50. K. Ting, *God Is Love*, 185.

51. Though fundamentalism morphed into various forms in the twentieth century, it took its primary shape in Evangelicalism. David Bebbington identifies the four features of Evangelicalism as conversionism (believing that lives can be changed), activism (expressing Christian conviction through evangelism, mission and service), biblicism (regarding the Bible as the source for truth), and crucentrism (stressing the sacrifice of Christ on the cross). Bebbington, *Evangelicalism in Modern Britain*, 3.

in the TSPM. Ting built a theology around God's love that utilized ideas from Teilhard's cosmic Christ and Whitehead's process theology. In 1982 he summarized his theological concerns in a series of questions:

> Is the world in the hand of the devil? What is the status of the world in the mind of God? How should Christians look at history? Should Christians only be concerned with questions of belief and unbelief and of life after death? Should Christians be concerned with issues of right and wrong? Should they differentiate good from evil? What is meant by being spiritual? Should Christianity negate and deny reason? What is the scope of God's care and love and of the work of the Holy Spirit? How does one assess the true, the good, and the beautiful outside the realm of the church? How should Christians think of the nation? Of patriotism? What is the place of the Bible in divine revelation? How should one look at the holiness of the Church in the face of the many evil deeds being exposed there? How can we recognize anew the holy love of God, his intentions in carrying out the ongoing work of creation, redemption and sanctification? In this providence of God, how should the role of Christ as revealed in Colossians and Ephesians be understood?[52]

Ting started with the premise that God is love. Love is not just *an* attribute of God; it is his supreme attribute. In his earlier theological training in the Anglican church, Ting had understood God in terms of his omnipotence, power, dominion, self-sufficiency, and changelessness. God was cast in the image of "Egyptian, Persian, Roman and Chinese potentates" and became a "reflection of an absolutization of human beings' own cravings, especially those of male human beings." But Ting came to reject this view. God's other attributes need to be "deabsolutized and subordinated to God's supreme attribute of love."[53] God is love first and foremost. This is K. H. Ting's gospel:

> "God is love." Love is not a sometimes attribute of God. Love is not merely an attribute of God among others. Love is the foremost attribute of all God's attributes. This *is* the gospel. . . . God is the cosmic lover. With a heart of merciful love he is constantly creating and redeeming. This teaching has been the decisive revelation of my own spiritual journey.[54]

52. K. Ting, *God Is Love*, 191.
53. K. Ting, *God Is Love*, 43.
54. K. Ting, *God Is Love*, 158–59.

Beginning with God as love, Ting then used ideas from Pierre Teilhard de Chardin and Alfred North Whitehead.

God embodies his love for humanity in Jesus Christ. Jesus is the great lover of humanity, the cosmic Christ. Leaning on Teilhard, Ting often utilized the same passages about Christ: John 1:1–4, 9,14; John 8:58; John 17:24; Eph 3:9–11; Col 1:15–20; Phil 2:6–11; Rom 5:15; and Heb 1:2–3. John described Jesus Christ as the divine Logos. Paul argued that Jesus sustains the universe. Colossians 1:15–17 is central in Ting's Christology: "For in him all things were created, in heaven and on earth, visible and invisible; whether thrones or dominions or principalities or authorities—all things were created through him and for him, and in him all things hold together." Christ is cosmic in nature. In him all goodness in nature and human history finds its fulfillment. Ting contended that if all creation embodies Christ, there must be goodness in human activities outside of Christianity. Adam's sin affected all humanity but the grace of Christ is victorious over this sin. All people are in solidarity with Christ. Ting concluded, "The benefit Christ brings to humanity surpasses the harm of Adam. Grace is greater than sin."[55]

He bemoaned the tendency of Christians to make the effect of Adam's fall universal while limiting the grace of Christ to those who believe in him. In his mind the evangelical view made the incarnation of the Son of God less efficacious than Adam's fall. The New Testament's greatest word is not sin but grace. Ting frequently cited Thomas Aquinas's comment that grace does not supplant nature but perfects it.[56] The incarnation removes the disparity between God and the world, grace and nature, belief and unbelief. Ting uses Teilhard's ideas to explain Jesus. He is the alpha and omega, the origin and culmination of God's creation. The universe is evolving to higher levels of complexity and consciousness culminating in the Omega Point.[57] The cosmic Christ is at work in "all human movements that are progressive, liberating, and humanizing."[58] These ideas gave Ting a theology that could work within United Front ideology, a way to embrace the CCP and remove the division between belief and unbelief. To summarize Ting's theology: the God of love works through the cosmic Christ in the process of creation.

55. K. Ting, *God Is Love*, 302.

56. K. Ting, *God Is Love*, 69 and 169. See Thomas Aquinas, *Nature and Grace*, I.Q1. A8.46.

57. Teilhard de Chardin, *Future of Man*.

58. K. Ting, *God Is Love*, 446.

God's creating through Christ proceeds into the present but is not yet complete. God has never stopped the process of creation:

> It is not that God carried on his work of creation for six days and then stopped and ceded its control to the successful rebellion of Satan, and then the redeemer came into the world to rescue some individuals out of it to be returned to God, leaving all others to eternal damnation. As creativity is inexhaustible and creation a long, ongoing process, Christ has been and is with God in all the creative work in the universe to this day.[59]

Christians should not set creation and redemption in opposition. Jesus Christ is both redeemer and creator. Paul wrote of creation's groaning in Rom 8, signifying the ongoing process of creation. "The world and the people in it are all products at various stages of completion who have appeared in the process of God's creation. A few individuals are not the only objects of redemption."[60] Christ fills the universe and manifests every latent spark of color. Reality is one gigantic process where matter and organisms are achieving higher levels of existence. The ultimate attainment of the image of God in humanity is a loving community, since the triune God exists in a community of love.

Ting utilizes Alfred North Whitehead's ideas to argue that humanity's "true destiny" lay in being "co-creators in the universe" and "partakers in the creative process."[61] Because the cosmic Christ continues to create the universe, Ting concluded that God is working through historical movements in the world, including Communism. This view of God and world provided Ting with a framework for theological reconstruction in China and for wide-ranging post-denominational unity. Christians could work gladly with Communists, Muslims, and Buddhists, celebrating the work of the cosmic Christ in their religions. The wall between belief and unbelief is torn down. These theological themes enabled Ting to affirm the present world, bring unity, and downplay the difference between believers and nonbelievers. While echoes of Teilhard and Whitehead are noticeable, can the same be said of any theologians from Union? The answer is yes in a broad sense and maybe in a more specific sense.

Broadly speaking, K. H. Ting saw his theological task as establishing a conversation between theology and culture. In this sense, he wrote and

59. K. Ting, *God Is Love*, 40.

60. K. Ting, *God Is Love*, 33.

61. K. Ting, *God Is Love*, 310.

spoke in the liberal tradition of Paul Tillich. Tillich argued that culture revealed humanity's fundamental existential questions, or "ultimate questions." For Tillich, the "courage to be" should supplant the dogma of the Christian creeds.

Russell Re Manning argues that Tillich's influence is as pervasive as it is subtle:

> While no "school" took his name, Tillich's ideas and terminology have, as it were, leaked out into the wider theological atmosphere, and it is constantly surprising just how much of Tillich's thought can be found lurking, often unacknowledged, in the background of a diverse range of debates.[62]

Tillich's primary conviction and, according to Re Manning, his most enduring legacy to contemporary theology was that theology must be done in dialogue. As Christian theology engages with culture, science, and other religious traditions, a "both/and" character emerges. Alister McGrath applies the term "liberal" to theologians in the tradition of Schleiermacher and Tillich who reconstruct belief in response to contemporary culture.[63] This is exactly what Ting did. He reconstructed Christian belief to adhere to United Front ideology.

Both K. H. Ting and Y. T. Wu developed a theology that was in dialogue with their times. Ting and Wu recast theology in light of contemporary culture. This is the essence of theological liberalism, and they had to learn it somewhere. Despite their silence on Union's influence, I believe the seminary transmitted this modernity to China, directly in its classroom and indirectly through the Christian colleges and YMCA. Modernity shaped Ting and Wu's theological method. Fundamentalism could not and did not adapt to the ideology of the CCP. But liberalism could. And it did, through Wu and Ting.

## Summary

Some Chinese Christians learned to distrust Christian dogma and adopt theological liberalism when they attended Union Seminary. Others learned these ideas through the Christian colleges and the YMCA, to which Union supplied key leaders. William Hung and Andrew Y. Y. Tsu recognized and

62. Manning, *Cambridge Companion*, xv.

63. McGrath, *Christian Theology*, 103.

gladly embraced Union's influence on their thinking. It was Union's esteemed professor Arthur Cushman McGiffert who caused Hung to reassess Christian beliefs and history. He salvaged his faith by detaching it from churches and abandoning the idea of becoming a pastor. Some Chinese Christians recognized Union's theology and rejected it. John Sung embodied this experience. I argued for a reexamination of the historiography surrounding Sung's time at Union and at the Bloomingdale asylum. The actual events differed from how Sung later remembered them; however, the assessment stands that Sung rejected Union and Union rejected Sung. Throughout the 1920s the community at Union—both faculty and students—mocked fundamentalism. Dietrich Bonhoeffer confirmed this observation and explained why in the 1930s. The last group of Chinese students at Union never acknowledged how Union impacted their theological perspective. These leaders, such as Y. T. Wu and K. H. Ting, rose to positions of prominence in the Three-Self Patriotic Movement. There is a curious silence regarding the seminary's impact on their thinking. I argued that there were political reasons for them to not acknowledge Union's influence. Whether or not Wu and Ting were influenced *at* Union, they were certainly influenced *through* the seminary. I now turn to the final chapter where I offer some observations about Union's influence on Chinese Protestantism and the irony therein.

# 10

# Conclusion

THIS BOOK ADDRESSES A deficiency in existing research on modern China: How have Chinese Protestants contributed to the development of twentieth-century China? John Stewart Barwick rightly notes: "Few historical works have been devoted to the subject of elite Chinese Protestants and their impact on Republican society." The dearth of academic research on this topic reinforces the wrong assumption that Chinese Protestants were, in Barwick's words, "entirely marginal to the development of modern China."[1] In the past century Union graduates played significant roles in China's development in religion, education, and politics. For example, in Republican China three of the four Chinese founders of Yenching University's influential Life Fellowship studied at Union. In Communist China, two Union graduates founded and led the Three-Self Patriotic Movement. Despite the clear connections between Union and Chinese Christianity, the seminary's influence on Chinese Protestantism has been virtually ignored.

Only one scholar has noticed and written on the connection. Xu Yihua argues that Union exerted "an extensive impact on the Christian church in China" through its training program for foreign missions, prestigious faculty, and recruitment of Chinese students.[2] During the years of Republican China, Union sent 196 graduates to China. Included in this list of Union graduates are 39 Chinese nationals.[3] When Union's Chinese graduates returned home, many of them held prominent positions in the church, the academy, and the state. Xu has rightly noted much of the seminary's influence on China; however, there seems to be more to the story. Union's connections to China are not difficult to see but they are difficult to understand and explain. The seminary's influence seems to be deeper, more

1. Barwick, "Protestant Quest for Modernity," 506.

2. Y. Xu, "Union Theological Seminary," 23.

3. Alumni Office of Union Theological Seminary, *Union Theological Seminary*. This number does not include the Chinese students who studied there for less than a year.

significant, and more interconnected. The preceding chapters explored and explained these connections.

This concluding chapter reiterates why my research matters and how it makes a unique contribution to the study of Chinese Christianity. Union's role in Chinese history comes into focus through combining Hunter's idea of "dense social network" and Granovetter's explanation of the "strength of weak ties." Union helped strengthen a relational network in China but did it have a theological impact? Chinese graduates responded in different ways to what they learned at Union: some embraced it and others rejected it. A third category of Chinese graduates downplayed Union's influence, even though their theology resonates with ideas taught at the seminary. In this final section I will admit some inherent limitations but present several avenues for future research.

## The Importance of this Research

The twenty-first century might well be considered the century of the dragon: the century when China became the greatest superpower in the world. Its economy is the world's second largest and is on pace to surpass the United States in ten to twenty years. In *China's Silent Army*, Cardenal and Araújo argue that China's global expansion is at its height. The Beijing-based journalists describe how China is casting the world in its image. The nation, its state-owned enterprises, and its vast diaspora are laying the foundations for a new world order in this century, "a world under China's leadership."[4] Not only has China's economy expanded rapidly in recent decades, so has the Chinese church. In 1949 there were 1 million Christians in China. Today there are at least 70 million. The core of the global church has swung to the South and East. In 1900 Europe and North America had 82 percent of the world's Christians. Today the West constitutes just 35 percent. China is poised to be the center of both the world economy and world Christianity. Scholars need to study and attempt to understand all facets of China: its history, politics, economy, and religion. Research on Christianity in China is imperative because the Chinese church flourishes like never before. This growth is shocking for two reasons. First, the Chinese church appeared to

4. Cardenal and Araújo, *China's Silent Army.* Cardenal and Araújo probably overstate their case. A nice counterbalance is provided by Shambaugh, *China Goes Global.* Shambaugh contends that China's influence is broad but not deep. Thus it is not as powerful as Cardenal, Araújo, and others imagine.

have died during the Cultural Revolution. Second, for centuries Christianity had failed in its attempts to establish deep roots in Chinese soil.

Christianity engaged the Middle Kingdom at four distinct periods in its history. Nestorian missionaries found favor with the Tang Court in the seventh century. In AD 638 Emperor Taizhong praised the "mysterious and transcendent" teaching of the Nestorian missionary Alopen that "saves creatures" and "should be propagated under heaven."[5] But two centuries later the Wuzong Emperor banned all foreign religions. Nestorian Christianity returned in the thirteenth century when Genghis Khan (1162–1227) married into the Keraiti royal family, a Turko-Mongolian tribe that had converted to Christianity. Under the protection of the Mongol rulers, both Nestorian and Catholic Christianity existed in China during the Yuan dynasty (1271–1368). But Christianity faded as the xenophobic Ming dynasty began. As in the Tang dynasty Yuan Christianity left little enduring mark on indigenous persons and institutions. Eventually the Ming leaders welcomed Matteo Ricci and other Jesuit missionaries in the seventeenth-century. The Jesuits, and later other Catholics, saw success in China. But the Rites Controversy led to the expulsion of missionaries in 1724. In these three distinct periods Christianity rose and fell with the tides of imperial favor. Establishing Chinese Christianity proved an enigma. Could an indigenous Christian faith grow in Chinese soil? Protestant missionaries would try a century later.

The British Empire used the opium trade and subsequent wars to pry China open in the 1830s. The Unequal Treaties enabled foreigners to travel throughout the entire land and to buy property in China. A trickle of Protestant missionaries, beginning with Robert Morrison in 1807, became a steady stream following the treaties. From 1860 to 1905 the number of missionaries in China grew from 100 to 3500 and the number of Chinese Protestants, from the hundreds to 100,000. Social chaos racked China at the start of the twentieth century: from the Boxer Uprising in 1900 to the collapse of the Qing dynasty in 1911. As the number of missionaries and Chinese Christians grew, it spawned the creation of new schools, hospitals, churches, and other institutions. Christianity had always struggled to become indigenous in China. The growing Sino-Foreign Protestant Establishment in twentieth-century China faced the perennial question: Could Christianity in China become Chinese Christianity?

5. Palmer, *Jesus Sutras*, 43.

This question of indigeneity dominated Chinese Christianity in late Qing and early Republican China. Would Western missionaries allow Chinese Christians to control their churches and institutions? Henry Venn and Rufus Anderson advocated the "Three-Self Principle," churches that were self-supporting, self-governing, and self-propagating. In 1892, at a Christian conference in Shanghai, missionary delegates agreed to these principles. However trouble came in finding reliable Chinese leaders. Christian converts came from the periphery of society and were not well educated. As the children of Chinese Christians attended missions' schools and studied in the West, they rose to positions of prominence. A good example is C. Y. Cheng, a second-generation Christian who studied in Glasgow for two years and returned to Beijing to pastor a church. In 1910 he captivated the delegates at the World Missionary Conference in Edinburgh with the challenge to give more control to native Christians. In the 1920s he became general secretary of the National Christian Council and general moderator of the Church of Christ in China, an ecumenical organization unifying sixteen denominations. Western missionaries were reluctant to give real control to Chinese Christians. When they did, as in the case of C. Y. Cheng, it was often to those who had been educated in missionary schools in China. Two of the most significant institutions in developing Chinese leaders were the Christian colleges and the YMCA. Union Seminary supplied leaders to both. The New York school formed a dense social network that would influence Protestantism in both Republican and Communist China.

## Union Seminary and China

In 1836 ecumenically minded Presbyterian ministers established Union Seminary. They wanted a new seminary to counteract the conservative tendencies at Princeton Seminary. The founders desired a seminary where men of "moderate views and feelings" could "cordially and affectionally rally" for theological study. They intentionally placed Union in the heart of New York City where students would be surrounded by the joys and problems of America's greatest city. Union became the epicenter of American theological liberalism. The heresy trials of Union professors Charles Briggs in 1892 and Arthur Cushman McGiffert in 1900 cemented Union's reputation as a place that challenged Christian orthodoxy and championed freedom of scholarship.[6] In the nineteenth century many Union professors

6. Xu notes: "Union's alleged political and theological liberalism was related more

studied in German universities renowned for merging modern ideas with historic Christianity. Theological modernism found fertile soil at Union. Historians have noted the seminary's commitment to liberal theology, but few have noticed the school's deliberate global focus.

From its founding Union sought be a seminary that impacted the entire world. In 1837 the "Society of Inquiry Concerning Missions" became the school's first student organization. The group, heartily endorsed by Union's leaders, met each month to discuss and pray about world missions. In a sermon in the 1880s George Lewis Prentiss boasted that Union alumni were among the "most useful ministers" in the nation and the "best missionaries among the heathen."[7] Union established the first professorship of missions in America in 1873. From 1838 to 1884 Union sent 196 alumni to serve as overseas missionaries. The most common fields of service were Turkey (27), Syria (21), China (20), India (12), and Persia (9). The number of Union graduates going to China swelled to 196 between 1911 and 1949. During this period, Union's class size averaged 97 students per year. Each year Union sent 5 graduates to China: over 5 percent of its graduating class every year for thirty-eight years. Scores of Union's graduates taught in missionary schools or Christian colleges.[8] Western missionaries struggled with how best to relate the Christian message to Chinese culture and often found themselves changed by their new home.[9] Union taught its students to use modern advances in psychology and biology to think differently about Christian dogma. They applied these lessons in China, using Confucius and Mencius rather than Darwin and Freud.

As they struggled with how best to adapt Christianity, Union graduates planted the seeds of the modernist-fundamentalist controversy in China. Those seeds sprouted in 1921 when Union's professor, Harry Emerson Fosdick, spoke at the missionary retreat centers of Peitaiho and Kuling. Fosdick's talks served as a counterpunch to talks given in 1920 by W. H.

to the seminary's spirit or style of free expression and its devotion to academic freedom than to its adherence to a single tradition of theological liberalism." While the seminary was not devoted to a "single tradition" of liberalism, its devotion to free expression led to championing theological liberalism. Y. Xu, "Union Theological Seminary," 21.

7. Prentiss, *Union Theological Seminary*, 100.

8. See Appendix B, "Union Alumni (1900–1950) in Chinese Higher Education."

9. "The untraditional, often syncretic, religious and cultural ideas that emerged out of the missionaries' experience in the East—the eventual unmaking of many missionaries—precipitated a major crisis within the missionary enterprise in the late 1920s and early 1930s." Xi, *Conversion of Missionaries*, xii.

Griffith Thomas. In "Modernism in China" Thomas described the modernist tendency among missionaries in China. He argued that modernist missionaries had abandoned evangelism for secular, educational work because they had no good news to preach. "The seminaries are being filled with men who are New Theology men and who have no message to give," one missionary complained to Thomas. "The students are filled with rubbish and then expected to preach, and what will they preach?"[10] The conservative missionaries were alarmed that Chinese Christians with the most critical views were those who studied in the West. Thomas wrote: "The 'returned student,' the man who has been to America and obtained a degree there. He often returns home to China with views of the Bible and Christianity which are definitely critical."[11] Some of the greatest purveyors of theological modernity in twentieth-century China were Chinese Christians who studied at Union. Thomas singles out the New York seminary as the source of theological liberalism in China. He rightly perceives the school's key role in training students in a modernist approach to Christianity.

During the years of Republican China, Union accepted more Chinese students than any other divinity school or seminary in America. The seminary provided scholarships to many of these students. Thirty-nine Chinese students enrolled at Union for a year or more between 1911 and 1949. Chinese Christians came to Union because of its reputation, because their professors in China recommended it and because it was in New York City. My observation that Union influenced Chinese Christianity is not unique; Thomas wrote about it in 1921. The seminary impacted China through sending missionaries, educating Chinese Christians, publishing works of its professors and alumni, and in providing a dense social network.

## Union's Dense Social Network

To understand Union's influence, I suggested a new approach that borrows ideas from James Davison Hunter and Mark Granovetter. By combining Hunter's theory of dense social networks and Granovetter's explanation of weak ties, the seminary's impact comes into greater focus. Hunter describes how active and interactive networks, "dense networks," shape cultures and change the world.[12] When networks of elites overlap, nation-shaping power

10. Thomas, "Modernism in China," 657.
11. Thomas, "Modernism in China," 644.
12. J. Hunter, *To Change the World*, 38.

is most concentrated. Granovetter explained the "strength of weak ties" in a 1973 article for *The American Journal of Sociology*.[13] Weak ties are important because they link disparate groups of close friends. Hunter and Granovetter argue for the unique power of social networks. I combined their theories, borrowing key ideas to apply to my archival findings. In so doing, the impact of Union comes to light.

Union graduates formed a dense social network in the years of Republican China. The seminary linked Shanghai and New York, connecting ambitious Chinese and powerful Americans. This Sino-American network worked bidirectionally, East to West and West to East. Chinese Christians gained access to a powerful social network of liberal Protestants. Likewise, these Americans formed ties with a network of Chinese Christian leaders who would shape China. Together the group formed a robust relational network that extended beyond pastors and professors to business leaders and politicians. Union Theological Seminary linked Chinese Christians with its professors, other Union graduates throughout China, and influential Americans. Timothy Tingfang Lew, William Hung, Y. T. Wu, K. H. Ting, and others formed strong and weak ties to men such as Henry Pitney Van Dusen, Harry Emerson Fosdick, Henry R. Luce, and John D. Rockefeller, Jr. In China this social web found clearest expression in the YMCA and the Christians colleges. Union's Chinese alumni rose to positions of prominence in China where they influenced the church and the state. In the following review of Chinese students who attended Union, I hope to reiterate the depth and interconnectedness of the seminary's social network in China.

## Timothy Tingfang Lew (Union, 1915–17)

Union's first Chinese student was Timothy Tingfang Lew. Like many other prominent Christians who attended Union, Lew grew up in a Christian family and studied at a Christian school in China. Between 1915 and 1920 he obtained degrees from Columbia University, Teachers College, and Yale Divinity School. He studied at Union for two years but transferred to Yale, where he graduated in 1918. While finishing his PhD at Teachers College, Lew taught at Union. He returned to China to teach in Beijing. Eventually he became dean of Yenching's School of Religion and assistant to the chancellor. In 1922 Lew and four other Union graduates helped establish

13. Granovetter, "Strength of Weak Ties" (1973).

Yenching's Life Fellowship. Lew founded and edited the group's influential periodical *Truth and Life*. His influence extended far beyond Beijing's classrooms. In 1925 he helped conduct the Christian funeral service for Sun Yat-sen in Beijing. Lew became a member of the KMT's legislative Yuan in the 1930s. Lew returned to Union in 1927 for a one-year teaching assignment in which he taught on principles of indigenization. Lew's network at Union gave him access to church leaders in Manhattan and other powerful Americans, such as Harry Emerson Fosdick and John D. Rockefeller, Jr. In 1926 Lew kept a list of Union alumni in China. The list represents Union's dense social network in the SFPE. It contained 101 names, including William Hung.[14]

## William Hung (Union, 1917–20)

William Hung studied at Union Seminary from 1917 to 1920. Hung met Timothy Tingfang Lew in 1916. Lew encouraged him to come to New York to pursue his two academic passions: history at Columbia and theology at Union. Two professors at Columbia and one at Union, who were all trained in Germany, transformed Hung's theological and historical methodology, as I described in the preceding chapter. Before returning to China, William Hung joined Henry Luce in traveling across the US to raise fund for Yenching University.[15] Hung's fundraising efforts with Luce deepened his connections to a matrix of wealthy Americans and ambitious Chinese. In 1924 Hung became dean of Yenching's College of Arts and Sciences. Hung, Lew, and Yenching's president, J. Leighton Stuart, became a triumvirate that ran the university throughout the 1920s. Hung's biographer contends that his leadership allowed Yenching to emerge from "an obscure college run by Western millionaires to a nationally recognized Chinese university that participated fully in the intellectual life of China."[16] Other Union graduates had vital roles in the SFPE and later in the Three-Self movement.

14. MRL 6: Timothy Tingfang Lew Papers, ser. 3, box 1, folder 13, Burke Library, Union Theological Seminary, NY. See Appendix F.

15. Luce's son founded *Time* magazine and became one of the most influential men in America. In 1936 Henry R. Luce founded the Henry Luce Foundation to honor his missionary parents. When he died in 1967, much of his fortune, estimated to be worth $100 million, went to this foundation. Today, it is one of the world's most important foundations in funding Asian studies.

16. Egan, *Latterday Confucian*, 110.

## Y. T. Wu (Union, 1924–27 and 1937–38)

Y. T. Wu studied at Union from 1924 to 1927 and again from 1937 to 1938. In 1924 when Wu first applied to the seminary, two of his three letters of reference came from Yenching professors who were Union alumni. A deep and interconnected social web appears again and again in Union's relationship with Chinese Christianity. In his 1936 application to return to Union, Wu explained the school's impact on him during a formative time. The seminary, he wrote, "really opened my eyes to the meaning and truth of religion in those years when I was initiated into Christian work." He hoped to return in 1937 to "come into contact again with the prominent minds and spirits which Union so helpfully offers."[17] Regardless of one's assessment of Wu, his immense role in twentieth-century Chinese Protestantism cannot be denied. In the 1920s/30s he held key positions in the Chinese YMCA, where he influenced generations of young minds across China. Wu spearheaded the creation of the Three-Self Patriotic Movement. For this he is both respected and reviled. For his close alliance with the Communist government, some Christians brand him as a heretic or an anti-Christ. In 1971 Lee Ming Ng aptly described Y. T. Wu as the "most controversial" and "least understood" of Chinese Christian leaders in modern China.[18] Wu's collusion with the CCP resulted from his views of Christianity. Union played no small role in imparting to Wu a hermeneutical framework, the theological and philosophical tools to do theology.

## K. H. Ting (Union, 1947–48)

In the 1930s Y. T. Wu posed a question to university students in Shanghai: "Is it enough for Christians to be concerned only with personal salvation, or should Christians be concerned about social reform?"[19] Wu challenged young Chinese Christians to bring the "whole Gospel of Jesus"—the personal and social gospel, the gospel of peace and revolution—to play into a pivotal time in China's history. This question transfixed K. H. Ting, who was studying theology at St. John's University. Ting grew up in a Christian family in Shanghai and attended St. Peter's Church where a popular priest,

17. Letter from Y. T. Wu to Daniel J. Fleming, August 27, 1936. Series 10A: 4. Folder 10, Burke Library, Union Theological Seminary, NY.

18. L. Ng, "Christianity and Social Change," 174.

19. K. Ting, *God Is Love*, 486.

Dong Jianwu, was a secret member of the Communist Party. As Philip Wickeri rightly points out, St. Peter's foreshadowed Ting's future career with its Communist sympathies, Christian piety, liberal theology, and commitment to self-government, self-propagation, and self-support.[20] Ting followed in Wu's footsteps in working with the YMCA, attending Union Seminary, and returning to China to help lead the TSPM. Ting had every reason to be a persona non grata after the establishment of the People's Republic of China on October 1, 1949: as a graduate of St. John's he was culturally alienated from traditional China and as an alumnus of Union Seminary he was connected with China's enemy, the United States. Despite these concerns Ting fought hard to return to China. He soon found a personal audience with the second most powerful man in China, Zhou Enlai. Historically, how are we to understand Zhou's willingness to meet with Wu and Ting? Would it not have been easier and more consistent with Communist ideology for the CCP to simply snuff out Christianity in new China? The answer, once again, lies in the dense social network in the SFPE. A former Union student helped connect Wu and Ting with Zhou: Gong Pusheng.

## Gong Pusheng (Union, 1941–42)

After graduating from Yenching University in the 1930s, Gong Pusheng joined the Chinese Communist Party.[21] In 1939 she met Zhou Enlai. Zhou told her: "You should go to America where you can tell the whole world about the Chinese people's war against Japan's invasion and win international support and sympathy. You need to make friends there and learn more about America."[22] Gong traveled to New York where she enrolled at Columbia and Union. Before finishing her MA in religion, she met Eleanor Roosevelt, Pearl Buck, and other well-known Americans. Gong embodies the elite network of Chinese students at Union who were connected to prominent people in both China and America. It was Gong who introduced K. H. Ting to his wife Siu-may Kuo. She also provided Wu and Ting with a direct link to Zhou Enlai and the corridors of power in Communist China.

Ting noted that Wu and other Christian leaders met with Zhou several times in 1950 for "earnest discussions during which he warmly praised the

20. Wickeri, *Reconstructing Christianity in China*, 25.

21. Gong's sister, Gong Peng, also graduated from Yenching, joined the CCP, and went on to a prominent role there.

22. *Jianghuai Morning News*, "Gong Pusheng."

Three-Self principle Christians had raised in the past."[23] The social network represented by Chinese Christians was simply too powerful and too connected internationally for the CCP to wipe out Chinese Christianity. Zhou used Wu to garner support for the CCP among Chinese Christians; Wu used Zhou to create an indigenous Chinese church, the Three-Self Patriotic Movement. Wu and Ting would ensure that the TSPM adhered to United Front ideology; Zhou would provide political cover for the TSPM, no easy feat under the capricious Mao Zedong. The Chinese Christians who attended Union were an ambitious group who recognized the benefits and power of working collectively. They not only helped lead institutions and organizations in China but they also formed secret societies and associations in America.

## CCH and CSCA

In 1917 Lew and Hung helped establish the Cross and Sword secret society in New York. Modeling themselves after the Jesuits, the founding members pledged to secrecy and to the motto: "We Unite for the Uplift of China." As the society grew, it soon contained men who would have prominent roles in the education, finance, and politics of Republican China. In 1918 a Cands member divulged the existence of another secret society of Chinese Christians in the America. David and Jonathan had formed in 1907 with the exact same motto. The two societies merged to form the Association for Accomplishing Ideals (*Cheng Zhi Hui* or CCH). The association had 270 members by 1936. Chinese Christians in Republican China instinctively organized into dense, organized social networks. The Chinese Students' Christian Association (CSCA) serves as another example. Founded in 1909, the CSCA acted as the Student Christian Movement for Chinese students at American colleges. The association was not a secret. But like the CCH its ranks included Chinese Christians with great social power. Filled with ambition, CSCA's members intended to play prominent roles in China's future development. Members of the CCH and CSCA formed a dense social network in Republican China. These organizations testify to the ambition and interconnectedness of Chinese Christians in America. Columbia University played a key role for Chinese Christians entering politics and business; Teachers College, education; and Union Seminary,

23. K. Ting, *God Is Love*, 490.

religious work. These three schools made Morningside Heights the hub of not only the SFPE but of much of Sino-American relations.

Union provided social connections like no other seminary in world. Chinese Christians in this social network had influence in the corridors of power. Andrew Y. Y. Tsu, who served as executive secretary of the CSCA, demonstrates this point in his relationship with China's highest leaders. After studying in New York, Tsu went on to prominent roles in the Christian colleges, in the Episcopal Church in China, and in the Nationalist government. On September 2, 1938, Madame Chiang Kai-shek wrote Tsu to thank him for the two prayer books that he had sent her husband, the generalissimo. She makes it clear that the Nationalist government wanted and needed the support of Chinese Christian leaders: "We need men like you to support the Government and to inspire confidence of the public both at home and abroad."[24] Chinese Christians affiliated with Union had access to power beyond the church into the academy, business world, and the state in both Republican and Communist China. As I explain in chapter 8, by 1948 four of the nine members of the CSCA's National Committee were members of the CCP.[25] Many of these leaders rose to positions of prominence in Communist China. Union's greatest impact on Chinese Christianity was relationally, through the network just described. But the school also influenced Chinese Protestantism theologically.

## Union's Theological Impact

Union Theological Seminary embraced a theology shaped by modernity. Many Union professors had studied in German universities, where scholars had transformed theology in the nineteenth century. Historical criticism sought to understand the Bible's primitive meaning in its original historical context. At the University of Tübingen, Bauer and Strauss offered a novel and skeptical approach to the study of the New Testament. *In the Life of Jesus Critically Examined* (1835), Strauss argued that the gospels were legends. The search for the "historical Jesus" began. Eventually Christian belief was reconstructed in response to contemporary culture. Union professors became a key voice of theological modernity, transmitting what they had learned in Tübingen, Halle, and Berlin throughout the United States. They

24. RG 275, box 1, folder 6, archives of the Episcopal Church, Austin, TX. Reprinted by permission.

25. Zhao, "Chinese Communist Party."

embraced modernism and dismissed fundamentalism. Union's international students learned an adaptive Christianity that could be changed in and through their home cultures. Union not only connected Chinese and American Christians, it also equipped them with an ecumenical faith and adaptable theology.

Chinese graduates of Union varied in their response to what they learned there. Some students, like William Hung, embraced Union's theological framework. They learned to distrust Christian dogma and adopted theological liberalism. Other Chinese students, such as the famed evangelist John Sung, rejected Union's theology.[26] The final group of Union graduates from China, such as Y. T. Wu and K. H. Ting, did not acknowledge Union's influence. Their silence on this matter is intriguing. Post-1949 political factors seemed to mitigate against them ever describing how their time at Union impacted their lives, careers, and theology. Doing so would have discredited them and perhaps done great harm to their careers in the TSPM. It is possible that Wu and Ting failed to appreciate the depth and importance of this Union-saturated network. However, given their political astuteness, it is more likely they refrained from discussing it due to the strong connections between liberal Protestants in America and the KMT. Union's accommodating theological framework enabled Wu and Ting to adapt Christianity to the CCP's United Front ideology. From Union directly and from institutions influenced by Union, such as the YMCA, Ting and Wu absorbed a theology that conversed with culture. They reconstructed Christian belief to adhere with the ideas and dictates of the CCP. Does this make them traitors to the Christian faith?

Some Christians say yes; others, no. I believe the answer depends on which Christianity you are referring to. If your Christianity seeks final authority in the Bible as the inspired word of God and adheres to orthodox Christian faith, the answer is probably affirmative. Jonathan Chao viewed Ting as "an unreconstructed liberal who was promoting theological reconstruction as the agenda of the Chinese Communist Party." Lin Xinyuan argues that Ting's cosmic Christology is simply a liberal universalism that "changes the gospel and confuses the truth."[27] But if your theology is more aligned to that of Union Seminary, seeking to adapt Christian dogma to

26. The events surrounding Sung's admission to the Bloomingdale asylum differ from how he later remembered them. However, the historical verdict stands that Sung rejected Union's liberal theology and Union scorned Sung's conservative theology.

27. Ruokanen, "K. H. Ting's Contribution," 110.

current philosophical and scientific trends, the answer might be no. In this latter case K. H. Ting is a hero of sorts. One of K. H. Ting's theological defenders in the West is Miikka Ruokanen, a theology professor at the University of Helsinki. Ruokanen acknowledges the criticism leveled against Ting but believes that such critique is based on an insufficient understanding of his theology. He attempts to illuminate Ting's "authentic intentions" in reconstructing Chinese theology.[28] Ting's reconstruction efforts aim to broaden the narrow and escapist theology of evangelical Christianity with insight from modern theologians. Ting has introduced theological ideas that are "widely accepted as legitimate expressions of Christian faith in the West" but are "in many ways in tension with the conservative revivalist and Evangelical ethos of Chinese Protestantism."[29] Wu and Ting consciously and unconsciously relied on non-Chinese sources to do theology. Their theological voices were far more informed by Alfred North Whitehead, Pierre Teilhard de Chardin, Harry Ward, Paul Tillich, and Harry Emerson Fosdick than they admitted.

Ultimately what Chinese Christians learned at Union, whether they admitted it or not, was how to adapt Christianity. Some Chinese Christians learned this lesson as students at Union. But others absorbed it before arriving in New York through Union-influenced organizations like the YMCA and Christian colleges in China. Ruokanen correctly notes that Ting's theological reconstruction relies on ideas from well-known Western theologians. Note the irony here. Ting defends the indigeneity of the TSPM but also introduces ideas from Western theologians. Xu Yihua describes this irony well:

> Leading the TSPM in its attacks against the church groups were, for the most part, former YMCA secretaries and St John's graduates. Herein lies another great irony. Although the TSPM leader found justification for their primarily in the rhetoric of anti-foreign nationalism, they themselves, more than any other elements within China's Protestant establishment, were products of Western institutions, particularly in education. Their eagerness to collaborate with China's Communist Party was in large measure a product of their liberal theological training and experience in social activism

28. One might ask what gives Ruokanen access to Ting's "authentic intentions" that other scholars do not have. Perhaps, other readers do understand Ting's intent and simply disagree.

29. Ruokanen, "K. H. Ting's Contribution," 111.

> they received in the YMCA, the Union Theological Seminary, and the Episcopal Church.[30]

K. H. Ting blasted the Beijing pastor Wang Mingdao for his refusal to join the indigenous TSPM. But it was Ting, not Wang, who was the product of the YMCA, St. John's University, and Union Seminary. In 1928 Wang wrote a diatribe against the YMCA, castigating it as a prime example of adulterated Christianity. The Y abandoned the gospel of salvation and replaced it with a modern substitute of "improving character, promoting mass education, reforming society, and serving the people." Wang insisted that China's problems came "entirely from sin" and that liberal social reform was "fake medicine."[31] China's hope lay not in social reform, in Western modernizations, nor in Communism but in individual repentance and acceptance of Jesus. Wang Mingdao epitomized the fundamentalism that Ting despised. Yet Wang's Beijing church was self-supporting, self-governing, and self-propagating, and his theology was not learned from any Western seminary. The irony is striking.

## Avenues for Future Research

To explain how Union Seminary impacted Chinese Christianity, I relied on primary historical data but I utilized an interdisciplinary approach that straddled the fields of history, theology, education, and sociology. One might fault it for being too broad but this view has allowed me to offer unique insight. Admittedly more focused and narrow research remains to be done. I foresee several avenues for future research.

1. *Studying the precise nature of Union's theological impact on individual Chinese Christians.* My research on Union's theological impact on Chinese Christians in chapter 9 merely surveyed the topic. Deeper study is needed on this topic. This would entail a more careful analysis of key thinkers at Union, such as Tillich, Niebuhr, and Fosdick, that could then be contrasted to the theology of Lew, Wu, Ting or other Chinese Christians who attended Union.
2. *Examining all of K. H. Ting's writings.* In the case of K. H. Ting a more detailed analysis should utilize all of his writings, not just those in the

30. Y. Xu, "'Patriotic' Protestants," 119.
31. Wang, "Eshizhong de husheng," 202. Cited in Xi, *Redeemed by Fire*, 120.

two English compilations that I utilized (*God Is Love* and *No Longer Strangers*). It is a weakness of this present study that I limited myself to these two English compilations to analyze Ting's theology; however, given the scope of research, this limitation seemed prudent. Since Ting died in 2012, now is an opportune time for research related to his life and theology.

3. *Investigating Union's role in the indigenization of Chinese Christianity.* A key theme throughout this study has been the challenge of indigenization: how "Christianity in China" struggled to become "Chinese Christianity." Christianity has become indigenous in recent decades. What role, if any, has Union played in that process? I touched on this question but hope to answer it more fully in future publications.

4. *Assessing Union Seminary's impact on Sino-American relations.* This book has focused on Union's impact on Chinese Christianity. But my archival findings unearthed important documents that go beyond religion in China. What impact did the network surrounding Union have on Sino-American geopolitics before, during, and after World War II? This question and others like it merit further study.

5. *Utilizing transnational history to study Union.* Transnational history examines the movement of people, ideas, technologies, and institutions across national boundaries. It differentiates from globalization and comparative history, seeing the former as too unidirectional and the latter, as too static in its view of nations. The transnational history method seeks to explain nations in terms of cross-national influences. Ian Tyrrell argues that formal empire is imbedded in transnational networks rather than vice versa.[32] Further study could bring sharper focus into our understanding of the role Union Seminary played in transnational history.

6. *Employing the combined ideas of Hunter and Granovetter in other fields.* I borrowed and combined the theories of Hunter and Granovetter. Could combining the ideas of "dense social networks" and "the strength of weak ties" lead to new insight in other areas of historical research? Union Seminary sat at the center of a dense social network of Chinese and American Christian between 1911 and 1949. But many other institutions could be studied for their influence in other realms at other times. I imagine a sociologist who could provide a

32. Tyrrell, *Reforming the World*, 5. See also Tyrrell, "What is Transnational History?"

more rigid and quantitative approach to utilizing these combined theories. I merely touch on their theories. More work can and should be done here.

I look forward to future research that will continue to explore Union's impact on China before and after 1949, be it from me personally or other scholars.

## Final Thoughts

A plaque next to the Van Dusen Gate at Union's entrance declares, "Through this gate let the world come to Union and Union go into the world." The seminary certainly fulfilled this goal in China in the twentieth century. Like an iceberg, some of Union Theological Seminary's influence has been above the surface and visible. This manifested itself in the number of Union alumni serving as missionaries in China, Chinese Christians who studied at Union, and through the publications and visits of Union faculty. But much of Union's impact has been below the surface and unseen, until now. The school exported progressive Christianity to the Middle Kingdom through a dense social network of American and Chinese Christians. Union Seminary liberalized Christianity in twentieth-century China through the Chinese Christian colleges, the Chinese YMCA, and the Three-Self Patriotic Movement.

# Appendix A

## Prominent Chinese Names in Publication

| Name (Alternate) | 汉字 | Years | Role/Affiliation |
|---|---|---|---|
| Chao, T. C. (Zhao Zichen) | 赵紫宸 | 1888–1979 | Yenching theology professor |
| Chen Duxiu | 陈独秀 | 1879–1942 | Co-founder of P. R. China |
| Cheng, C. Y. (Cheng Jingyi) | 誠静怡 | 1881–1939 | Prominent pastor |
| Chiang Kai-shek (Jiang Zhong Cheng) | 蔣中正 | 1887–1975 | ROC premier & generalis-simo |
| Cixi (Tz'u-his) | 慈禧 | 1835–1908 | Empress dowager |
| Confucius (Kongzi) | 孔子 | 551–479 BC | Philosopher |
| Ding Chufan (Chu Van Ding) | 丁楚范, | 1884–1963 | Ting's father |
| Dong Jianwu (H. C. Tung) | 董 健吾 | | St. Peter's priest |
| Gong Peng (Kung Peng) | 龚澎 | 1914–70 | Yenching; CCP leader |
| Gong Pusheng (Kung Pu-sheng) | 龚普生 | 1913–2007 | Yenching; CCP leader |

| Name (Alternate) | 汉字 | Years | Role/Affiliation |
|---|---|---|---|
| Hong Xiuquan (Hung Hsiu-chuan) | 洪秀全 | 1814–1864 | Taiping leader |
| Hu Shih (Hu Shi) | 胡适 | 1891–1962 | Philosopher |
| Huie, Caroline | | 1897–1970 | Tsu's wife |
| Huie Kin (Xu Qin) | 许芹 | 1854–1934 | New York City pastor |
| Hung, William (Hong Ye) | 洪业 | 1893–1980 | Yenching professor |
| Hsu, P. C. (Xu Baoqian) | 徐寶谦 | 1892–1944 | Life Fellowship founder |
| Kuo, Siu-may (Gong Xiumei) | 郭秀梅 | 1916–95 | K. H. Ting's wife |
| Liang Qichao (Liang Ch'i-ch'ao) | 梁启超 | 1873–1929 | Poet & writer |
| Lew, Timothy Tingfang (Liu Tingfang) | 劉廷芳 | 1892–1947 | Yenching professor |
| Li Jinglan (Li Lizi) | 李静栏 | 1886–1986 | Ting's mother |
| Li, K. C. (Li Jiaqing) | 李嘉青 | | Ting's grandfather |
| Lin, Paul T. K. (Lin Ta Kuang) | 林达光 | 1920–2004 | CCSA general secretary |
| Lu Xun (Zhou Shuren's penname) | 鲁迅 | 1881–1936 | Writer |
| Hung, William (Hung Ye) | 洪业 | 1893–1980 | Yenching professor |

| Name (Alternate) | 汉字 | Years | Role/Affiliation |
|---|---|---|---|
| Mao Zedong (Mao Tse-tung) | 毛泽东 | 1893–1976 | Chairman of PRC |
| Mozi (Mo Tzu) | 墨子 | 470–391 BC | Philosopher |
| Pu Huaren (Paul H. J. Poo) | 浦化人 | | St. Peter's priest |
| Song, Meiling (Soong May-ling) | 宋美齡 | 1898–2003 | Chiang's wife |
| Soong, T. V. (Song Ziwen) | 宋子文 | 1891–1971 | Financier & ROC politician |
| Sung, John (Song Shangjie) | 宋尚節 | 1901–44 | Evangelist |
| Ting, K. H. (Ding Guangxun) | 丁光训 | 1915–2012 | TSPM & CCC leader |
| Ting, Stephen Yenren (Ding Yan Ren) | 丁言仁 | 1948– | K. H. Ting's son |
| Tsu, Andrew Y. Y. (Zhu Yuyue) | 朱友渔 | 1885–1986 | St. John's professor |
| Wang, C. T. (Wang Zhengting) | 王正廷 | 1882–1961 | CSCA founder |
| Wu, Y. T. (Wu Yaozong) | 吴耀宗 | 1893–1979 | TSPM founder |

# Appendix B

## Union Alumni (1900–1950) in Chinese Higher Education

| Name, Union Graduation Year | Position, Department | Years |
|---|---|---|
| **Nanking University (1910, Nanjing)** | | |
| Wilson, Wilbur '02 | Professor | 1896–1927 |
| Griffing, John '13 | Professor of agriculture | 1919–27 |
| Hummel, William '16 | Professor of religious education | 1908–27 |
| Hamilton, Clarence '21 | Professor of philosophy & psychology | 1914–27 |
| Marx, Edwin '26 | Professor of English | 1918–22 |
| Jones, Francis '30 | Professor | 1930–37 |
| Riggs, Charles '31 | Professor of agricultural engineering | 1932–44, 1946–47 |
| Young, John '35 | Director of religious education | 1930–34 |
| **Ginling College (1913, Nanjing)** | | |
| Graves, Stella '30 | Teacher | 1934–37, 1946–48 |

| Name, Union Graduation Year | Position, Department | Years |
|---|---|---|
| **Yenching University (1912, Beijing)** *(including Yenching School of Religion)* | | |
| Winans, Edward 1919 | Professor | 1914–18 |
| Porter, Lucius 1908 | Professor & dean of philosophy | 1918–22, 1947–49 |
| Burgess, John 1909 | Professor & chair of sociology | 1919–29 |
| Hung, William 1920 | Professor of history | 1922–28 |
| Mead, Lawrence 1913 | Professor of English | 1928–39 |
| Smith, Emest 1916 | Professor | 1929–43 |
| Hung, William 1919 | Dean of College of Arts | 1924–27 |
| Cheng, Andrew Chih-yi 1924 | Professor of New Testament | 1927–33 |
| **University of Shanghai (1906, Shanghai)** | | |
| Wilcox, Floyd 1913 | Professor & dean of education | 1926–28 |
| Hipps, John 1921 | Professor & chair of religious studies | 1935–41, 1945–49 |
| Carver, George 1938 | Professor & head of English | 1931–41 |
| **St John's University (1879, Shanghai)** | | |
| Roberts, William 1912 | Teacher & college pastor | 1914–23 |
| Tsu, Yu-yue 1921 | Professor of sociology & chaplain | 1912–20, 1935–37 |
| Ting, K. H. 1948 | Lecturer of religion | 1942–46 |

| Name, Union Graduation Year | Position, Department | Years |
|---|---|---|
| **Canton Union Theological Seminary (1888, Guangzhou)** *(Lingnan University)* | | |
| Henry, James '07 | Professor, president, & provost | 1909–48 |
| Sboop, Charles '18 | Professor of religious education | 1918–38 |
| Len, Paul Yuey '30 | Professor of sociology | 1930–33 |
| Cheng, Andrew Chih-yi '24 | Professor | 1933–34 |
| Chyung, Wai-king Taai '31 | Asst. professor of New Testament & religious education | 1939–43 |
| **Fukien Christian University (1915, Fuzhou)** | | |
| Stowe, Everett '28 | Teacher | 1928–43 |
| Leger, Samuel '16 | Professor of sociology | 1940–44 |
| **Huachung University (1922, Wuhan)** | | |
| Chyung, Wai-king Taai '31 | Professor of education, psychology, & Bible | 1943–45 |
| Fulton, Robert '38 | Asst. professor | 1947–50 |
| **West China Union University (1910, Chengdu)** | | |
| Starrett, Oscar '22 | Teacher & administrator | 1931–34 |
| **Cheeloo University (1902, Jinan)** *(Shantung Christian University)* | | |
| Lair, Howell '22 | Professor & associate president | 1915–51 |
| Stanley, Charles '13 | Professor & dean | 1930–41 |

| Name, Union Graduation Year | Position, Department | Years |
|---|---|---|
| Cady, Lyman 1923 | Professor of religion & Christian ethics | 1920–38 |

**Soochow University (1911, Suzhou)**

| | | |
|---|---|---|
| Heam, Walter 1923 | Professor of religion & religious education | 1923–27 |
| Williams, Melville 1936 | Associate professor of sociology | 1929–40 |

**Hangchow University (1897, Hangzhou)**

| | | |
|---|---|---|
| McMullen, Robert 1936 | Provost | 1932–38 |

# Appendix C

## Top Last Schools Attended in China for Students in American Colleges and Universities, 1854–1953[1]

| School in China | Affiliation | Location | Student# | Degree# |
|---|---|---|---|---|
| Tsing Hua University | Amer. Boxer | Beijing | 1,119 | 906 |
| St. John's University | Protestant | Shanghai | 790 | 569 |
| Central University | Protestant | Wuhan | 744 | 518 |
| Chiaotung University | Chinese govt. | Shanghai | 571 | 391 |
| Yenching University | Protestant | Beijing | 522 | 362 |
| Lingnan University | Protestant | Guangzhou | 472 | 330 |
| National Peking University | Chinese govt. | Beijing | 431 | 254 |
| University of Nanking | Protestant | Shanghai | 416 | 282 |
| Shanghai College | Protestant | Shanghai | 313 | 212 |
| Fuhtan University | Shanghai | | 265 | 152 |
| Southwest Associated | Chinese govt. | Kunming | 228 | 137 |

1. Data from *Survey of Chinese Students*, 25, 36–37, 51–52. Tabulated in Bieler, *"Patriots" or "Traitors,"* Appendix D, 381.

## TOP LAST SCHOOLS ATTENDED IN CHINA

| School in China | Affiliation | Location | Student# | Degree# |
|---|---|---|---|---|
| Soochow University | Protestant | Suzhou | 220 | 148 |
| Chung Shan University | Chinese govt. | Guangzhou | 219 | 121 |
| Ginling College | Protestant | Nanjing | 196 | 127 |
| Chekiang University | Chinese govt. | Zhejiang | 178 | 122 |
| Wuhan University | Chinese govt. | Wuhan | 145 | 96 |
| Nankai University | Chinese priv. | Nanjing | 135 | 95 |
| Normal University | Chinese govt. | Beijing | 128 | 92 |
| Political Science University | | | 118 | 67 |
| Peiping Catholic University | Catholic | Beijing | 115 | 89 |
| Fukien Christian University | Protestant | Fuzhou | 114 | 77 |
| Utopia University | | | 108 | 52 |
| Peiyang Engineer. Coll. | Chinese govt. | Tianjin | 99 | 73 |
| Kwanghua University | Shanghai | | 91 | 41 |
| Hua Ching University | Protestant | Wuchang | 90 | 63 |
| TOTAL | | | 7,827 | 5,376 |

| | |
|---|---|
| Number of alumni from Chinese Christian colleges in US | 3,877 (49.5%) |
| Number of alumni from Chinese govt. univ. in US | 2,299 (29.4%) |
| Number of US degrees to alumni of Christian colleges | 2,688 (50.0%) |
| Number of US degrees to alumni of Chinese govt. univ. | 1,286 (23.9%) |

# Appendix D

## American Colleges and Universities Granting Degrees to Chinese Students, 1854–1953[1]

| College/University | Total Number of Degrees[2] |
|---|---|
| Columbia University | 1,834 |
| University of Michigan | 1,300 |
| Massachusetts Institute of Technology | 734 |
| Harvard University | 647 |
| University of Illinois | 603 |
| New York University | 596 |
| University of Pennsylvania | 511 |
| University of Chicago | 463 |
| Cornell University | 387 |
| University of Minnesota | 366 |

1. Data from *Survey of Chinese Students*, 40–50. Tabulated in Bieler, *"Patriots" or "Traitors,"* Appendix G, 382.

2. In total 366 colleges and universities are listed in the survey. The total number of degrees is 13,797: 4,590 BA; 7,221 MA; 1,727 PhDs; 33 honorary degrees; 104 certifications and diplomas; and 122 other.

| College/University | Total Number of Degrees[2] |
|---|---|
| University of Washington | 306 |
| Ohio State University | 283 |
| University of California | 269 |
| Stanford University | 265 |
| University of Southern California | 175 |
| Northwestern | 168 |
| Iowa State Agricultural | 145 |
| Oberlin | 135 |
| Iowa State University | 116 |
| University of Missouri | 110 |
| California Institute of Technology | 91 |
| University of Colorado | 90 |
| Boston University | 88 |
| Oregon State University | 83 |
| Princeton University | 82 |
| Purdue University | 82 |

# Appendix E

## Luce Dinner for Churchill

DINNER IN HONOR OF The Right Honorable Winston S. Churchill, O. M., C. H., M. P., given by Mr. Henry R. Luce on Friday, the twenty-fifth of March, nineteen hundred and forty-nine, at the Ritz Carlton New York[1]

| THE HEAD TABLE | TABLE 2 |
|---|---|
| Bernard Baruch<br>John J. McCloy<br>Francis Cardinal Spellman<br>Sir Oliver Francis<br>Governor Thomas E. Dewey<br>Henry R. Luce<br>Winston S. Churchill<br>Charles E. Wilson<br>Laurence A. Steinhardt<br>Russell C. Leffingwell<br>Governor Alfred E. Driscoll<br>Dr. George A. Buttrick | Theodore L. Bates<br>John A. Coleman<br>James A. Farley<br>John Farrar<br>Malcolm Forbes<br>George L. Harrison<br>Thomas S. Lamont<br>Samuel W. Meek<br>Iva Patcevitch<br>Thomas J. Ross |
| **TABLE 3** | **TABLE 4** |
| Frederick Lewis Allen<br>Chester I. Barnard<br>Alexander Brackenridge<br>Thomas D'Arcy Brophy<br>Allen W. Dulles<br>Curt E. Forstnern<br>C. D. Jackson<br>Dr. Robert L. Johnson<br>Carleton H. Palmer<br>Robert R. Young | Frank W. Abrams<br>Hamilton Fish Armstrong<br>Gen. William J. Donovan<br>James H. S. Ellis<br>Dr. Harry Gideonse<br>John F. Kennedy<br>H. H. S. Phillips, Jr.<br>Vincent Riggio<br>Harold V. Smith<br>Dr. Paul A. Wolfe |

1. Eugene E. Barnett Collection, box 14 (1948–49), folder 1949, Rare Book and Manuscript Library, Columbia University in the City of New York.

| TABLE 5 | TABLE 6 |
|---|---|
| Ned E. Depinet | Gen. Julius Ochs Adler |
| Gen. James H. Doolittle | Allen Billingsley |
| Ferdinand Eberstadt | George T. Christopher |
| John H. Hancock | Allen Grover |
| Marlon Harper, Jr. | Robert Lyon Hamill |
| Thomas J. Hargrave | Arthur W. McCain |
| Paul V. McNutt | Irving S. Olds |
| Torkild Rieber | David O. Selanick |
| Dr. Ralph W. Sockman | Dr. Philip Young |
| Charles L. Stillman | |

| TABLE 7 | TABLE 8 |
|---|---|
| Dr. John Sutherland Bonnell | Eugene E. Barnett |
| Dr. Harry Woodburn Chase | James F. Brownlee |
| Reginald O. Coombe | W. Randolph Burgess |
| J. L. Johnston | Bernard F. Gimbel |
| James M. Mathes | Roy Howard |
| Charles B. McCabe | Gerald M. Lauck |
| Edward J. Noble | Barry T. Leithead |
| Fairfield Osborn | James A. Linen |
| Francis DeWitt Pratt | Paul M. Mazur |
| | Theodore G. Montague |

| TABLE 9 | TABLE 10 |
|---|---|
| Hugh Baillie | Frederick H. Bedford, Jr. |
| J. Stewart Baker | Francis Brenan |
| Bart Bydorn | Clay Buckbout |
| Austin S. Igleheart | Bertran B. Geyer |
| William Harding Jackson | James Hill, Jr. |
| Chester LaRoche | James L. Madden |
| Dr. Robert J. McCracken | Geoffrey Parsons |
| James D. Mooney | Dr. Willard Cole Rappleye |
| Earl Newsom | Raymond Rubican |
| Edward V. Rickenbacker | Herbert Bayard Swope |

| **TABLE 11** | **TABLE 12** |
|---|---|
| Bernard Barnes | Winthrop W. Aldrich |
| Robert A. Chambers | Sen. Raymond E. Baldwin |
| Gardner Cowles, Jr. | John W. Davis |
| Roy K. Ferguson | Charles Dollard |
| Walker Howing | Charles Edison |
| Edwin L. James | Roy Larsen |
| Eric Johnston | Father Laurence J. McGinley |
| Prof. Allan Nevins | Stanley Resor |
| F. B. Ryan, Jr. | Gen. David Sarnoff |
| Philip C. Smith | Robert W. Woodruff |

| **TABLE 14** | **TABLE 15** |
|---|---|
| Arthur A. Ballantine | Morris Hadley |
| Herbert Brownell, Jr. | William R. Herod |
| Wallace K. Harrison | Henry Luce III |
| Harrison K. McCann | Thomas S. Matthews |
| P. L. Prentice | Joel S. Mitchell |
| D. Kimtpon Rogers | Dr. Reinhold Niebuhr |
| Dr. George N. Shuster | Alan M. Scaife |
| Capt. Christopher Boamen | Myron C. Taylor |
| Sir T. Ashley Sparks | Sir William Wiseman |

| **TABLE 16** | **TABLE 17** |
|---|---|
| John S. Billings | Lord Camrose |
| Stuart M. Crocker | John Foster Dulles |
| Clarence Francis | Andrew Heinkell |
| N. Baxter Jackson | Herbert A. Kent |
| Admiral Tomas C. Kinkaid | Nelson A. Rockefeller |
| Louis B. Mayer | Clarence Strait |
| Sen. Brian McMahon | George C. Waldo |
| Robert Sherwood | Thomas J. Watson, Jr. |
| Ward Wheelock | Maj. Gen. Roscoe B. Woodruff |

| | |
|---|---|
| **TABLE 18**<br>John E. Bierwirth<br>Robert C. Clothier<br>Rear Admiral Walter S. De Lany<br>Richard de Rochemont<br>John W. Hanes<br>Amory Houghton<br>Paul Lockwood<br>Whitelaw Ried<br>W. Dickinson Wilson | **TABLE 19**<br>Ken Cooper<br>Clarence Dillon<br>Dr. Frank D. Frankenthal<br>Maurice T. Moore<br>Charles S. Munson<br>Dr. J. Robert Oppenheimer<br>William S. Paley<br>Winthrop Rockefeller<br>Bishop Henry K. Sherrill<br>Thomas J. Watson |
| **TABLE 20**<br>F. Abbot Goodhue<br>William T. Griffin<br>Sen. Robert C. Hendrickson<br>Rovert Lehman<br>Peter Paul Luce<br>Malcom Muir<br>Philip D. Reed<br>Beverly Randolph Robinson<br>Carrol M. Shanks<br>Joseph J. Thorndike, Jr. | **TABLE 21**<br>Luis de Flores<br>Father Robert I. Garmon<br>Daniel Longwell<br>Charles Marz<br>Gerard Swope<br>Francis Henry Taylor<br>Juan T. Trippe<br>Dr. Henry P. Van Dusen<br>Maj. Gen. Robert M. Webster |
| **TABLE 22**<br>William B. Carr<br>Dr. Everett Case<br>Thomas W. Dewart<br>Frederick H. Ecker<br>Artemus L. Gates<br>Gen. Willam H. Harrison<br>William E. Knox<br>Michael A. Morrissey<br>Spyros P. Skouras<br>Jack I. Straus | **TABLE 23**<br>Henry Alexander<br>Howard Black<br>Sir Francis Evans<br>Francis M. Flynn<br>Frank M. Folsom<br>Eberson Foote<br>Morehead Patterson<br>J. Arthur Rank<br>William S. Rodgers<br>Emil Schram |

# Appendix F

## China Alumni Association of Union Theological Seminary

Compiled by Timothy Tingfang Lew, November 1926[1]

**Albertson, Wilford Beaton**; Union 1913–1914 BD; Burser of W C Union Univ

**Anderson, Sidney R.**; Union 1 year; Supt Society Features Moore Church

**Anderson, Olive L.** (Mrs. S R); Union 1 year

**Baxter, Alexander**

**Beach, Frederick Paul**; Fukien Christian University, Foochow; Union 1909–1910 "Graduate"; Prof. Edu. Psych (FCU); Cooperating Gen. Sec. Fukien Christian Board Education

**Boyd, Herbert Alexander**; Union 1910–1912 BD; Canadian Presby; Evangelistic Educational

**Boynton, Charles Luther**; Union 1903–1906; National Christian Council, Shanghai

**Braskamp, Otto**; Union 1920–1921; Ichowfu, Shantung; Evangelistic work- Presby.

**Brown, Homer Grant**; Union 1910–1913 "Graduate"; W. China Union University, Chengtu

**Burgess, John Stewart**; Union 1908–1909; Prof. Soc. Yenching University

**Cady, Lyman Van Law**; Union 1922–1923 STM; Assoc. Prof. Religion and Ethics, Shantung Christian Univeristy, Tsianfu

1. MRL 6: Timothy Tingfang Lew Papers, ser. 3, box 1, folder 13, Burke Library, Union Theological Seminary, NY. List reproduced uncorrected from original with information relevant to thesis; that is, I excluded educational credentials apart from Union.

**Carhart, Charles L.**; Union 1886–1889 "Graduate"; Pastor, Union Church, Pastoral Service for English speaking community, Hankow

**Cartwright, Frank Thomas**; Union 1922–1923; Evangelistic, Editorial, Foochow

**Chandler, Robert E.**; Union 1918–1919; Foreign Gen. Sec. NC Kung Li Hui, Gen. Sec. N C Mission, Edu and Evangelistic in Tientsin, Secretarial N C Kung Li Hui

**Chang, Zeh-ling**; Union 1918–1919; Principal, Lowrie Institute, Shanghai

**Cheng, Andrew C. Y.;** Union 1926–1927

**Cheng, Ching-yi;** Union 1922–1924; National Christian Council, Secretary, Shanghai

**Chow, Tien**; Changsha, Hunan

**Cressy, Earl H**; Union 1917–1918; Sec. E. C. Christian Edu. Association & Sec. for Higher Education in G C E A, Shanghai

**Cross, Rowland M**; Union 1914–1915, 1923–1924 STM; Am. Board; Gen. Sec. of N china Mission Kung Li Hui, Peking

**Davis, W Ward**; Union 1923–1924; Am. Presby. North, Exe. Sec. The Community Guild, Siangtan, Hunan, Institutional Church

**Day, Steward**; Union 1921–1922 BD; Student Pastor Talmage Middle School, Changchow

**Ekeland, T. L.**; Union 1923 BD; Lutheran United Mission, Kwangchow, Honan

**Eyestone, James Bruce**; Union 1920–1921 STMSup. Edu. Work Mingtsing Dist., Principal of Ner Wm Cline Mem Jr. Mid School; Mingtsinghsien, FuFairfield,

**Wynn Cowan**; Union 1st sem 1917–1918; Dean of Oberlin Shansi Mem. School, Taiku, Shansi

**Field, Frank Edson**; Union 1900–4; Presby. Board For. Mis., Prin. Laughlin Academy, Tsining, Shantung

**Fitch, George Ashmore**; Union 1906–1909 "Graduate"; Inter. Committee Y.M.C.A., Gen. Sec. Foreign Y.M.C.A., Shanghai

**Gage, Brownell**; Union; Yale in China Office-Provost, Yale Foreign Mis. Soc., Changsha

**Gleysteen, William Henry**; Union 1900–1904 BD; Presby. Board; Prin. Truth Hall Academy, Peking

**Green, Stephen William**; Union 6 months; Teacher, Prin. Proctor School, Changsha

**Griffing, John B.**; Union 1912–1913; University of Nanking, Head Dept. Cotton Improvement Land & Rural Edu.

**Hayes, Robert M.**; Union 1911–1913; Sec. of S.V.M., Y.M.C.A., Shanghai

**Hearn, Walter Anderson**; Union 1919–23 STB; Prof. Religious Edu., Soochow University

**Henry, James McClure**; Union 1904–1908 BD; President Canton Christian College, Canton

**Henry, Robert Timmons**; Union one term; Kong Hong Institutional Church, Soochow

**Hildreth, Ellison Story**; Union 1907–1909 BFMS; Evangelistic, Chaochow

**Hipps, John Burder**; Union 1920–1921 STM; Prof. Old Testament, Dean Theology Dept Shanghai College, Shanghai

**Holroyd, Ben Edgar**; Union 1916–1917; Prof. English University of Nanking

**Hood, Cooper George**; Union 1908–1911 "Graduate"; Presby., Evangelistic, Nanhsuchow

**Hou, Entang Hsueh-cheng**; Union 1916–1917; Government, Teacher; Pang Chuang, Te Chow, Shantung

**Howe, Edwin C.**; Union 1920–21 BD; Relig. Edu. Union Mid. School, Paak Hok Tung, Canton

**Hsu, Pao-chien**; Union 1921–1924; Prof. Philosophy, Edu. & Religion, Yenching University, Peking

**Hsu, Ti Shan Kough**; Union 1923–1924; Instructor of History of Religion, Yenching University, Peking

**Hu, Samuel Hsueh Cheng**

**Hubbard, Hugh Wells**; Union 1911–1912; Am. Board allocated to Y.M.C.A. work, Student Sec. Y.M.C.A.

**Hummel, William F.**; Union 1915–1916 ME; Teacher, University of Nanking

**Hung, William**; Union 1917–1920 STB; Asso. Prof. History and Dean College of Arts & Sciences, Yenching Univ, Peking

**Hylbert, L. C.**; Teachers Col (NY) 1917–1918; Promotional and Evangelistic, Shanghai

**Innerst, J. B.**; United Brethren Miss., Canton

**Jan, Timothy Y. W.**; Union 1918–1921; Y.M.C.A. Peking

**Johnson, Obed Simon**; Union one semester 1917; Teacher Church History, Union Theol. College, Canton

**Lair, Howell Portman**; Union 1921–1922 STM; Prof. Religion, Teacher of English, Bible, Relig. Educ. History of Relig., Dean of School of Arts and Science, Shantung Christian University, Tsinanfu

**Leete, William Rockwell**; Union 1909–1912 BD; Student Evangelistic Worker, Tientsin

**Leger, Samuel H.**; Union 1913–1914 BD; Teacher Foochow Union Theol. Sem., Foochow

**Lew, Timothy Tingfang**; Union 1915–1919; Dean, Faculty Religion, Yenching University, Peking

**Lin, Homin Leopold**

**Lo, Yii Tang**

**Lo, Shih-chi**; Union 1920–1921; Am. Bapt. North; Exe. Sec, Shantung

**Lobenstine, Edwin Carlyle**; Union 1896–1897; NCC, Secretary, Shanghai

**Luce, Henry Winters**; Union 1892–1894 BD; Presby representative in Yenching Univ; Vice President-Yenching University, Peking

**MacRae, John Donald**; Dean School of Theol., Acting President, Shantung Christian University, Tsinanfu, Shantung

**March, B. F.**; Yenching Univ, Peking

**Mead, Lawrence Myers**; Union 1911–1913; Y.M.C.A.-Edu. Sec., Peking

**Miner, Edwin Demetrius**; Union one year; Fukien Christian University, Foochow

**Morris, DuBois Schanck**; Union ?; Am. Presby; Evangelistic work, Anhwei

**Nance, Walter Buckner**; Union 1903 MES; President Soochow University, Soochow

**Nasmith, Augustus I**; Union 1908–1909; Evangelistic, Hangchow

**Neff, Clarence A.**; Union 1910–1913 "Graduate"; Teaher Soci. Science, Fukien Christian University, Foochow

**Peabody, Stephen C.**; Union 1920–1923 BD; Men's Evangelistic work, Peking

**Porter, Lucius C.**; Union 1907–1908 & 1915–1916; Head Dept. Philosophy, Dean Yenching School of Chinese Studies, Yenching University, Peking

**Preston, Thomas James**; Union 1896–1897 & 1905–1906 BD; Presby Board; President Hunan Union Theol. School, Changsha, Hunan

**Price, Frank Wilson**; Union 1922–1923; Presby South; Prof Relig. Edu., Hangchow Christian College

**Rawlinson, Frank J.**; Union 1925–1926; Am. Board; Editor; Chinese Recorder, Shanghai

**Reid, Gilbert**; Union 1879–1882 BD; Director-in-Chief Inter. Institute of China, East Imperial City, Peking

**Reumann, Otto G.**; Union 1914–1916; Am. Board; Relig. Education, Foochow

**Roberts, William Payne**; Union 1911–1912 ACM; Nanking

**Robinson, Harold W.**; Union 1916 "Graduate"; Am. Board; Studetn work, Paotingfu

**Scheufler, Karl Wm.**; M.E.; Yenpng, Fu

**Sears, Laurance M.**; Union 1920–1923; Princeton in Peking; Student work Sec. Y.M.C.A., Peking

**Scott, Roderick**; Union 1922–1923; Dean and Prof. Fukien Christian University, Foochow

**Shaw, Ernest Thornton**; Union 1915–1916, 1926; Co-operator in Relig Edu., Peking

**Shoop, Charles Wilson**; Union 1917–1918; For. Mis. Soc. U.B. in Christ; Supt. United Brethren Mis., Canton

**Simkin, Robert Louis**; Union 1903–1906, 1914–1915 BD; Teacher Relig. W China Union University; Principal Union Bible School at WCUU, Chengtu, Sze

**Sites, Mrs. Evelyn Worthem**; Union 1917–1918 MEN; Evangelistic; Foochow

**Smith, Ernest Ketcham**; Union 1915–1916; Chinese Government; Prof. English, Tsing Hun College, Peking

**Stenley, Charles Alfred**; Union one year; Gen. Mission Adm., Tientsin

**Starrett, Oscar G**; Union 1919–1920 MEM; Gen. Sec. Shensi Gai Institutional Church, Chengtu, Sze

**Storrs, Charles Lysander**; Union 1920–1921; Principal Han Mei Academy; Shaowu, Fukien

**Tewksbury, Malcolm Gardner**; Union spring term 1919; Presby. North; Evangelistic; Tsinan

**Thomson, James Claude**; Union part of 1915–1916; Prof. of Chemistry, University of Nanking

**Topping, William Hill**; Union 1914–1917 BD; Am. Board; Dist. Evangelistic; Diongloh Fukien

**Tsu, Y-Yue**; Union 1920–1921 Fellowship; PUMC, Peking; Sec of Religious & Social Work, Peking

**Wallace, Edward Wilson**; Union 1912, 1921 (2 ½ years); United Church of Canada; Asso. Gen. Sec CCEA, Shanghai

**Wang, Chwen Yung**

**Wang; Shan-chi**; Union 1916–1919 BD; Methodist Church, Pastor and Editor of Books, Nanchang

**Wickes, Dean Rockwell**; Union 1919–1920; Am. Board; Bible and Theological teaching, Lintsing, Shantung

**Wilcox, Floyd C**; Union 1911–1913 BD; Educational Depart., Shanghai Baptist College

**Willetts, Alfred G**; Shanghai Baptist College, Shanghai

**Wilson, Wilbur F**; ME; University of Nanking, Nanking

**Winans, Edward Jones**; Union 1918–1919; MEM; Principal Hui Wen Middle School, Tientsin

**Woo, Y. K.**; Union 1921–1922; National Committee YMCA; Ex. Sec. Pub Dept; Shanghai

**Wu, Yao Tsun**

# Bibliography


Adeney, David H. *China: The Church's Long March*. Ventura, CA: Regal, 1985.

Aikman, David. *Jesus in Beijing*. Washington, DC: Regnery, 2003.

Allen, Roland. *Missionary Methods: St. Paul's or Ours?* Reprint, Grand Rapids: Eerdmans, 1959.

———. *Spontaneous Expansion of the Church and the Causes Which Hinder It*. Reprint, Eugene, OR: Wipf & Stock, 1997.

Alumni Office of Union Theological Seminary. *The Union Theological Seminary Alumni Directory, 1836–1958*. New York: N.p., 1958.

Anderson, Gerald. "Peter Parker and the Introduction of Western Medicine in China." *Missions Studies* 23 (2006) 203–28.

Anderson, Gerald H., et al., eds. *Missions Legacies: Biographical Studies of Leaders of the Modern Missionary Movement*. American Society of Missiology 19. Maryknoll, NY: Orbis, 1994.

Angelova, Kamelia. "Vintage Photos: Take a Tour of Manhattan in the 1940s." *Business Insider*, July 11, 2011. https://www.businessinsider.com/new-york-city-1940s-photos-2011-7.

AP. "Andrew Tsu of China, Anglican Bishop, 100." *New York Times*, April 15, 1986. http://www.nytimes.com/1986/04/15/obituaries/andrew-tsu-of-china-anglican-bishop-100.html.

Askew, David J. "The Nanjing Incident: Recent Research and Trends." *Electronic Journal of Contemporary Japanese Studies* (April 2002) 1–21.

Austin, Alvyn. *China's Millions: The China Inland Mission and Late Qing Society, 1832–1905*. Grand Rapids: Eerdmans, 2007.

Barnouin, Barbara, and Yu Changgen. *Zhou Enlai: A Political Life*. Hong Kong: Chinese University Press, 2006.

Barr, James. *Fundamentalism*. London: SCM, 1977.

Barwick, John S. "Liu Tingfang." Biographical Dictionary of Chinese Christianity, n.d. http://bdcconline.net/en/stories/liu-tingfang.

———. "The Protestant Quest for Modernity in Republican China." PhD diss., University of Alberta, 2011.

Bays, Daniel H. *A New History of Christianity in China*. Oxford: Wiley-Blackwell, 2012.

Bays, Daniel H., and Ellen Widmer, eds. "'The Call': The Student Volunteer Movement for Foreign Missions." In *China's Christian Colleges: Cross-Cultural Connections, 1900–1950*, edited by Daniel H. Bays and Ellen Widmer, 1–2. Stanford, CA: Stanford University Press, 2009.

———. "Introduction." In *China's Christian Colleges: Cross-Cultural Connections, 1900–1950*, edited by Daniel H. Bays and Ellen Widmer, xiii–xx. Stanford, CA: Stanford University Press, 2009.

Bebbington, David. *Evangelicalism in Modern Britain: A History from the 1730s to the 1980s*. London: Unwin Hyman, 1989.

Beeching, Jack. *The Chinese Opium Wars*. London: Hutchinson & Co., 1975.

Bethge, Eberhard. *Dietrich Bonhoeffer: Theologian, Christian, Contemporary*. Translated by Eric Mosbacher. London: Collins, 1970.

Bhaskar, Roy A. *The Possiblity of Naturalism*. London: Routledge, 1979.

———. *A Realist Theory of Science*. London: Verso, 1975.

Bieler, Stacey. *"Patriots" or "Traitors": A History of American-Educated Chinese Students*. London: Sharpe, 2004.

Bitton, Nelson. "Cheng Ching-Yi: A Christian Statesman." *International Review of Mission* 30 (1941) 513–20.

Bondanell, Peter, ed. "Antonio Gramsci." In *Cassell Dictionary of Italian Literature*, 276–78. New York: Continuum International, 2001.

Bonhoeffer, Dietrich. *Barcelona, Berlin, New York: 1928–1931*. Vol. 10 of *Dietrich Bonhoeffer Works*. Translated by Douglas W. Stott. Minneapolis: Fortress, 2008.

Boorman, Howard L., and Richard C. Howard, eds. *Biographical Dictionary of Republican China*. 4 vols. New York: Columbia University Press, 1971.

Bosanquet, Mary. *The Life and Death of Dietrich Bonhoeffer*. London: Hodder and Stoughton, 1968.

Brinkley, Alan. "Henry Luce: The Master of Changing Media Landscape." *History News Network*, June 20, 2010. https://historynewsnetwork.org/article/128108.

———. *The Publisher: Henry Luce and His American Century*. New York: Knopf, 2010.

Brown, Terrry M. "Metacosmesis: The Christian Marxism of Frederic Hastings Smyth and the Society of the Catholic Commonwealth." PhD diss., University of Toronto, 1987. http://anglicanhistory.org/academic/brown1987/.

Bullock. Mary Brown. *The Oil Prince's Legacy: Rockefeller Philanthropy in China*. Stanford, CA: Stanford University Press, 2011.

Burnett, Richard E. "Historical Criticism." In *Dictionary for Theological Interpretation of the Bible*, edited by Kevin J. Vanhoozer, 290–93. Grand Rapids: Baker, 2005.

Cardenal, Juan Pablo, and Heriberto Araújo. *China's Silent Army: The Pioneers, Traders, Fixers and Workers Who Are Remaking the World in Beijing's Image*. Translated by Catherine Mansfield. New York: Crown, 2013.

Carlyle, Thomas. *On Heroes, Hero Worship and the Heroic in History*. Gutenberg, May 5, 1840. http://www.gutenberg.org/files/1091/1091-h/1091-h.htm.

Carpenter, Joel A. *Revive Us Again: The Reawakening of American Fundamentalism*. Oxford: Oxford University Press, 1997.

Chao, T. C. "On the Strengths and Weaknesses of the Chinese Church." *Life Monthly* 3 (1923) 1–8.

Chassin, Lionel Max. *The Communist Conquest of China: The History of the Civil War 1945–1949*. Translated by Timothy Osato and Louis Gelas. London: Weidenfeld and Nicolson, 1966.

Ch'en, Jerome. *China and the West: Society and Culture 1815–1937*. London: Hutchinson, 1979.

Chen, Su. "Lyon and His Comrades: Indigenizing YMCA in China 1895–1925." Paper presented at the annual conference of the Association for Asian Studies, Toronto, March 15–18, 2012.

Cheng, Pei-kai, et al. *The Search for Modern China: A Documentary Collection*. New York: Norton, 1999.

Chow, Alexander. *Theosis, Sino-Christian Theology and the Second Chinese Enlightenment: Heaven and Humanity in Unity*. New York: Palgrave Macmillan, 2013.

Coffin, Henry Sloane. *A Half-Century of Union Theological Seminary*. New York: Scribner, 1954.

Cohen, Paul A. "Christian Missions and Their Impact to 1900." In *The Cambridge History of China*, edited by John K. Fairbank, 10:543–90. Cambridge: Cambridge University Press, 1978.

———. *History in Three Keys: The Boxers as Event, Experience, and Myth*. New York: Columbia University Press, 1977.

Cotey, Gladys Ada Carrier. "Generations of the Van Dusen Family." *The New York Times*, July 24, 2011. http://www.nytimes.com/2011/07/24/nyregion/generations-of-the-van-dusen-family.html.

Cowan, Alison Leigh. "The Van Dusens of New Amsterdam." *The New York Times*, July 22, 2011. http://www.nytimes.com/2011/07/24/nyregion/the-story-of-the-van-dusen-family-one-of-manhattans-oldest.html?pagewanted=all&_r=0.

Cram, Ronald Hecker. "Harrison S. Elliot." Biola University, n.d. http://www2.talbot.edu/ce20/educators/view.cfm?n=harrison_elliott.

Crouch, Andy. "How Not to Change the World: A Call to 'Faithful Presence.'" *Books and Culture*, May–June 2010. https://www.booksandculture.com/articles/2010/mayjun/hownotchangetheworld.html.

Crowley, James Buckley. *Japan's Quest for Autonomy: National Security and Foreign Policy, 1930–1938*. Princeton, NJ: Princeton University Press, 2016.

Custers, Peter. "Introducing Gramscian Concepts: Towards a Re-Analysis of Bangladesh's Political History." *Aritro*, October–December 2000. http://www.petercusters.nl/index.php?topic=gramsci.

Daily, Christopher. *Robert Morrison and the Protestant Plan for China*. Hong Kong: Hong Kong University Press, 2013.

de Bary, Wm. Theodore, and Irene Bloom. *From Earliest Times to 1600*. Vol. 1 of *Sources of Chinese Tradition*. New York: Columbia University Press, 1999.

Dikötter, Frank. *The Age of Openness: China Before Mao*. Hong Kong: Hong Kong University Press, 2008.

———. *Mao's Great Famine*. London: Bloomsbury, 2011.

Dikkötter, Frank, et al. *Narcotic Culture: A History of Drugs in China*. London: Hurst, 2004.

Domhoff, G. William. *The Higher Circles: The Governing Class in America*. New York: Random, 1970.

Doubrovskaia, Dina V. "The Russian Orthodox Church in China." In *China and Christianity: Burdened Past, Hopeful Future*, edited by Stephen Uhalley and Xiaoxin Wu, 163–78. Armonk, NY: Sharpe, 2001.

Doyle, G. Wright. *Builders of the Chinese Church: Pioneer Protestant Missionaries and Chinese Church Leaders*. Eugene, OR: Wipf & Stock, 2015.

Duke, David Nelson. *In the Trenches with Jesus and Marx: Harry F. Ward and the Struggle for Social Justice*. Tuscaloosa: University of Alabama Press, 2003.

Dunch, Ryan. "Science, Religion, and the Classics in Christian Higher Education to 1920." In *China's Christian Colleges: Cross-Cultural Connections, 1900–1950*, edited by Daniel H. Bays and Ellen Widmer, 57–82. Stanford, CA: Stanford University Press, 2009.

Egan, Susan. *A Latterday Confucian: Reminiscences of William Hung (1893–1980)*. Cambridge, MA: Harvard University Press, 1987.

Elegant, Simon. "The War for China's Soul." *Time Magazine*, August 20, 2006. http://www.time.com/time/magazine/article/0,9171,1229123,00.html.

Fairbank, John King, ed. *The Missionary Enterprise in China and America*. Cambridge, MA: Harvard University Press, 1974.

Fenby, Jonathan. *The Penguin History of Modern China: The Fall and Rise of a Great Power, 1850–2008*. London: Allen Lane, 2008.

Fenn, William. *Ever New Horizons: The Story of the United Board for Christian Higher Education in Asia, 1922–1975*. North Newton, KS: Mennonite, 1980.

Ferreira, Johan."Did Christianity Reach China in the Han Dynasty?" *Centre for Early Christian Study* 2, n.d. www.cecs.acu.edu.au/HanChinaChristianity.pdf. Site discontinued.

Fosdick, Raymond B. *John D. Rockefeller, Jr.: A Portrait*. New York: Harper & Brothers, 1956.

Fu, Poshek. *Passivity, Resistance and Collaboration: Intellectual Choice in Occupied Shanghai, 1937–1995*. Stanford, CA: Stanford University Press, 1993.

Gant, George F. Review of *The Story of the Rockefeller Foundation*, by Raymond B. Fosdick. *The Journal of Politics* 15 (1953) 300–304.

Gernet, Jacques. *China and the Christian Impact: A Conflict of Cultures*. Translated by Janet Lloyd. Cambridge: Cambridge University Press, 1985.

Gillett, Charles R., ed. *Alumni Catalogue of the Union Theological Seminary in the City of New York, 1836–1926*. New York: Union Theological Seminary Press, 1926.

Godsey, John D. "Dietrich Bonhoeffer." In *The Modern Theologians: An Introduction to Christian Theology in the Twentieth Century*, edited by David F. Ford, 1:43–61. Oxford: Basil Blackwell, 1989.

Gramsci, Antonio. *The Antonio Gramsci Reader: Selected Writings 1916–1935*. Edited by David Forgacs. New York: New York University Press, 2000.

———. *Selections from Prison Notebooks*. New York: International, 1971.

Granovetter, Mark S. "The Strength of Weak Ties." *The American Journal of Sociology* 78 (1973) 1360–80.

———. "The Strength of Weak Ties: A Network Theory Revisited." *Sociological Theory* 1 (1983) 201–33.

Gulick, Edward V. *Peter Parker and the Opening of China*. Cambridge, MA: Harvard University Press, 1973.

Hancock, Christopher. *Robert Morrison and the Birth of Chinese Protestantism*. London: T&T Clark, 2008.

Handy, Robert T. *A History of Union Theological Seminary in New York*. New York: Columbia University Press, 1987.

Harr, John Ensor, and Peter J. Johnson. *The Rockefeller Century: Three Generations of America's Greatest Family*. New York: Charles Scribner's Sons, 1988.

Harvey, Charles E. "John D. Rockefeller, Jr., and the Interchurch World Movement of 1919–1920: A Different Angle on the Ecumenical Movement." *Church History* 51 (1982) 198–209.

Harvey, Thomas Alan. *Acquainted with Grief: Wang Mingdao's Stand for the Persecuted Church in China.* Grand Rapids: Brazos, 2002.

Hauerwas, Stanley, and William H. Willimon. *Resident Aliens: A Provocative Christian Assessment of Culture and Ministry for People Who Know That Something is Wrong.* Nashville: Abingdon, 1989.

Hayford, Charles W. *To the People: James Yen and Village China.* New York: Columbia University Press, 1990.

Hendricks, Luther V. "James Harvey Robinson and the New School for Social Research." *The Journal of Higher Education* 20 (1949) 1–11.

———. *James Harvey Robinson: Teacher of History.* New York: King's Crown, 1946.

Henry Luce Foundation. "History." Henry Luce Foundation, nd. https://www.hluce.org/about/history/.

Herzstein, Robert Edwin. *Henry R. Luce, Time, and the American Crusade in Asia.* Cambridge: Cambridge University Press, 1984.

Huebner, Jon W. Review of *A Latterday Confucian*, by Susan Egan. *The Australian Journal of Chinese Affairs* 24 (1990) 415–17.

Hunter, Alan, and Kim-Kwong Chan. *Protestantism in Contemporary China.* Cambridge: Cambridge University Press, 1993.

Hunter, James Davison. *To Change the World: The Irony, Tragedy, and Possibility of Christianity in the Late Modern World.* New York: Oxford University Press: 2010.

Hutchinson, Paul. "The Conservative Reaction in China." *The Journal of Religion* 2 (1922) 337–61.

International Churchill Society. "Never Despair: May 1945–1965." International Churchill Society, Sept. 15, 2008. http://www.winstonchurchill.org/learn/biography/timelines/never-despair-may-1945-1965.

Ireland, Daryl R. *John Song: Modern Chinese Christianity and the Making of a New Man.* Studies in World Christianity. Waco, TX: Baylor University Press, 2020.

———. "John Sung: Christian Revitalization in China and Southeast Asia." PhD diss., Boston University, 2015.

———. "John Sung's Malleable Conversion Narrative." *Fides et Historia* 44 (2013) 48–75.

Jenkins, Philip. *The Next Christendom: The Coming of Global Christianity.* Oxford: Oxford University Press, 2007.

Jian, Youwen. "Foreword." In *Geming de Jidujiao* [A revolutionary Christianity], by Harry Ward, 1–8. Shanghai: Zhonghua Jidu jiao wen she, 1926.

*Jianghuai Morning News.* "Gong Pusheng—Revolutionary and Diplomat Extraordinaire." *Jianghuai Morning News*, September 25, 2010.

Jones, Francis Price. *The Church in Communist China: A Protestant Appraisal.* New York: Friendship, 1962.

Jones, Francis Price, and Wallace C. Merwin. *Documents of the Three-Self Movement.* New York: National Council of Churches of Christ, 1963.

Kobler, John. *Luce: His Time, Life and Fortune.* London: Macdonald, 1968.

Kuhn, Isobel. *Stones of Fire.* London: China Inland Mission, 1951.

Kuo, Siu-may. *Journeying through the Bible.* Nanjing: Nanjing University Press, 1990.

———. *Venturing into the Bible.* Nanjing: Nanjing University Press, 1989.

Kuyper, Abraham. *Lectures on Calvinism.* Grand Rapids: Eerdmans, 1931.

Laaman, Lars. "H499: Christianity in China (1600–1949)." Unpublished lecture notes, School of Oriental and African Studies, University of London, 2010–2011.

Lambert, Emma. "Luce, Henry (1898–1967)." *St. James Encyclopedia of Popular Culture*, updated May 5, 2023. https://www.encyclopedia.com/media/encyclopedias-almanacs-transcripts-and-maps/luce-henry-1898-1967.

Latourette, Kenneth Scott. *A History of Christian Missions in China*. New York: Macmillan, 1929.

———. *The Twentieth Century outside Europe*. Vol. 5 of *Christianity in a Revolutionary Age: A History of Christianity in the Nineteenth and Twentieth Century*. London: Eyre & Spottiswoode 1962.

Lauby, Paul T. *Sailing on Winds of Change: Two Decades in the Life of the United Board for Christian Higher Education in Asia, 1969–1990*. New York: United Board for Christian Higher Education in Asia, 1996.

Lautz, Terrill E. "The SVM and Transformation of the Protestant Mission to China." In *China's Christian Colleges: Cross-Cultural Connections, 1900–1950*, edited by Daniel H. Bays and Ellen Widmer, 3–22. Stanford, CA: Stanford University Press, 2009.

Lee, Lily Xiao Hong. "Gong Pusheng." In *Biographical Dictionary of Chinese Women: The Twentieth Century, 1912–2000*, edited by Lily Xiao Hong Lee and A. D. Stefanowska, 179–82. Armonk, NY: Sharpe, 2003.

Leitch, Alexander "Henry Pitney Van Dusen." From *A Princeton Companion (*Princeton, NJ: Princeton University Press, 1978). http://etcweb.princeton.edu/CampusWWW/Companion/van_dusen_henry.html.

Lew, Timothy Tingfang. "The Psychology of Learning Chinese." PhD diss., Teachers College, 1920.

Leys, Simon. *The Burning Forest: Essays on Chinese Culture and Politics*. New York: Holt, Rinehart, and Winston, 1986.

Li, Xinyuan. *Theological Construction—or Destruction? An Analysis of the Theology of Bishop K. H. Ting*. Streamwood, IL: Christian Life, 2003.

Lin, Paul T. K., and Eileen Chen Lin. *In the Eye of the China Storm: A Life between East and West*. Toronto: McGill-Queen's University Press, 2011.

Lin, Yü-sheng. *The Crisis of Chinese Consciousness: Radical Anti-traditionalism in the May Fourth Era*. Madison, WI: University of Wisconsin Press, 1979.

Lindsay, D. Michael. "Evangelicals in the Power Elite: Elite Cohesion Advancing a Movement." *American Sociological Review* 73 (2008) 60–82.

Ling, Samuel. *Chinese Intellectuals and the Gospel*. Phillipsburg, NJ: P & R, 2000.

Liu, Jiafeng. "Same Bed, Different Dreams: The American Postwar Plan for China's Christian Colleges, 1943–1946." In *China's Christian Colleges: Cross-Cultural Connections, 1900–1950*, edited by Daniel H. Bays and Ellen Widmer, 218–40. Stanford, CA: Stanford University Press, 2009.

Liu, Yu. "The True Pioneer of the Jesuit China Mission: Michele Ruggieri." *History of Religions* 50 (2011) 362–83.

Lodwick, Kathleen L. *Crusaders against Opium: Protestant Missionaries in China*, 1874–1917. Lexington: University of Kentucky Press, 1996.

Long, Charles Henry, and Anne Rowthorn. "Roland Allen, 1868–1947: Missionary Methods: St. Paul's or Ours?" In *Missions Legacies: Biographical Studies of Leaders of the Modern Missionary Movement*, edited by Gerald H. Anderson, 383–90. Maryknoll, NY: Orbis, 1994.

Luo, Zhufeng, ed. *Religion under Socialism in China*. Translated by Donald E. MacInnis and Zheng Xi'an. London: Sharpe, 1991.

Lutz, Jessie G., and R. Ray Lutz. "Karl Gützlaff's Approach to Indigenization: The Chinese Union." In *Christianity in China: From the Eighteenth Century to the Present*, edited by Daniel H. Bays, 269–91. Stanford, CA: Stanford University Press, 1996.

Lutz, Jessie Gregory. *China and the Christian Colleges, 1850–1950*. London: Cornell University Press, 1971.

———. *Opening China: Karl F. A. Gützlaff and Sino-Western Relations, 1827–1852*. Grand Rapids: Eerdmans, 2008.

Lyall, Leslie T. *Come Wind, Come Weather: The Present Experience of the Church in China*. London: Hodder & Stoughton, 1961.

———. *John Sung*. London: China Inland Mission, 1954.

Ma, Jia. *Discerning Truth through Love: The Biography of Bishop K. H. Ting*. Hong Kong: Chinese Christian Literature Council, 2006.

MacFarquhar, Roderick, and Michael Schoenhals. *Mao's Last Revolution*. London: Belknap, 2006.

Machen, J. Gresham. *Christianity and Liberalism*. Grand Rapids: Eerdmans, 1923.

Maltz, Albert. *The Cross and the Arrow*. New York: Little, Brown and Company, 1944.

Manning, Russell Re, ed. *The Cambridge Companion to Paul Tillich*. Cambridge: Cambridge University Press, 2009.

Mao, Zedong. "Farewell, Leighton Stuart!" In *Selected Works of Mao Tse-tung*, 4:433–40. Beijing: Foreign Languages, 1969.

Marsden, George M. *Fundamentalism and American Culture: The Shaping of Twentieth-Century Evangelicalism, 1800–1930*. Oxford: Oxford University Press, 1980.

———. *Understanding Fundamentalism and Evangelicalism*. Grand Rapids: Eerdmans, 1991.

Matthews, Shailer. *Jesus on Social Institutions*. New York: Macmillan, 1928.

McGiffert, Arthuer Cushman. *A History of Christianity in the Apostolic Age*. New York: Charles Scribner's Sons, 1897.

McGrath, Alister E. *Christian Theology: An Introduction*. 2nd ed. Oxford: Blackwell, 1994.

———. *Nature*. Vol. 1 of *A Scientific Theology*. London: T&T Clark, 2003.

———. *Theory*. Vol. 3 of *A Scientific Theology*. London: T&T Clark, 2003.

Metaxas, Eric. *Bonhoeffer: Pastor, Martyr, Prophet, Spy*. Nashville: Thomas Nelson, 2010.

Miller, Glenn T. *Piety and Profession: American Protestant Theological Education, 1870–1970*. Grand Rapids: Eerdmans, 2007.

Miller, Robert Moats. *Harry Emerson Fosdick: Preacher, Pastor, Prophet*. Oxford: Oxford University Press, 1985.

Mills, C. Wright. *The Power Elite: New Edition*. Oxford: Oxford University Press, 2000.

Mungello, D. E. "An Introduction to the Chinese Rites Controversy." In *The Chinese Rites Controversy: Its History and Meaning*, edited by D. E. Mungello, 3–14. San Francisco: The Ricci Institute for Chinese-Western Cultural History, 1994.

Ng, Lee Ming. "Christianity and Social Change: The Case in China, 1920–1950." PhD diss., Princeton Theological Seminary, 1971.

Ng, Peter Tze Ming. *Chinese Christianity: An Interplay between Global and Local Perspectives*. Religion in Chinese Societies 4. Leiden, Neth.: Brill, 2012.

———. "T. C. Chao and Yenching School of Religion—A Case for the Study of Indigenization of Christian Higher Education in China." Paper presented at the annual conference of the Association for Asian Studies, Toronto, March 15–18, 2012.

Niebuhr, H. Richard. *Christ and Culture*. San Francisco: Harper and Row, 1956.

Palmer, Martin. *The Jesus Sutras: Rediscovering the Lost Scrolls of Taoist Christianity.* New York: Ballantine, 2001.

Parker, Michael. *Kingdom of Character.* Lanham, MD: University Press of America, 1998.

Patterson, George N. *Christianity in Communist China.* London: Word, 1969.

Patton, David. *Christian Mission and the Judgment of God.* London: SCM, 1953.

Piven, Frances Fox. "Can Power from Below Change the World?" *American Sociological Review* 73 (2008) 1–14.

Polo, Marco. *The Travels of Marco Polo: The Complete Yule-Cordier Edition.* Edited by Henri Cordier. Translated by Henry Yule. 2 vols. New York: Dover, 1993.

Prentiss, George Lewis. *The Union Theological Seminary of New York: Historical and Biographical Sketches of its First Fifty Years.* New York: Randolph and Co., 1889.

Polkinghorne, John. *Belief in God in an Age of Science.* London: Yale University Press, 1998.

Putney, Clifford. *Muscular Christianity: Manhood and Sports in Protestant America, 1880–1920.* London: Harvard University Press, 2001.

Qiao, Songdu. *Qiao Guanhua and Gong Peng: My Father and My Mother.* Beijing: Zhonghua, 2008.

Ramsey, Arthur Michael. *From Gore to Temple: The Development of Anglican Theology between* Lux Mundi *and the Second World War.* London: Longmans, Green, and Co., 1960.

Rauschenbusch, Walter. *Christianity and the Social Crisis.* New York: Macmillan, 1907.

———. *A Theology for the Social Gospel.* New York: Macmillan, 1917.

Richmond, Annette B. *The American Episcopal Church in China.* N.p.: The Domestic and Foreign Missionary Society of the Protestant Episcopal Church in the United States of America, 1907.

Robert, Dana L. *Occupy until I Come: A. T. Pierson and the Evangelization of the World.* Grand Rapids: Eerdmans, 2003.

Rosen, Susan Grant. "The Union Medal and the Union Plaque." *Union News* (Summer 1995) 14–15.

Ruokanen, Mikkaa. "K. H. Ting's Contribution to the Contextualization of Christianity in China." *Modern Theology* 25 (2009) 107–22.

Ruokanen, Miikka, and Paulos Huang, eds. *Christianity and Chinese Culture.* Grand Rapids: Eerdmans, 2010.

Sachs, William L. *The Transformation of Anglicanism: From State Church to Global Communion.* Cambridge: Cambridge University Press, 1993.

Sandeen, Ernest R. *The Roots of Fundamentalism: British and American Millenarianism, 1800–1930.* Chicago: University of Chicago Press, 197.

Sanneh, Lamin O. *Disciples of All Nations: Pillars of World Christianity.* Oxford: Oxford University Press, 2008.

———. "Prospects for Post-Western Christianity in Asia and Elsewhere." *The Brown Journal of World Affairs* 12 (2006) 117–28.

———. *Whose Religion Is Christianity? The Gospel beyond the West.* Grand Rapids: Eerdmanns, 2003.

Schaff, Philip. *Germany: Its Universities, Theology and Religion.* Philadelphia: Lindsay and Blackiston, 1857.

Schaff, Philip, and Johann Jakob Herzog. *The New Schaff-Herzog Encyclopedia of Religious Knowledge.* 12 vols. Edited by Samuel Macauley Jackson. New York: Funk and Wagnalls, 1914.

Schubert, William E. *I Remember John Sung*. Singapore: Far Eastern Bible College Press, 1976.

Schwartz, Michael, and Beth Mintz. *The Power Structure of American Business*. Chicago: University of Chicago Press, 1985.

Seagrave, Sterling. *The Soong Dynasty*. New York: Harper & Row, 1985.

Shambaugh, David. *China Goes Global: The Partial Power*. Oxford: Oxford University Press, 2013.

Shaw, Yu-Ming. *An American Missionary in China: John Leighton Stuart and Chinese-American Relations*. Cambridge, MA: Harvard East Asian Monographs, 1992.

Showalter, Nathan D. *The End of a Crusade: the Student Volunteer Movement for Foreign Missions and the Great War*. Lanham, MD: Scarecrow, 1998.

Smith, James K. A. "How (Not) to Change the World." *The Other Journal*, September 8, 2010. https://theotherjournal.com/2010/09/how-not-to-change-the-world/.

Smith, James K. A., and James Davison Hunter. "Neither Triumphalism nor Retreat: A Conversation about Faith Presence with James Davison Hunter." *The Other Journal*, September 20, 2010. http://theotherjournal.com/2010/09/22/.

Sneller, Christopher D. "'Take Away Your Opium and Your Missionaries': The Opium Wars (1839–60) and the Chinese National Psyche." *Bible in Transmission* (2012) 20–22.

Song, Shangjie. *The Diary of John Sung: Extracts from His Journals and Notes*. Compiled by Levi Song. Singapore: Genesis, 2012.

———. *The Journal Once Lost: Extracts from the Diary of John Sung*. Compiled by Levi Sung. Singapore: Genesis, 2008.

Spence, Jonathan D. "Claims and Counter-Claims: The Kangxi Emperor and the Europeans (1661–1722)." In *The Chinese Rites Controversy: Its History and Meaning*, edited by D. E. Mungello, 15–30. San Francisco: The Ricci Institute for Chinese-Western Cultural History, 1994.

———. *The Memory Palace of Matteo Ricci*. New York: Penguin, 1983.

———. *The Search for Modern China*. New York: Norton & Company, 1990.

Stanley, Brian. *The World Missionary Conference Edinburgh 1910*. Grand Rapids: Eerdmans, 2009.

Stranahan, Patricia. *Underground: The Shanghai Communist Party and the Politics of Survival, 1927–1937*. Lanham, MD: Rowman & Litttlesfield, 1998.

Stuart, John Leighton. *Fifty Years in China*. New York: Random House, 1954.

*A Survey of Chinese Students in American Universities and Colleges in the Past One Hundred Years*. New York: National Tsing Hua Research Fellowship Fund and China Institute of America, 1954.

Swanberg, W. A. *Luce and His Empire*. New York: Scribners, 1972.

Teilhard de Chardin, Pierre. *The Future of Man*. New York: HarperCollins, 1964.

Thomas, W. H. Griffith. "Modernism in China." *The Princeton Theological Review* 19 (1921) 630–71.

Tiedemann, R. G. "Indigenous Agency, Religious Protectorates, and Chinese: The Expansion of Christianity in Nineteenth-Century China." In *Converting Colonialism: Visions and Realities in Mission History, 1706–1914*, edited by Dana L. Robert, 206–41. Grand Rapids: Eerdmans, 2008.

Ting, K. H. "The Dilemma of the Sincere Student." *The Canadian Student* 25 (1947) 81, 92–93.

———. *God Is Love: Collected Writings of K. H. Ting*. Colorado Springs, CO: Cook Communications Ministries International, 2004.

———. *No Longer Strangers: Selected Writings of K. H. Ting*. Edited by Raymond L. Whitehead. Maryknoll, NY: Orbis, 1989.

———. "Youth and Religion." *Chinese Theological Review* 10 (1994) 7–9.

Ting, Siu May. "The World Begins Now and Here." *The Canadian Student* 25 (1947) 48–49.

Tingfang, Liu. "Jidujiao de shehui fuyin" [The Christian social gospel]. *Ta Kung Po (*December 14, 1933) 14.

Tryon, Harold H., ed. *Union Theological Seminary in the City of New York, Alumni Catalogue, 1836–1947*. New York: Union Theological Seminary Press, 1948.

Tsu, Andrew Y. Y. *Friend of Fishermen*. Ambler, PA: Trinity, 1951.

Tsu, Caroline Huie. "Huie Kin." In *Friend of Fishermen*, by Andrew Y. Y. Tsu, 22–24. Ambler, PA: Trinity, 1951.

Twain, Mark. "To My Missionary Critics." *North American Review* 172 (1901) 520–34.

———. "To the Person Sitting in Darkness." *North American Review* 172 (1901) 161–76. https://www.jstor.org/stable/25105120.

Tyrrell, Ian R. *Reforming the World: The Creation of America's Moral Empire*. Princeton, NJ: Princeton University Press, 2010.

Utley, Uldine. *Why I Am a Preacher: A Plain Answer to an Oft-Repeated Question*. New York: Revell, 1931.

Volf, Miroslav. *Exclusion and Embrace: A Theological Exploration of Identity, Otherness, and Reconciliation*. Nashville: Abingdon, 1996.

Wang, Chengting T. "Making Christianity Indigenous in China." *The Chinese Recorder* 52 (1921) 323–28.

Wang, Wei-fan. "Tombstone Carvings from AD 86: Did Christianity Reach China in the First Century." Lyon Catholic University, n.d. https://www.eecho.fr/wp-content/uploads/2021/06/WONG-tombstone-carvings-from-ad-86_Christianity-in-China.pdf.

Wang, Zhixin. "The Indigenous Church and Indigenous Christian Writing." *Wen She Monthly* 1 (1926) 21–34.

Ward, Harry. *Geming de Jidujiao* [A revolutionary Christianity]. Shanghai: Zhonghua Jidujiao wen she, 1926.

Wei, Francis C. M. "The Chinese Moral Tradition and Its Social Values." PhD diss., University of London, 1929.

West, Philip. *Yenching University and Sino-Western Relations, 1916–1952*. Cambridge, MA: Harvard University Press, 1969.

Westad, Odd Arne. *Restless Empire: China and the World Since 1750*. New York: Basic, 2012.

Whyte, Bob. *Unfinished Encounter: China and Christianity*. London: Fount, 1988.

Wickeri, Philip L. *Reconstructing Christianity in China: K. H. Ting and the Chinese Church*. Maryknoll, NY: Orbis, 2007.

———. *Seeking the Common Ground: Protestant Christianity, the Three-Self Movement, and China's United Front*. Maryknoll, NY: Orbis, 1988.

Widmer, Eric. *The Russian Ecclesiastical Mission in Peking during the Eighteenth Century*. Cambridge, MA: East Asian Research Center, 1976.

Witte, John, Jr., and Frank S. Alexander, eds. *The Teachings of Modern Protestantism on Law, Politics, and Human Nature*. New York: Columbia University Press, 2007.

Wolsterstorff, Nicholas. *Until Justice and Peace Embrace*. Grand Rapids: Eerdmans, 1983.

Wood, R. Derek. "The Treaty of Nanking: Form and the Foreign Office, 1842–43." *Journal of Imperial and Commonwealth History* 24 (1996) 181–96.

Wu, Chang-shing. "Idea and Practice of Religious Education and Social Change in China: A Study of Timothy Tingfang Lew (1891–1947)." PhD diss., Chinese University of Hong Kong, 2001.

Xi, Lian. *The Conversion of Missionaries: Liberalism in American Protestant Missions in China, 1907–1932*. University Park: Pennsylvania State University Press, 1997.

———. *Redeemed by Fire: The Rise of Popular Christianity in Modern China*. New Haven, CT: Yale University Press, 2010.

Xing, Jun. *Baptized in the Fire of Revolution: The American Social Gospel and the YMCA in China: 1919–1937*. London: Associated University Presses, 1996.

Xu, Edward Yihua. "Liberal Arts Education in English and Campus Culture at St. John's University." In *China's Christian Colleges: Cross-Cultural Connections, 1900–1950*, edited by Daniel H. Bays and Ellen Widmer, 107–24. Stanford, CA: Stanford University Press, 2009.

Xu, Xiaohong. "The Institutional Transformation of Moral Governances: The YMCA and State Making in Revolutionary China." Paper presented at the annual conference of the Association for Asian Studies, Toronto, March 15–18, 2012.

Xu, Yihua. "'Patriotic' Protestants: The Making of an Official Church." In *God and Caesar in China: Policy Implications of Church-State Tensions*, edited by Jason Kindopp and Carol Lee Hamrin, 107–21. Washington, DC: Brookings Institution, 2004.

———. "St John's University, Shanghai as an Evangelising Agency." In *Studies in World Christianity* 12 (2006) 23–49.

———. "Union Theological Seminary and the Christian Church in China." *The Journal of American-East Asian Relations* 14 (2004–2006) 11–24.

Yang, Huilin. *China, Christianity and the Question of Culture*. Waco, TX: Baylor University Press, 2014.

Yao, Kevin Xiyi. *The Fundamentalist Movement among Protestant Missionaries in China, 1920–1937*. Lanham, MD: University Press of America, 2003.

Yarbrough, Robert W. "Tübingen School." In *Dictionary for Theological Interpretation of the Bible*, edited by Kevin J. Vanhoozer, 822–23. Grand Rapids: Baker, 2005.

Ye, Weili. *Seeking Modernity in China's Name: Chinese Students in the United States, 1900–1927*. Stanford, CA: Stanford University Press, 2001.

Yeo, K. K. *Chairman Mao Meets the Apostle Paul*. Grand Rapids: Brazos, 2002.

Zhao, Xiaoyang. "The Chinese Communist Party and the Late Period of the Chinese Students' Christian Association in North America." Paper presented at the annual conference of the Association for Asian Studies, Toronto, March 15–18, 2012.